# THE PENNY WORLD

# THE
# PENNY WORLD

BY

# EDWARD BLISHEN

SINCLAIR-STEVENSON

First published in Great Britain by
Sinclair-Stevenson Limited
7/8 Kendrick Mews
London SW7 3HG, England

*British Library Cataloguing in Publication Data*

Blishen, Edward, *1920–*
The penny world.
1. English literature. Blishen, Edward, 1920–
I. Title
828.01409

ISBN 1-85619-003-X

Photoset by Rowland Phototypesetting Limited
Bury St Edmunds, Suffolk
Printed and bound in Great Britain by
Clays Limited, St Ives, plc

To
EVE AND PETER LIKEMAN

# Acknowledgements

Nine lines from 'A Cooking Egg' are reprinted by kind permission of Faber & Faber Ltd from *Collected Poems 1909–1962*, by T. S. Eliot.

# PROLOGUE

'Good Lord!' said the gentleman from Leamington, gazing at the gentleman from Khajuraho: who in this setting was remarkable less for his intimate entertainment of the young woman bent forward in front of him than for the finger with which he was stabbing at her spine. 'You're not going to photograph that?' Our guide, Mr Pathan, was anxious that we should understand the significance of the finger. There were, as calculated by the Chandela, such and such a number of erogenous zones (I forgot the figure at once, as I'd forgotten the number of divine creatures in the Hindu pantheon, but it was large), and this sandstone gentleman, bald, a little paunchy, was taking the opportunity of stimulating Zone No... it might have been fifteen. Much depended on the calendar, the stars, the weather. 'I've been counting,' said the gentleman from Leamington. 'In the past five minutes you have taken twenty-seven photographs.'

My own astonishment, I thought, lay in wondering how my fellow-traveller refrained from such excess, let alone thought it worthy of comment. He too was bent forward (but not with erotic intent), putting his weight on his shooting stick – one stick only, in a corner of the world where he might more suitably have sported a dozen. This was no place for single items! If the park brimming with temples through which the Worldwide party was making its way had been in want of a

1

name, an obvious suggestion would have been Profusion. The soaring surfaces around us boiled over with human beings in half-relief, somewhere between pink and sepia in colour: all of them . . . lascivious. Yet *that* vocabulary had become difficult to use. About the man with the prodding finger and his collaborator there was no hint of the unwillingness to be discovered that would have marked the activity for the gentleman from Leamington, if it had been possible to imagine him indulging in it. (For a moment I did imagine it, and him converted to sandstone: but the shooting stick, inseparable from him, marred the tableau).

In the midst of all that photography (perhaps I *had* taken twenty-seven, and now was taking the twenty-eighth, a cheerful scrimmage involving elephants: but then how *not* attempt some record of these astonishing blithenesses?), I was overwhelmed by a simple amazement. Of course, we'd read about the temples of Khajuraho: Kate and I, on our way to India to celebrate forty years of marriage, had resolved not to join in any sniggering that arose. We foresaw a typical middle-class Anglo-Saxon incapacity to examine the temples without a good deal of nudging and so on. As it turned out, there had certainly been levity in the Worldwide party, but it was mixed with a disdain that would have been familiar to socially unpopular persons in suburbs back home. It appeared to be felt that the carvings represented a barely credible period when history had been transformed into a saucy postcard. 'Good Lord!' said the gentleman from Leamington once more. Well, good Lord indeed! Here a young woman with breasts as round as apples, and thighs and legs that constituted, as it were, a fine form of human lettering, was about to lift her sari. (Yes, a lively human alphabet – delicious Ss danced across the sandstone, accompanied by pliant Cs. Over there, an intricate copulation of Us!) The existence of the sari was indicated only by the delicate line that represented its hem, and which she now – and forever – held in the slim fingers of each hand. Mr Pathan, who could have made the Song of Solomon sound like an academic tract, was explaining that this was no plain matter of taking off a sari. Undressing was a set of philosophical propositions. Quite general concepts were being illustrated. So said Mr Pathan: while this charming woman persisted with the teasing act she'd begun nine hundred years earlier.

What to make of it, so beautiful, so candid, peered at now with such astonishment! Here seemed to have existed a people who made exultant public art out of what we regarded as private indelicacy. They'd proclaimed the pleasure of making love in series in which some were upside down and some were not, and they'd repeated the series across the faces of one immense place of worship after another. What sort of people were they? Did they, or some of them, pay a price for such unashamed acceptance of the flesh?

I found Laura at my side: a cool figure in a sari of her own, which neither in plain fact nor as a philosophical gesture was she removing.

Laura was our escort. She was a necessarily substantial, amused person, with the perhaps perverse passion for management without which no one would be drawn to this occupation. What on this scene it required was deep experience of Indian bureaucracy and of the local habits of arbitrary delay, postponement and cancellation: the ability to do and say the mysteriously right things in the mysteriously right order; and the patience to hang on, smiling, when the right things turned out to have become the wrong things, or there'd emerged some enormous indisposition to permit anything whatever to proceed. Laura looked at ease among the carvings. Not one of them was likely to demand that she produce the passports of the entire party accompanied by a novel range of back-up documents, most of which were in New Delhi, or London, or had been confiscated at this or that airport. She and I seemed to be gazing mildly together now at an inverted man, wearing a ruby or two and being enjoyed by upright women, one on each side, who for the occasion had flung on the odd bracelet.

'I find these people impossible to imagine,' I said.

'They've given you plenty to go on,' said Laura.

'Oh well, physically . . .' I said.

Laura said: 'I find it difficult not to believe they were happy. Which I guess is nonsense.'

Well, I guessed it was nonsense, too. If sexual hangups were a great cause of human distress, their removal would still leave a number of famous hurdles for human beings to fall at. And the question remained: would the absence of shame in an entire community lead even to general sexual felicity? I remembered a book title I'd glimpsed at the Frankfurt Book Fair, where I was helping to make a programme for the corner of the BBC's external services in which I worked. *Guilt Without Sex*, it seemed to say. I'd gone half a million books beyond it in those choking literary alleys before what I'd seen sank in: but though I kept my eyes anxiously open, I never caught sight of it again . . . And what would happen, in any case, if one of the women making the upside-down man happy had feelings about him that made her wish the other woman away? Or could you set up a sexual culture so relaxed that passionate preferences did not emerge? I felt I'd known Laura too short a time to ask her opinion. The gentleman from Leamington would not quite do, either. And Kate, who would do, and had been my sandstone companion for so long (I imagined her in a vague ruby or so), was not in sight.

We'd come to India to round off all those years of marriage, but I was not at all surprised to find that it was not much of a rounding-off sort of place. The fact was that being close to seventy, as we both were, had all the marks of a much-earlier phase in our lives: adolescence. That was a time when you felt gauchely new to the place, terribly eager to cut an impressive figure and terribly aware that you were not able to do so: and when the world seemed to be boiling under your feet. Nothing was what it had seemed, and everything you clapped eyes on was in a state of beautiful and alarming transition. For Kate and me, that had all been . . . fifty years ago, or more. We'd danced, trudged, groaned, laughed, wept, blushed our way through the intervening half century, and here we were, reaping the harvest of that long, grave, improving experience.

4

At nearly seventy (the fact was) you felt a gauche newcomer, anxious to command admiration and very much aware that you could not do it: and the world seemed to be boiling under your feet. Everything was engaged in turning into something else. Well, oldest friends, for example.

Mr Pathan said: 'Worldwide, I will leave you for half an hour to make findings for yourself. I expressly suggest a sighting of the whole park from the furthest point you are able to reach.'

There was Tom Sadler: always, amusingly, an indoors man. One of one's youthful jokes. Tom, even when we were at school together, had had a liking for being indoors rather than out. 'Oh, not fresh air!' he'd say – even in the spring of that awful year 1940, when we were waiting for a hesitant hell to declare the shape it meant to take. He'd laugh, and we'd laugh, and with difficulty we would get him out, and he would make a pantomime of his being inexperienced in this matter of walking. Our school had not known what to do with Tom. It had thought him over-sweet – and he was: but I now saw *that* as part of the defensiveness that seemed an amusing trait, then, not the tragic flaw I now thought it was. The school had taken it for granted that boys had a natural love for that submission to mud, rain, wind and sometimes snow, that was involved in playing Rugby football. I looked back now and saw that Tom's natural hatred of all that was not a whim: the term that for so many decades thereafter it had been possible to apply to his general aversion from outsideness. It was in fact a true hatred, and it had grown less and less of a joke: and Tom now, I'd sometimes thought, himself near to seventy, would be happy only if he could barricade himself inside his house, with his wife, and children, and his children's children, and stay there, for some sort of ever.

One aspect of this secondary adolescence: that what had seemed whims, oddities, eccentricities, turned out to be deep-rooted distortions of personality. On the young tree, a decorative strangeness in the bark: now, a tumour, a tremendous fungoid growth.

5

But here came Kate: pursued heavily by Michael Reemer. In this mild party of tourists, Reemer had quickly emerged as the odd man out. Well, the phrase was too ordinary. He was the oddest man, and he was most extravagantly out. Austrian by birth, a professional historian who might, on the other hand, have been an unprofessional one, and who generated a mysterious impression of being also some sort of miscellaneous tycoon, he thrived on challenging discussion, and found himself among people who, not eager for challenge when at home, were distinctly opposed to it when on holiday. If he could not be throwing down gauntlets, or striking persons on the cheek with the glove of some disagreeable contention, he was wretched. A group would be breakfasting, talking happily about nothing at all, and Reemer would, as it seemed, ride up to the table, anxious to talk about something most abrasively particular. You could hear the snorting of his intellectual charger. Let us, he seemed to be suggesting as he leapt out of the saddle, let us be at exciting odds with one another over politics, education, religion! If he were to eat his usual large breakfast, there must be disputative roughage to help it down! Mr and Mrs Dreary, whose real names we had not picked up, were specially unable to endure this. They were often his victims, and cowered with insipid anger under his assault. They had come to India ready to scorn it. The highlight of the trip for them, so far, had lain in their gratified dislike of the Taj Mahal. That had been an attempt to impress them by an abuse of marble. Given to a low and dispirited level of comment on anything whatever, they were deeply offended by Michael Reemer, who commented only in italics or capital letters. 'That is *marvellous*!' he would cry, if someone had made a breakfast-time remark of a faintly aggressive kind. 'That is MARVELLOUS!' These exclamations were designed to spur others on to be more marvellous still, to make remarks to which powerful exception might be taken. Here came bacon, pancakes, bananas; but how to digest them without a strong dash of offensive utterance, no matter from whom, some bridling

6

or flushing or refusal, frankly, to go along with whatever it was!

'There is no sign,' he said now, glaring at the nearest face of the temple, 'that these people ever engaged in intellectual activity.' He fixed me with a furious eye. He had found me easily fixable in this fashion, and pinned many of his most awkward assertions to some such glare, his eyeball to mine. I thought his students must have fought to occupy a back seat in the lecture theatre, out of his optic range.

'They are certainly not reading books,' I conceded. He laughed scornfully: mine had clearly been a shallow comment.

'Nor,' he said, holding up one finger after another, 'are they playing chess: studying, or practising any form of mathematics: engaged in discussion of any kind . . .' He made the face of a man unwilling to continue to fill in the vacant places in another's imagination. 'I ask you,' he said. 'What are they doing?'

'Tell him,' said the gentleman from Leamington, with unexpected coarseness.

'On the whole,' I said, 'they are' – Laura drifted into earshot – 'pleasuring one another.'

'It is,' said Michael Reemer, 'I accept that it is, the correct description, in the correct words. Here are a rather large number of extremely solid examples of architecture – of a bizarre kind – with *built-in* graffiti – observe the cunning of that . . . And as our friend has implied' – he smiled at me in an unfriendly fashion – 'this immense achievement is dedicated to – what? *Copulation.*'

'You clearly prefer mathematics or chess,' I said.

'I say,' said the gentleman from Leamington. But suddenly Mr Pathan was with us again.

'You are not seeking a distant view,' he said reproachfully.

'Good Lord,' said the gentleman from Leamington. 'So we are not.'

I thought, inevitably, of T. S. Eliot's 'Birth, and copulation, and death' – inevitably, that is, as someone who'd grown up at a time when Eliot's verse had reached the sixth forms of even rather philistine grammar schools, so that my head had been haunted by it for more than five decades: quite apart from the effect that, falling perversely in love (in 1937: I had reason to know that was the year) with the anti-heroine of one of his poems, I'd resolved as soon as possible to share a penny world with a woman who, if it was unlikely that she would precisely be called Pipit, would at least consent to co-exist with me behind a screen. Kate had turned out to be called Kate: but in our earliest desperate lodgings, eleven years after that resolve of mine, we'd eaten, sat to read or listen to music, and on at least one decisive occasion made love, behind a screen, given to us by Kate's mother as a barrier against what must have been the cruellest draughts in East Finchley . . . I couldn't imagine why Michael Reemer was so contemptuous of great buildings that had dedicated their surfaces to one of the supreme human experiences. I was myself an avid reader, would have played chess if I could, and often in the depths of my spirit apologised to Miss Baker, who round about 1929 at Barley Road School had made me a *petit maître* in arithmetic, for not being given to the practice of any form of mathematics: but I did not believe that any of these activities was intrinsically superior to the grave human engagement celebrated in that energetic sandstone.

Well, damn it – what did I mean, 'energetic'? *Joyous* was the word! Whatever doubts I had about the complete felicity of that early Hindu society, this was still a wonderful salute to carnal delight! (Among other things, it made all my attempts to define it seem mealy-mouthed, unsuitably polite.) Being born in London in 1920, and staying there ever since, meant that I'd travelled through several strata of moral geology, and was now barely able to recapture the sensations of sexual ignorance and panic I'd known in childhood and youth (from the influence of which imaginative emancipation and happiness in love would never entirely set me free). In that setting, this moment in 1988 was like a tremendous last-minute carnival, a fabulous loosening: as well as a spectacular late riposte to *joyless* one-time mentors – among them, Percy Chew, the grammar-school headmaster; Sergeant Clinker, who drilled us weekly and took the opportunity of advising us against the use of, interchangeably, catapults and cocks; and my father, who attributed most of the world's ills to an undue interest in what was 'below the navel'. (It was never quite clear to me if the navel itself was implicated in this anathema).

The idea of being happy physically, as opposed to the idea of being physically miserable – *that* shift was one measure only of the movement within those seventy years of existence Kate and I were soon to celebrate. And it was *movement* of which, after being around all that time, I was suddenly and exhilaratingly aware: enormous sensations of things having unfolded, or collapsed, sometimes over and over again . . . Bursting change! Well, we ourselves had been designed and redesigned, latterly at a furious rate: so that sometimes, looking in the mirror, I could not believe what mere months had made of my increasingly helpless physical plasticine!

Kate had taken my arm and was drawing me away across that curiously polite park, populated by those curiously impolite sun-coloured pyramids of carved stone, so that when he reappeared and called us together, we could meet Mr Pathan's eye. He'd been the gentlest of our guides, so far. In Jaipur we'd been a chain-gang for Mr Pram, who'd given us tasks ('You will notice this', 'You will notice that') and, terrifying of moustache, had grilled us on re-assembly. ('You will not have failed to notice . . .' But we had). Mr Pathan made wooing suggestions, like that one of taking a distant view of the temples, and when we failed him was most beautifully sad.

Kate said: 'Do you feel what I feel – something like . . . being a very long way from home, and yet close to it?'

Michael Reemer drifted past. He had the gentleman from Leamington by the elbow.

'Until she took over,' he was bellowing, 'I was ashamed to show my British passport . . .'

'Good Lord,' said the gentleman from Leamington, whom we had reason to know would be seething with political chagrin.

'Never would have guessed,' he'd confided, 'how wearing it could be – I mean, nearly a decade of simple detestation –'

'Not only is it good to be here', said Kate, 'but I'm thinking of several places I'm glad *not* to be. Where are you glad not to be?'

I thought of a number of detestable scenarios. I could be back in a studio with young Mr Broom, who'd wanted my interviews for the book programme to be abruptnesses each exactly four minutes twenty-eight seconds long. On the other hand –

'I'm glad,' I said, 'not to have failed to notice that Arnold Pribble is on the platform, so that I have to travel with him all the way into London.'

# PART ONE

# 1

'Right! Right! Right! Right!' he said. Then, since I was still talking: 'Right! Right! Right!' He thought I was near the end of what I had to say. 'Right, right, right, right, *right*,' he said, smiling immensely.

'But it was a long time ago', I added.

'Right,' said Arnold.

He'd always had the habit of expressing, in this whip-cracking way, his agreement with whatever you were saying: it was a device for hurrying you on, so he could speak instead. Sometimes his eagerness for that, and his lack of eagerness to hear what you had to say, were such that he ran ahead of himself: that stampede of barks of approval would race forward to cover what you'd not yet uttered, the next sentence and the sentence after that.

'Of course,' he said now, grasping my knee in a gesture that I recognised to be a substitute for clapping a hand across my mouth, 'of course, Nell never watches.'

He knew I'd been talking about radio, because it was he who'd introduced the topic. The leap to television, by way of this statement that his wife never watched it, was characteristic. Conversation with Arnold was full of fissures opening up inside the subject you thought you were discussing. It was like crossing an ice-field that was breaking up fast. I didn't believe him about Nell, anyway. I'd noticed he had this trick of

13

attributing to her opinions she'd clearly never held, deeds she'd never performed, simply in order to give a conversation a certain direction. He was ruthless in his exploitation of her, though I must say she seemed to enjoy being subjected to such misuse. Any of his inventions along this line would bring a glow to her face – belonging, I'd sometimes thought, to the bedroom rather than Arnold's study, or their living room, or wherever we'd be sitting.

Before his recent retirement, Arnold had been a successful journalist, writing about economics: was always at conferences, summits, critical encounters between ministers. I didn't read or much understand that sort of thing, and had experience of the flow of his opinion only once or twice a year, over dinner; or, as now, owing to my having stepped on to the platform with insufficient furtiveness, on the train from Barley Wood. I'd never been able to make much of what he had to say, at this professional level. He seemed to take it that you knew everybody and everything. I'd said once, thinking I was teasing him, that if reference books were subject to a selective blight that destroyed all the dictionaries of contemporary biography, he'd be able to replace them out of the contents of his own head; but he seemed to think this no more than a sober appraisal of his mastery of the modern scene. 'Strasbourg,' he'd say. 'Of course, the devious Grundeis!' Attack on your knee. 'You want to know what was said about PSB?' (There were always in his talk thickets, and sometimes forests, of initials.) 'Oddly, oddly, *oddly*' – if this was at his place, he'd thrust a dish of peanuts at you; elsewhere, he'd sketch out the gesture of someone offering you peanuts – 'nothing, nothing, *nothing*.' Immense laughter. A nudge, as if you'd been the author of whatever joke had been made. 'But sharp of you,' he'd say. Over the years I seemed to have built up with him a considerable reputation for acuteness in his own field simply by never managing to deny that I had such and such a thought in mind, usually about someone I'd never heard of.

We were passing through the first of the three stations on this line that, within the last few years, had been burnt down.

14

It had become a feature of local existence, the blazing railway station. Barley Wood itself, one weekend, had been jubilantly consumed: the jubilation being evident from the large number of beercans found among the ruins. The station was central, surrounded by houses, including ours; the unnatural light caused well after midnight by the flames, the sounds of burning, including that of falling roof beams, might have been expected to bring the entire neighbourhood to the spot in its nightwear. Given so much beer, there would presumably have been some sound of carousal too; laughter certainly, perhaps music. Did one dance whilst causing conflagrations on railway property? But no one seemed to have noticed. I didn't know what to make of this. Too much, perhaps, to suppose we'd become a people incapable of being woken by the glare and crackle of burning railway stations. But what else to think?

And dammit, there I was, being Mr Growserish again, perilously close to brandishing my indignant citizen's umbrella as that apoplectic character from Toytown had done on the wireless long ago. 'Disgrrrraceful!' Because you'd come a long way through change after change (well, I'd known Barley Wood station when it was *gas-lit* – my son Tom, who in a year or so would celebrate his fortieth birthday, had as a baby wept from horror at the flarings and mutterings of the gas-jets), there was this tendency to see any difference between past and present as a worsening.

It was what I'd been trying to say to Arnold just now, and he'd been trying to get me to say quicker, quicker, so he could talk instead. He'd asked how I found radio, these days – well-known loss of morale at the BBC – the Government hated it, of course – assembly-line of programmes – pretty dismaying, eh? Arnold's journalistic habit was to have a set of trim ideas about anything whatever, picked up perfectly reputably through reading and listening – all very bright and interested; yet I found I took against this readiness of opinion and crisp informedness of his. He reminded me of a rather nicer man I knew, a young producer in the BBC's World Service, an uncommonly modest highflyer, who had the helpless intellectual habit of providing a theory to cover any phenomenon, however trivial. He'd worked briefly in the corner of the BBC that I worked in as an outside contributor, and I'd been fascinated to observe how Peter's elaborate mind was unable to refrain from high-level analysis of some failure by a secretary to bring up from the canteen the required number of cups of coffee. He would seem to be attempting to set the negligible incident within some extended historical framework – an everyday act of forgetfulness being related to large fluctuations of memory and the failure of memory. I think he did not believe anything was simple, and the appearance of simplicity in an event made him anxious to expose it as the complexity it really was. One secretary, a young woman delightful for her skirts, said to him after one of his explorations of the scarcely explorable: 'Peter, you're a love,' and kissed him boldly. His blush had barely faded before he was wondering aloud, pleasantly, at her choice of a kiss to make the point she was making, though he confessed that he'd not yet worked out, not so much what that point was, but why it needed to be made at this juncture.

Arnold's air of certainty that *this*, and nothing but *this*, was what was happening in radio, and that all who kept themselves abreast with affairs agreed that it was so, made me wish to present some other view. Instead, I found myself saying what had been in my mind recently, how glad I was to have begun broadcasting in the early 1950s, in the schools department, where every script had been minutely discussed, mostly in terms of its being speakable or not, and there'd been rehearsals and . . . And that was where I'd brought myself to a halt, saying it was a long time ago. I didn't want to be swept away by the facile choler of Mr Growser inside me. I knew Arnold was only too ready to abuse today for being today. The last time we'd caught the same train he'd launched an attack on graffiti; which had made me imagine one of those actions I was, alas, too infuriatingly good-natured, or perhaps supine, to commit. I wanted to lean forward and say that across the

16

surface of almost everything I'd ever said to him over the years Arnold had scrawled his 'Right! Right! Right!' 'Oral graffiti, wouldn't you agree! I'd say you operate the most promiscuous aerosol in the history of vandalism!' – and I'd make a gesture as of someone withholding peanuts from another.

I noticed at that moment that on the railway embankment we were passing someone had painted, in thrilling blue, across ten yards of concrete, PISS OFF EVERYONE.

Arnold was saying: '. . . as you'll not need to be told, going down and down and down . . .' I nodded. Where was he now? Was this some fresh allegation about Nell – had he found it convenient, in the context of what he was saying, to claim that she'd taken up potholing? It would not be his wildest invention. But even if I hadn't been thinking of other things, I found it easy nowadays not to hear what was being said to me. I wanted to laugh sometimes, catching myself, talked to across a dining table or from seat to seat in a railway carriage, turning my head this way and that, subtly altering its inclination, enlarging or reducing the size of the horn my hand made at my ear; altogether as if I were some rough-and-ready radar dish.

The train was slowing now alongside one of the windiest platforms in London. *That* wasn't Growser speaking. British Rail's recent efforts of modernisation had seemed to be devoted to the preservation and improvement of this great gathering-place of the city's draughts. Where it was at its worst, they'd placed seats, offering for much of the year a peculiarly cruel form of uncomfortable comfort. A bit of Growser in *that*, perhaps. I rose.

'This is where I get off,' I said.

'Right! Right! Right! Right!' said Arnold.

And here I was, in the Underground – and Growser at my elbow, ready to shout his head off as these tiring tunnels encouraged him to do.

Well, there'd been the misery, two or three years long, of splendid improved new escalators being installed; and the misery since then, of the splendid improved new escalators

17

being constantly out of service. There'd been the dilapidation and, on top of that, the dilapidation of the creeping measures taken to remove the dilapidation. (We were ruled by those who travelled by car, Growser would rage, and knew nothing of public transport, equating it with an alien race who, in using it, did not use the car.) Then there was the overcrowding – this morning was a prime example of it, so that everyone looked forward to an ultimate disaster, when our surge down to the platforms where too few trains were awaited by too many would result in the front ranks pitching forward onto the lines. It was all too melodramatic, *that* fear of yours, you'd thought; until in those everyday intestines of the town, fire had exploded and human beings with it.

Even Mr Growser fell silent at the thought of that.

There were times, and this morning was certainly one of them, when travelling on an up escalator that chanced to be working, I imagined that the escalator coming down (which chanced not to be working, so that those on it had a preposterous air of agitation, each step they took seeming to make them laboriously and joltingly rise and fall – so startling was the absence of the expected silky descent) was being used by satirists and other great persons whose amazement at the scene I longed to witness. Jonathan Swift would be in the lead, and they'd tail off, upwards, by way of William Morris, Samuel Butler and . . . *there* was John Dryden! And William Langland, just visible as he stepped onto the top stair! There'd be time for a quick word with Swift, who'd ask for a brief account of the society that tolerated such wearisomeness. His own had not been averse to causing discomfort, he'd say, but there was a difference between cruelty and cruelty; this of ours seemed that of people ingenious enough to avoid it, if they wished to. But, I'd say, the very matter of our being a society had been questioned. The Dean would open an amazed mouth, but I'd have been driven onwards by a helpless scrum of fellow-travellers.

As it happened, this morning at the foot of the escalator there was an Irish harpist, and the sweetness of the sounds he made had a remarkable effect on the shabby scene. Those on the down escalator (not an obvious satirist among them) wore looks of astonished pleasure. The small sounds, magnified by the sheer space, filled the cavernous air with tiny, happy dances. Having passed a noticeboard announcing the authority's implacable opposition to the performance of music anywhere on the Underground, people were melted. I found myself smiling as if I were suddenly on some ideal holiday, I wasn't sure where, but I thought a pleasant green mountain came into it somewhere. And as two policemen added themselves to those trudging downwards and the atmosphere of delight turned slowly but distinctly to hisses (which made the policemen assume the sheepish expression of those who know they are foolishly engaged), I observed that the cloth the young musician had spread at his elbow sparkled with silver.

# 2

Young Mr Broom said: 'I want simple and direct questions.'

I liked him. A quiet, earnest man. He had taken charge of the book programme I presented. The problem was that he insisted on a view of our task with which I had no sympathy at all. By 'simple and direct' he meant rapidly editable, and making no prolonged claim on the listener's attention. It had been quite suddenly decided that listeners no longer had the elastic minds that broadcasting had once assumed in them; they were now persons suffering from gravely limited mental endurance, together with a simply vast general ignorance. They switched on for a book programme, but could not be expected to know who Shakespeare was, or Henry James.

'Not too much *literature*,' young Mr Broom had murmured, as if the producer of the daily weather forecast had said: 'And not too much about sunshine or rain and that sort of thing . . .' 'I want at most four . . . or five *simple*, *direct* questions.'

He had a perhaps nervous, certainly tactless, tendency to say he *wanted* things. It was, come to that, a simple, direct tactlessness. If I had been only my father's son, I'd have roared at him out of the rage that filled me. How *dared* he talk like that to someone who'd been doing the programme for a dozen years and more, and broadcasting since . . . Great inward spluttering! But I was also my mother's son, and was worried about young Mr Broom being shy and uncertain under that

. . . Good Lord, *disgraceful insolence*! And perhaps there *was* a case for greater simplicity and a going straighter for the target; and perhaps, as an interviewer, I *was* too oblique, too inclined to spread myself, too apt to abandon such questions as I'd prepared in favour of following up unexpected responses. Too exploratory.

I'd grown to love interviewing – having read a book, to talk of it with the author, with a kind of impressionism that arose from my being interested in it, because I'd read it, and the author being interested in it, because he or she had written it. You had a limited time, it was a limited encounter (though not the terrible little snapped exchange Mr Broom *wanted*), and the pleasure was to attempt to capture, in that brevity, the characters of book and author, together, the nature of this marriage between producer and product.

Mr Broom was morose, this morning, because of that interview we'd recorded with the Irish novelist, in her mid-eighties, one of the youngest women I'd ever met, and not to be contained within any simplicity, perfectly immune to directness. We'd gone to the London flat where she was visiting. An essential part of the interview (Mr Broom fidgety) had lain in talking to her in the kitchen, and having some little comedy of convenient seating in the living room (so that the microphone could be moved by the producer from one speaker to the other). I don't know how we got on to the subject of peeing, but she said she and her brother, seventy years earlier, had had contests to see who could pee further, and of course he'd always won. It seemed he'd taken advantage of her not at that stage understanding that, if creation had had such competitions in mind, it had fitted him for them better than it had fitted her. I'd thought, as a brother, how I must have exploited my sister Betty in similar fashion. Well, not in our case in such micturatory Olympics, but in the keeping of diaries, for example. I kept my own (doomed little diarist from about eight years onwards), and insisted on keeping Betty's too, on the grounds that she would fail to rise to the interesting challenge of it. (Mr Broom looked at his watch.) That was the only one of my interviews (when we'd got down to it) in which the answer to a question had begun: 'Dear heart . . .' I knew Mr Broom would cut this out, as not being a form of address listeners would expect, given their current tendency to puzzlement and panic. I'd said I thought she must be a happy writer; but she said no, she dreaded the act of writing – 'When I'm writing, I'm *Mrs Grim*!' She talked beguilingly, but neither simply nor directly, of her earliest novels, written under a pen-name because she very much wanted to go on being danced with by attractive young men, and your attractive young man in Ireland in the 1920s was unlikely to dance with a young woman who'd been so unfeminine as to publish a book.

Mr Broom had said that was fine, though I knew he meant he'd much rather have had a quick confession on her part (responding to questions from me delivered much like bullets by a firing-squad) that she was Irish, and eighty-five, and that the plot of her new novel was as follows. 'Let the young person go,' she'd murmured, and Mr Broom had not hesitated to leave; and she said then that I was clearly in need of a sip of whisky (or two), and no, she would not leave me to sip alone.

It was fine, said Mr Broom again, now, but there had been twenty minutes of it, when all he wanted was four minutes and twenty-eight seconds, and we'd laughed a lot, which was all very well but made editing *very* difficult: and he'd like to say again that what he *wanted* was a sawn-off approach, not your roundaboutness and your questions growing out of answers and your assumption that because this was a programme about books, listeners were interested in . . . He did not have time to say 'books', because I was suddenly swamped by my father, and went off and resigned. I returned to find Mr Broom startled and distressed and, swamped by my mother, went off and withdrew my resignation, confusedly making it plain that I meant to carry on as before (if only because I could not have done the other, chilly thing), and that it was, of course, *his* programme, and I did see that it might be a problem, taking it over when it had such a ponderous sitting tenant as I was.

22

My mother squeezed my hand: *That bloody tolerance of yours*, said my father.

It was true, of course, that it was Mr Broom's programme. The producer, in the end, was accountable. It was like some complication of marriage; for a good many years, a succession of courteous producers had made it possible for me to feel we were both, presenter and producer alike, the programme's true spouse. Tactfully, no indecorous sense of the marital bed being over-occupied was allowed to emerge. But while Mr Broom remained, the scene was bound to be one of sordid struggle; I attempting to remain in bed, Mr Broom trying to relegate me to what he saw as a more suitable setting, the floor. I'd go on enjoying myself still, despite him. But it would be enjoyment framed with rage.

And dammit, I did like him. He was so eager to make something of the programme! He wanted it tight, and precise, and unshadowy.

'We'll aim at something . . . middling-complex, half-direct,' I said. He made a face.

'I want you to know that I do respect your work,' he said. Oh Lord, what could I say? I liked his taste in jackets, but it might not help to mention that now. I could tell him about Kate saying . . . But his face was not at the moment framed for jokes.

It had been one of those occasions, increasingly occurring, when a simple word eluded me. It happened to us both, and sometimes became entangled with that other problem: that you'd be dashing upstairs with some clear urgent aim and, at the very moment of arrival, discover you hadn't the faintest idea what you were doing. Your head had emptied. At the end of that purposeful bounding from stair to stair you were stranded, and your ordinary healthy sense of intention replaced by utter foolish blankness. It could happen the other way round: resolute in the bedroom, you'd end up bewildered in the kitchen. Running down to reproduce the situation in which the forgotten aim had been conceived, I had even passed Kate running up with a similar intention.

23

In that recent case of the lost word, it had been a matter of naming the . . . She was wearing it.

'Don't tell me,' I said. 'I'll get it. At the moment, what I'm thinking of is . . . jacket. But it's not a jacket, is it?'

'Oh dear,' said Kate. 'Then it would have been Ravel's *Jacket*.'

It certainly wasn't the moment to mention boleros to Mr Broom, given the Latin-American novelist who was coming in to be interviewed at the end of the week. 'A surprising man, as subtle as you'd expect,' I'd said. 'You have to play a game with him if you want an interview worth having.' And then I'd observed the horror on Mr Broom's face, and realised I'd sketched out the worse of all scenarios. An interview as a game – Ye Gods! However would you edit that?

Well, I thought as I walked through the long open office the whole department shared, like a great working dormitory, editing had always been the crux of it. The willingness of the producer to labour over the transformation of the raw matter of an interview, shaping it into an item approximately five minutes long. Everywhere in that office, producers doing something like this: sitting at their editing machines, cut off by earphones from the world, stopping, using a razor, sealing an edit, reflecting, going back and then back again to assess a passage.

I was still thinking of them as I plunged back into the Underground. What did that collective intent anxiety of theirs suggest? Surely it was that of a whole tribe of wireless operators sending out SOSs from whole fleets of sinking ships.

# 3

No. If anyone was sinking, it was I.

Kate had lately seemed to fear that I was actually, physically, doing that. I was letting my head droop, she delicately hinted. Bending, somewhat, as I ate. Her delicacy was never enough to prevent anger from flaring up, at once. Partly that was because my father had discussed me so frequently in terms of my spine, the length of my pace when walking ('Don't drag your feet!'), what he saw as my actual eagerness to have the whole apparatus, to which he'd devoted a great deal of concern and money over the years – to have it, from the head he personally kept shorn to the feet in passionately shiny shoes ('You can't call *them* polished! Do them again!'), reduced to a slump of flesh, a . . . Well, what he feared, I suspect, was that one day he'd look across the breakfast table and find he was father to a hunchback. 'That boy's going to end up a hunchback!' I don't think he ever believed that hunchbacks were unlucky victims of some original mishap in their making. They were persons whose fathers had failed in their duty of barking at regular intervals: *'For God's sake, stand straight!'*

Now, for a horrid moment or so, I'd sulkily suggest that Kate's reference to my posture was partly an effect of some fault of vision in herself. She'd always had this weakness in making a distinction between those who slumped and those who bore themselves perfectly well; I'd noticed it over the years, but not mentioned it till now out of hopeless kindness. Kate would retort that the time had come when she must point to a defect of character in me that she'd been silent about too long, out of a mistaken wish to protect my feelings: I couldn't take criticism. I would laugh hollowly, especially if I'd just had a book out and hardly dared to open a newspaper for fear of its either not being reviewed, or of its being reviewed.

We would pass on swiftly to general hints that affection had been foully withdrawn, there'd been a collapse of the good taste that had made it possible for one to like and admire the other . . . At which point we'd find the mechanical little comedy impossible to endure without laughing. 'Oh what idiots!' It worried us, though, that these squibs of fury lay so close to the skin: one unwary word, and you were a walking November the fifth, with rockets of rage shooting out of your head. Growing old, you seethed with the unresolved apoplexies of childhood and youth.

And anyway, how odd, now I thought of it, that my father should have denounced me for drooping, and my schoolfriend Ray Bolton's mother should have arraigned me for standing pretentiously upright. I remembered the schoolboys' quarrel we had had one long summer holiday, when quarrelling was the last pleasure left to resort to, and how we'd exchanged, between our house and his in the next road, with much snapping of letter boxes, communications in which we glanced at each other's frailties; and Ray had written, 'My mother says you walk about stiffly as if you had a poker down your back. She says lots of people say that. She says you are haughty, and she doesn't know what you've got to be haughty about.' Well, of course, I had nothing whatever to be haughty about. It was difficult to scrape together a reason for being haughty if you were a fifteen year old liable to have his hair cut without warning by a father for whom this was only a first step; it would be followed up with a ruthless inspection of your wardrobe, an inquiry in depth into your recent behaviour at a moral level, and the suggestion that if you thought Williams, the English master, wanted you to go to university for your sake, you were to be pitied for naïvety. Williams was simply interested in his own career, which would benefit if he managed to secure the dispatch in that pretentious direction even of entirely unsuitable material like yourself. Disqualified, in the first place, by slumping.

'But,' Ray had said when we had engineered a reconciliation (neither wishing to go alone to a film we'd enormously looked forward to), 'you are a bit stuck-up . . . I don't mean *I* think you are stuck-up, but some people might think you are, when you talk about books. You know? I mean, you are a bit rough on me when I don't know who wrote the book I'm reading.'

Poor Ray! I remembered the priggish rage that caused me, his never knowing if he was indebted for his current literary pleasure to Charles Dickens or Jeffrey Farnol. Because I didn't want to quarrel (at any rate, not until it became a necessary way of passing time on a long holiday), I'd try not to ask Ray about authors – but some dogged little rage in me, caused by the difficulty I had in understanding how anyone could be incurious about such a matter (how *could* you not care?) would again and again make me cry, 'Who wrote it then?' And we'd be prickly, and a weekend would be spoilt.

Nearing seventy, I found so often that . . . Oh, it was like discovering an unexploded bomb many years after the end of war. As recently, when Kate, with perfect wisdom – and, as it happened, with absolute delicacy – had got rid of the piano.

I'd had no access to a piano for a long period, fifteen years or so, after we were married. Then we'd moved to a new house and it seemed the moment to bring the piano back into our lives. Well, strictly, into mine. Perhaps the children might learn; perhaps Kate would take it up again. I, of course, would continue playing where I'd left off. The piano would take its place among our furniture, amounting to some kind of assertion. *Here is music*, it would say, quietly and pleasantly, but firmly.

It turned out to be an assertion much grander than I'd hoped. Well, baby-grander. It was black, and had belonged to a young composer, selling it because . . . It wasn't quite clear why he was selling it. Slow to hear truly what I heard, I thought after a month or so that it was because the sound was plummy and limited. A good upright would have been better. But it had this splendid shape, and this impressive blackness, and enabled me to fumble with Beethoven again, and falter with Chopin, and make ragged dashes at Schubert, and fervently mangle Liszt. I was happy, for a while; but then the dreadful distance between my performances and any halfways decent notion of what the music should sound like made itself more and more apparent. I began to hate the musical ignorance that now seemed as much part of my fingers as their bones were. Indeed, they were nothing but disobedient bones. I played less and less. And as the years passed, Kate sensibly began to urge (one tiny, kind hint followed at a humane distance by another) that better uses could be made of the space occupied by what had become a large useless black piece of non-furniture. I held some position, never clearly stated, as of one possessing secret information that at any moment the piano would turn out to be marvellously serviceable. Oh, one shouldn't prejudice this possibility, and I'd rather talk of something else. I made as little as I could of what had become my true reasons for keeping it. First, that it still said, *Here is music*, although this was plainly untrue, or might have been replaced with the less attractive statement: *Here is a means, which small grandchildren can barely believe is offered to them, of making horrible noises either deafeningly bass or ear-achingly treble*. My second reason for wishing to keep it was that its top, closed, made a marvellous and romantic surface on which to place Christmas cards, or glasses and bottles at a party. It was as if Beethoven silently underwrote our silliest moments.

Kate wore me down, subtly, sensibly. She had plans for the space. Over the years she contrived to build up, as against the growing obviousness of my poor reasons for keeping the piano, the greater obviousness of her good reasons for getting rid of it. No one could have proceeded with more tender determination. And late in the day she hit upon a reason more difficult than the rest to deal with. She pointed out that the piano would be serving music, as it was designed to do, better in some household inclined to play it, than in a household with the strongest inclination to refrain from doing so. In short, I was holding a piano captive and standing between it and its natural destiny.

The end came quickly. No, I murmured, I wouldn't mind, I really wouldn't mind. Within days Kate had run down a family of small children, seven or eight of them, I vaguely gathered, all musically promising, all desperate for a piano. They would be coming to take it away . . . on Saturday.

I didn't know what was happening to me. If anything, it was like providing accommodation for a waterspout. Somewhere inside me, this formed and gushed upwards. It wept its way through my breast and then reached my eyes. I was sobbing. I had been hijacked by sobs. Altogether I was being possessed by a great stormy despair that was wholly beyond my understanding. I wept an apology, and made my way into the garden. I sobbed among the bushes. And when I could, furious with myself, I went back into the house to apologise to Kate. She must not be upset. I had indeed said I was ready to let the piano go. I had not changed my mind about that. It did not appear to be my mind that was involved. I was in the grip of some deep emotion that seemed to have no context, had forced itself upon me without a moment's warning. It was a ridiculous uncontrollable weeping of the same order as sneezing.

This speech of mine was a curious one: half of it a level, sensible statement, half of it . . . well, ridiculously I could stand aside and define those sounds myself . . . heart-rending sobs. 'I haven't cried like this since I was a boy', I said to Kate, speaking out of the composed side of myself, truly surprised, and very distressed to have alarmed her.

Not since I was a boy. In the end, that seemed to me to be the clue. Here I was, in my sixties, a man with some worldly experience, a distinct sense of irony, given to critical self-observation; and I was shaken with grief like an adolescent. It seemed to me that indeed the tears were not those of the ageing man; inside me, an old self (in fact, a very young self), who might have been considered long dead, was making himself felt as if he still, absolutely, incorrigibly, existed.

I worked it out slowly. He was the boy with the desperate need to feel he belonged to the worlds of literature and music. He lived in a household with no experience of these, and a habit of mocking them. My father, who bought a piano at last out of the vaguest notion that it was an element in the polite middle-class life he believed I and my sister were headed for, had a detestation of the music I sought to play on it which he once expressed in the complaint, 'All you ever play is bloody funeral marches!' My struggle for another sort of life must have had, at its centre, preposterously, this possession of a piano, and the defiant (and appalling) performance on it of the music my father abhorred. And in a sense it wasn't an argument about music; it was a war between passionately different political viewpoints. To my father, this music stood for all the incomprehensible things that, if known about, appeared to strengthen his enemies, the educated. To me, feverishly half-educated, this music was a promise that I might not have to live as my father had done, warring endlessly with the very notion that one might traffic in ideas, or in ambitious forms of entertainment or delight.

And, *damn it*, after all these years of living – imperfectly but distinctly – as I had yearned to do, still the way the quarrel had revolved round the possession of a piano had been capable of reducing me to tears; to the actual sobbing, not of a man in his sixties, but of a sixteen year old. I know what an adolescent breaking his heart sounds like, and that's what I sounded like.

What other wild old weather lay within us, waiting for a freak coincidence of winds to blow and storm again?

30

# 4

The foolish things you found you were asking yourself! 'Are my dreams becoming narrower?' the grumbling in my head demanded as I walked down Kingsway, bound for young Mr Broom and his dissatisfactions. I could tell the second fruit stall on the left, tucked between the church and the bank, had Gallia melons for sale: the smell was coming towards me, a whole sweeter world in the air. 'I mean, they were always B features, but now they're monotonously about losing things and never finding them again.'

Last night's, for example. As usual, the geography had been elastic. I'd lost my way, but there was no telling what my way was. It was a sort of town, but invented itself as I went. At some rough turnstile, in the shadow of a building that was half palace, half department store, I took my shoes off, and waded through mud. My destination was obvious. It was at the end of a wavering vista, and I set off towards it: but, with exquisite exactness, the entrance to a tunnel appeared before me: I stepped into it and straight onto a spiral staircase, that rose into what suggested itself as much more than the usual amount of upper air. I now remembered that I had left my raincoat behind. I turned, but was at once on the edge of a vast slope of mud, over which floodwater ran white and deep, racing towards a mud-brown sea that filled the space towards the infinitely distant horizon and (since an horizon couldn't accommodate the horrifying sense of unlimitedness) beyond. There was nothing but water, and I was walking with others towards what promised to be a shallow stretch but immediately declared itself as unfathomably deep. I realised that I had lost my shoes. Absurdly, at that distant dry moment, I had taken my shoes off and then forgotten them, and now I was walking towards that endlessness of furiously flowing water, and was shoeless.

It was the need to pee that woke me. Always I tried to disobey the summons. If I curled up in a certain fashion the need would vanish. Then I'd remember that it wouldn't: and, surly, I got out of bed. The sense of surliness seemed to be something I was wearing. I was heavily clad in it.

I hated the way the middle of the night did this to you. I didn't care for being surly; but if the middle of the night wanted you surly, surly you'd be. As I peed in the hesitant manner that had lately become natural, although perhaps it had been going on for years, I was able to remember the last few feet of the dream. I thought of it as a film, always, a spool in the mind. Usually when I stood there, begging my bladder to get on with it, the film effaced itself, there was just a tantalising flutter of movement, the last and most useless traces of a narrative. But if you could remember the last few feet and grab hold of them and pull, cunningly enough, it might come back. This time it did. I thought with bleak irony that at least on this occasion I hadn't lost my luggage. Usually I had masses of it, suitcases vaguely galore, and I'd put it down in a pause in that endless walking that dreams imposed upon you, and had gone on, and later realised I hadn't got it; and would try to return for it, but the geography remained restlessly inventive and made no provision for return journeys to exact spots. In dreams, there was a terrifying absence of exact spots. Well, the point about life was that you had this constant illusion of being able to navigate from one particular place to another. If you lost your raincoat (that repetitively mislaid raincoat!) there was, at worst, the Lost Property Office. Dreams made it clear that, when you moved an inch beyond superficial realism, Lost

Property Offices . . . lost their purpose. They simply could not be found. If found, they certainly would not contain any property that had actually been lost. Unable ever to go back, doomed incessantly to invent, a dream would fill a Lost Property Office with anything but the precise lost property that people had come looking for. Property that was lost in a dream was irretrievably lost. If ever it was found again, it would be in an Irretrievably Lost Property Office . . .

I'd made my way back to bed. The route through the upper floor of the house was short and profoundly familiar, but I had an awful sense of its being, in its plain way, no better than the tortuous journeys one made through dreams. Here was the bedroom door. Here was the need to attempt to close it with a steady slowness, so as not to wake Kate. Too often, caution led to the sharp snap you were aiming to avoid. Not that it ever woke Kate. I was married to an extremely skilful sleeper. I wouldn't go so far as to lay on an experiment (at least I didn't think I would, though perhaps the collapse of good sense threatened in ageing would tempt you even to that), but I'd thought it might be interesting to establish whether fireworks would wake Kate. There'd been an enormous hurricane and trees had crashed down along the lane we lived in, and the wind had howled immensely, and Kate had continued to sleep. I'd ask her once if she realised that she would never make the heroine of a Gothic novel, because no amount of bad behaviour on the part of the elements, backed up by vampires, would restore her to consciousness in time to take part in the action; and she was displeased.

Back in bed I'd thought that the awful thing about the night was that the world, which made sense only if you used it, was being unused. Everywhere around me, houses, roads, considerable stretches of fields; and nobody doing anything with them. What was the point of it all when for large stretches of time, as the ageing person with a failing bladder became aware, it served no purpose whatever! In Barley Green Road, which in a few hours would be so busy as to suggest some form of social insanity, the traffic lights would be carefully blinking through their repertoire, red, amber, green, and little interest would be shown. It was precisely what went on in dreams. In them, the busy apparatus of the day was allowed to provide substantial images, but what dreams said was that all activity was beside the point. In the end, for all of us, it would be drowning by floods that had always lain in wait, or arrival at some busy traffic system, with immense blinkings, and great gesticulations by direction boards and signposts: but nothing, nothing would be happening.

Surely other people had truly inventive dreams of which they could be proud, *Gone with the Wind* every night, with *Les Enfants du Paradis* to give the programme weight? The inward scriptwriter was of the best quality. My dreams showed no evidence of having been written at all. They were the work of some inward hooligan, in fact, who took the incidents and furniture of my life, past and present, and threw it around, carelessly. If dreams were reviewed, mine would be wearily slammed . . . raincoats, briefcases, elastic landscapes, the mixture as before.

Kate said dreaming about losing things was an obvious expression of anxiety. In that case I was simply anxious, a person dedicated to anxiety, a full-time worrier, and not much more.

And then I'd drifted half asleep again, and a scene appeared that was out of my past, out of wartime. It was the river, the Thames, we were driving alongside it in an immense lorry, the actual lorry of that time monstrously expanded, it was full of wheat, we were delivering it to the docks, the river was full of small neat fish, there was a tremendous smell of . . . It was a huge sweetness in the air . . . And I woke, and remembered a precise morning when we'd made that journey, perhaps it was 1944, and as we looked down at the river we saw a school of condoms swimming steadily towards Westminster. I had never held, let alone used, a condom – this at twenty-four! – would I never cease to rage at the absurdity of my sexually desolate youth? – and Jim Mead, driving our lorry, told me what they were. Accident or air raid must have spilled a consignment of them into the Thames. Then we came to the warehouses, of great height, lanes lined with them, like back-to-back castles, and from them came the simple smell of . . .

Oranges!

In the war, I think, no oranges arrived there, but we believed at the time that the smell, laid down over a century or more, was ineradicable. Lately Kate and I had gone sniffing for it, and it wasn't there any more.

I thought in that snatch of a dream about the river I'd actually avoided losing anything; but then remembered the fish. The fish were clearly a substitute for the condoms, and the allegation the dream was making was fairly clear.

I'd once lost something like five thousand condoms.

# 5

*Row row row the boat*
*Gently down the stream*
*Merrily merrily merrily merrily*
*Life is but a dream . . .*

The thesis was offered, with blinks and what I can only call bold blushes, by a grandson, who attended a nursery that seemed to have made him, at three, a small Cecil Sharp, a collector of wisps of song. Some were famously jocular, buoyant, impertinent, but he brought to them all a quality as of faintly incredulous melancholy. He'd sing a version of 'Daisy, Daisy', remarkably abbreviated, that broke my heart. Kate was teaching him 'Any Old Iron'. Her singing of *that* had always been the first sign that anarchy was brewing in our household, the Lord of Misrule was at the door; she'd taught it to our sons, and was now inducting a new generation, but this grandson was putting his mark on it; singing it most sweetly in a fashion that would have made 'The Ashgrove', by comparison, seem boisterous.

With a reservation or two, I agreed with my descendant about the entanglement of life and dream. Certainly in respect of the scarcely rational way in which people appeared and reappeared. I'd been reading my diaries for 1940, for example, in which there was constant reference to my friend Tom Sadler; I hadn't seen him for years, and now, like any figure conjured up by a dream – the process clear enough: you'd touched a button that had caused related buttons to operate – he made himself visible. And to increase the impression of buttons being sensitive to other buttons, our encounter occurred in Barton's new shopping precinct.

I'd been trying to work out which of the shops was standing on the site of Sergeant Clinker's house. He'd drilled us in a persecutory way at the grammar school in the early 1930s, before the new school was built and its having a gymnasium made him irrelevant. Underneath the precinct lay the historically unthrilling foundations of the Royal Army Pay Corps barracks; Sergeant Clinker had lived there in a grace-and-favourish way, though he'd have been impatient with so flighty an account of his right of residence. To any airiness of language he was quite terrifyingly opposed; almost any remark addressed to him by a boy was declared out of order for some whiff of verbal perfume he'd discern in it.

'Shall we talk like men?' he'd say, rather often to Tom Sadler, who had a natural sweetness to which the sergeant took special exception.

'Why does he pick on *me*?' Tom would ask.

'Just growl. He likes that. Growl at him,' I remember a classmate saying once, impatiently. You growled at the sergeant, cut language to the bone, took care not to smile. Smiled at, he'd recoil as if you were making a direct attempt to enrol him in those boyish depravities from which he believed Friday afternoon drill provided our one healthy respite. But Tom had no gift for being curt and unsmiling. His habit was to be roundabout, and to seek the affection of an interlocutor with polite phrases, twinklings, small jokes. For Tom, every day was St Valentine's Day, and every other human being was his Valentine. With the moral elasticity of an eleven or twelve year old, I managed to be Tom's friend, and at the same time to feel something of the scorn that was felt for him by the sergeant, and by our classmates who were made impatient by

Tom's failure to talk to the sergeant as he required to be talked to.

The dreadful intolerance of the young for those who lack skill in dissimulation!

The new precinct (that itself surely a dissimulatory use of a word, with its holy undertone) would have enraged the sergeant. And there were moments, nearly sixty years on, when I felt closer to him than I'd have wished. He'd have hated the way the precinct begged to be loved and favoured, its air of cajolery, the insistence with which it smiled at those who'd ventured into, and might even safely venture out of, the web it had stickily prepared. I thought the foundations of the sergeant's home must have lain under a new shop offering a cavernous display of greetings cards. Alongside the making of cards in improbable quantities seemed to go now the making of occasions when they might be purchased. There were three such shops here, all everlastingly crammed. Huge numbers of my fellow-townspeople appeared to feel a non-stop need to send cards to everyone they knew.

But perhaps the shops had already created an appetite for sending cards to strangers?

But I couldn't believe *that* insanity would last, and I thought the new shop like others in the precinct might well have opened with a closing-down sale. In the new Barton, shops seemed like lemmings. Regularly, large numbers of them threw themselves to their deaths; in terms of the assertions that filled their windows, as eager in their going as in their coming. Such a terrific enthusiasm of collapse!

It was now that Tom appeared; suddenly, in the crowd, a familiar stranger. Odd how you feel about transformations in those you've known most of your life! A tall slender boy had taken the opportunity of my looking the other way to become a bent, bulky old man. He'd been moving in that direction when I'd last seen him, ten years or so earlier; but now the disguise was complete. Though it wasn't a disguise so much as the submission of the original body to uncouth expansions and distortions. Some darkness dragged at his face; if he smiled now, it would be against its whole drift. I saw him recognise me and then attempt to cancel the look of recognition. But I said: 'Tom!'

'First time in this place. And last time,' he said.

'But where have you been? Why haven't I seen you around for so long?'

'Oh, I don't go in for being around,' said Tom. 'I stay away from things as much as I can.'

'Family's well?'

'Yes.' He was evasive, as if he might have murdered them all and buried them in the back garden. 'Yes.'

'You never liked going out, I know – but this is ridiculous. Have you got time now for a drink and a talk?'

I might have invited him to come along and be hanged.

'No. No,' he said. 'You do that – go and talk. I hear you doing that on the radio.' It was an accusation. He was already moving away. 'I like to get home as quickly as possible.'

And he'd gone.

This was someone I'd known for over half a century, and who, in the spring of that appalling year, 1940, had overcome his reluctance for what he then called 'bloody hiking' and walked with me into the country on several weekends, along lanes and across fields, all waiting for the war to declare its hideous shape.

On the afternoon of Saturday 18 May 1940, I 'spirited myself away with TS, into a spendthrift summer of fields and glowing trees and cuckoos, and dingy little boats on the poisonous waters of Johnson's Lake, and the couples in the grass, making T and me so hungry'.

I have these diaries, which then I made for myself out of typing paper cut small and bound, alas, in the wrenched-off covers of despised books of appropriate size. (So that from 15 March to 10 April my diary might have been taken to be *Saints in Society* by Margaret Baillie-Saunders, and from 20 May to 13 July *The Making of Modern Egypt*, by Sir Auckland Colvin.) I was a reporter on a weekly newspaper, the *Monmouth*

*Hill Gazette*, and had been elaborately jilted by Tess Grayson, whom I'd loved very much indeed for a year and a half, and still loved, and who had suddenly married a man of whom she'd spoken once or twice, disparagingly. Had, she'd told me, to endure going out with him, in his despicably splendid sports car, and had spilt ice cream – and, later, coffee – over his naval uniform. Well, he was a lieutenant-commander, how absurd! Very public school! No poetry in him at all! Being with him, so complacent, made her long to be with me, so . . . (She failed to define what it was that made me his superior, but it was understood between us: it was a matter of my being ill-at-ease, all over the place, and, as to poetry, fairly stuffed with it.) On the tail of her latest comment of this kind came the news of her marriage. It was provided by her father, in the form of a copy of a newspaper containing an account of it. He'd been deeply opposed to our association: 'Cub reporter', Tess said he'd called me, with such an emphasis as amounted to the allegation that I was, in fact, an immature creature of a species not human, and for that reason alone unfit to enter into alliance with the Graysons. *'Dear cub!'* she'd written as the circumstances of war slowly assembled themselves in the weeks after September 1939, and had almost at once given herself to a man in respect of whose clothing she appeared to have the instincts of a vandal.

The usual agonies of being rejected (in my case leading to an outbreak of a disorder called angio-neurotic oedema, the effect of which was to convert the sufferer into a single stupendous blister) were compounded when I received a message from Tess, assuring me that the wedding had been a form of deliberate mistake. There'd been enormous pressure from her family, she'd feared that countering it might be too much for an unworldly person like myself, and I should hang on; there would be further developments of a kind that might well restore my cheerfulness. With this maddening hint that she'd married as a mere trick for changing and strengthening her finger-hold on the cliff-face of love, she went off to Scotland, where, in one of the more militant lochs, her husband had a command

40

she was vague about; being bound, it seemed, not only by the oath of marriage but by another requiring her to say almost nothing about anything. 'But hush-hush has never been our way, and soon, soon, *soon* we'll be able to say whatever we like to each other – and not a bit of gold braid in sight.'

It didn't seem much of a forecast of the year that was unfolding, as I made my little diaries and hid myself inside them.

How easy to see it now as the comedy it was! But first love, I suspect, may be clothed from head to foot in farce, and often is, but still be profoundly earnest: in some important sense, true; a wise form of idiocy and a silliness of which one's glad to have been part. Fifty years later, looking back, you see the comic bones of it. But these diaries restore to me those old emotions that drew, in the first place, so much on the sheer energy and novelty of being young! In no time at all we forget what that was like! We're composed, then, of possibilities; inhabiting a world that is a prospectus entirely, with everything to be arranged. And those are our first adult seasons! That most terrible year, 1940, provided a summer of very great beauty, and from the diary I rediscover the extent to which, when so young, you *are* the weather. The absurd boy I was is difficult to disentangle from the skies (full of barrage balloons, 'like elephants aloft'), the leaves, the flowers of a season on which he commented with a dazzled sort of dread: 'This ripening summer,' he wrote, 'means the deepening war.'

He was not happy reporting. The *Monmouth Hill Gazette* was edited by Mr Trout, a man most deeply banal. He regarded the newspaper as a pillar of patriotism and wove his own testy loyalties into reports of any occasion that seemed less than rowdily supportive of the war effort. When the reports were mine, he claimed the right to put his mark on them. We clashed about this again and again, and particularly when it came to a meeting addressed by a pacifist Member of Parliament, Reginald Sorensen.

I'd gone to that with Jenny Lawrence, from the rival newspaper. To Jenny I was drawn for her companionship (we

41

covered the district together, despite the rivalry between our papers), and for her hair, which was thick and fair, and her bright face, and her legs, and, with indescribable vagueness, for the rest of her, I guess, my ignorance of which was quite as profound as if I'd had no even academic understanding of what it amounted to, in terms of this or that arrangement of physical items. My affair with Tess Grayson, for all its intensity, had been passion without practice. Odd to remember how easily it could be so then, when practice was accompanied by such perils and sexual secrecy was so intense. I also recoiled from poor Jenny on the grounds of her being shallow. 'You look through her and there's no vista of feeling,' my diary grumbled. 'She talks like a newspaper. She chatters till I wish someone would take her tongue and hold it.' I'd note at one and the same time that her cheeks were 'warm and damp for kissing', and that she used a range of verbs of motion that made me feel murderous. 'Let's chug,' she'd say. We'd 'leer along' and 'surge forth'. She'd end a remark with the phrase 'said she'. Again and again she'd cry: 'Life's but an empty –', and leave it at that. As we made our way through the woods that happily intervened between Monmouth Hill and the police court that we covered three mornings a week, I loved the way her hair was thrown about by the merest breeze and the charming bewilderment of her fingers as she tried to keep it in place; and I grew sullen at what I told my diary were her 'malarial verbs'.

That night she'd kept a seat for me at the back of the little Quaker meeting house. Sorensen was introduced and began with a tribute to this quiet place we were in. Before he could say another word, it became – and for the rest of the evening remained – an unquiet place.

There were shouts, on the edge of hysteria. The meeting ought not to be held. Treason. Go to Germany. Fifth column. Hitler money. You're dealing with a bestial race. Our sons. Your war record? Ought to be shot. 'I felt I must run out,' I wrote, 'and Jenny at my side was only fretful and cynical. She wanted to be given the opportunity to laugh. She tried to make

42

me laugh. It was a spectacle of the whole world as it now is and not to be laughed at. Sorensen struggled on to say: "What Jesus urged was that we should not merely love our friends but also our enemies." The hall became one huge rough laugh. "Foolishness!" someone shouted. "Then Jesus was a fool," said Sorensen. There were growls of agreement. "Look," said a man, leaping to his feet. "We don't want religion. Get down to facts. We don't want religion: we're at war."

'The second speaker was a last-war colonel, a simple un-dramatic man, who spoke quietly of Paschendaele. Another generation must not be betrayed into such horror. "I am a very worried man," he said. But they would not listen. "Fifth column, fifth column!" they chanted. "Treason, treason! You ought to be shot!"

'Afterwards, Jenny wanted to shake it off. She wanted us to resume our usual selves, making our way quickly back to ease and apathy. But I could not . . .'

Poor Jenny, tethered to that earnest boy! And yet there was so much during that year that belonged to moral Grand Guignol, was hideous, raw and simply tragic. The diarist expressed what can't have been an uncommon feeling: 'I shall go mad, I think, from this pursuing sense of responsibility for what is happening; I feel weighed to earth by the misery of millions. It is a lovely morning and the children in the street outside sound intoxicated – their rushing feet, their screams, their chuckles: with a desperate effort it is possible to listen with something like normal quietude – for a second. Then I remember that Holland has gone, broken to pieces, into that monstrous stomach. In five days, so much destruction! Has anyone the right to look on from some little window, as I seem to be doing? But where should I be?'

In my dreams I saw the advancing beast, he was black and deformed and had a red eye, he was trampling the quiet woods that Jenny and I ran through on our way to police court. But it was all internecine, somehow; *our* eyes, too, were reddening. 'I am haunted by a vision of man impaling himself upon man, battering himself to blood and bones against himself.'

Jenny longed for us to be jolly. Mr Trout growled like the voices at Sorensen's meeting, but gave way to last to my claim that, since it was I who had been there, I was a trustee for the report. It should not be written from the point of view of the interrupters. I said I could find other work; and Mr Trout had no wish to lose a reporter from his shrunken staff. He liked to remain comfortably all day at his desk, slowly preparing and delivering his editorial broadsides. I noted that the searchlights that prowled the night sky had a beauty of their own; a main stalk of light from which others grew, tall petals. Jenny and I passed a policeman talking to a man who was holding a long green ladder with exactly the ease with which a clerk would hold a pen.

'I reckon they'll soon be on the run,' the man was saying, and it was a statement that dragged so much against all likelihood at that dreadful juncture that I hear the tone of it still and feel the dismay it caused us. We were on our way to talk to the widow of a local shopkeeper, just dead. She sat in a room above the shop that was the living room, plainly enough; but there were shelves lined with ledgers and the dining table was piled high with bills and order forms. The widow sat in the middle of it, making out accounts for wines and spirits, and commented on her husband's death: 'The king is dead,' she said. 'Long live the king.' As we left, 'You can print that if you like.' But we didn't.

My father spoke of his own war. It was all right. You were young, you didn't care, you took it as it came.

'You're all together, you've got guns, you don't see any danger'.

He'd always talked like that of his two years in the trenches, ended with a shell fragment in the back: but I guessed never really ended – not even when he overcame the nervous break-down he had in 1924, when even the open air brought on his dread of being buried alive. I'd read somewhere a survivor's account of the Battle of the Somme – he said he remembered a sound like that of an enormous thumb being drawn across the surface of an immense wet pane of glass. It went on and on and on, and was the sound of injured and dying men screaming and groaning in No-Man's-Land. My father had a dark nature. His childhood had been harsh and there'd been nothing much in him to soften him, but I thought the war couldn't have been the experience of comradely indifference he claimed. There'd have been roughnesses he'd have loved, but I didn't think the terror had ever left him.

Now he was telling my mother and me how to get through 1940. She'd heard him lay out the rough stuff of his philosophy many times before, but was adept at appearing freshly interested; only her hand ruffled again and again the dress over her knee. Turning squarely to her, which meant he was speaking squarely to me, he said: 'If once you get it into your noddle that there is not much in this life worth living for, you won't worry.' Then, his invariable pay-off line: 'I just do what I'm told to . . . Time for bed.'

I turned away to write it up in my diary, together with a reflection on the need to train people to appreciate silence. Among other things, this diarist driven half mad by the events he was recording was a bossy youngster and much given to pointing to the urgent need to train people to do this or that. A very special thread in his half-madness seemed to be his belief that the midnight expression of these earnestnesses brought them very close to being realised.

And on Saturdays he walked into the country with Tom Sadler, who had a nervous view of life, as if he thought Sergeant Clinker was the larger part of it, and in some form or other would always be around to pick on him. Together they were amazed by the blueness of skies, the greenness of trees, the whiteness of clouds, and the inaccessible youth and womanliness of young women.

# 6

In no way, said Kate, could Jane Austen have interpreted the scene before us.

White was very white here, the colour of the apartments we were staying in, and blue very blue, the colour of the sea fifty yards away, as we sat on our terrace and looked down on the pool. Beside it lay a young woman, with a pleasantly slender body and a voice like a foghorn, and she was wearing the scant bottom half of a bathing costume. Beside her lay a young man, clad as slightly. As they talked he ran a reflective hand around her body, making little tours of it, here and there lingering. He halted at times at such a spot that you'd think silence must be enforced, a sort of sensual awe – you could have stopped me in mid-broadcast, I thought, with some analogous touch – but the klaxon of her chatter continued. Their bodies were, clearly, something else.

They were both . . . heavens, nowadays one tended to think it was pre-cancerously brown. Kate and I had always sought to be brown, on some analogy with attractive egg-shells and from a dislike of our white winter bodies; but she'd had one or two tiny perilous growths, and now was wistfully cautious. We were winter-holidaying; I was escaping from Mr Broom.

Well, Kate went on, tell me where, trying to make sense of this *conversazione* between two young English people, Jane Austen would have begun. I said she would clearly take some

46

time to adjust to the absence of gowns and suiting (though surely breasts had not been particularly hush-hush in her time?), but it wouldn't be more than half an hour – and a deal of *sal volatile*, said Kate – Really? *Jane Austen*? Well, at some point, she'd be drawn to the comedy of the contrast between the charming body and the charmless voice, and between his idle conversation and his busy hand. It would be the culture shock to end all culture shocks, if she were Jane Austen or not, said Kate, and we'd probably be left with a dead great lady on our hands.

Birds for which we had no name, white-collared with yellow streaks among their feathers, were making a nest in a Moorish-style light fitting above our heads. Having chosen their own five-star apartment on the site of ours, which at most was three-star, they seemed unable to adjust to our presence. At every approach, with beaks sprouting grasses, feathers, scraps of toilet tissue, they'd hover, freshly aghast, find some compromise of a perch, watch out of the corner of eyes that in fact had nothing but corners, and at last make some desperate, crooked flight home. One was hanging in the air now and in our own unadjusted way we wondered anew how to convey to it that it was among friends. Difficult not to feel ridiculously hurt, being treated with such spectacular caution.

I thought of the woman who out of the blue recently, following some reference in a broadcast, had sent me a final chapter she'd written for *Middlemarch*, in which she'd tried to imagine how Dorothea Brooke and Will Ladislaw would have discussed Dorothea's sexual experience with the pedantic Casaubon. In what language did mid-Victorians talk about such things, she'd wondered. It struck me now that George Eliot might have made herself quite quickly at home with the scene by the pool – but then again . . . Our own experience, Kate's and mine, over our twentieth-century lifetimes had bridged immense alterations of behaviour. If Tom Sadler and I some Saturday afternoon in the spring of 1940 had stumbled out of our time and found ourselves staring down at that bright pool . . . !

But how impossible to read *Middlemarch* without wondering if those ancestors of ours had been pursued to the most intimate places and moments by euphemisms and indirectnesses? Did they have any use of a bold, frank language? And if they'd had it, could they have continued to be masters and mistresses of a language indirect and allusive and sometimes marvellously charged?

This morning we'd walked to a beach on the other side of the town, where enormous development had occurred. Twenty years ago, a fishing village; now, a foolish rapacity of apartments crammed on apartments, hotels thrusting their fat white elbows into other hotels. Regiments of lounging-chairs stretched across the beach. Here breasts were . . . They were two a penny, I'd said. Toplessness gave them still a look as of ultimatums. Two women were walking in the thin sheet of water as it slid up the sand, one with remarkably large breasts, the other with remarkably small ones; and, defying that quite endearing comedy of contrast, they had an air of being banners, slogans, defiant declarations. Though part of my feeling that that was so must be rooted in the plain fact that I was born in 1920 and that some of my earliest seaside experiences had been in the company of my Great Aunt Ada. I had a photo of us somewhere; Ada and her friend Nellie Martin, sitting on east coast pebbles and wearing what now looked like black duvets, both with hats that might have been made by dipping rather large birds' nests in tar. They wore buttoned-up boots and their necks were funerals of lace. I am sitting between them, their seven-year-old confidant, while they examine the question: Did the rot begin with lipstick? That was perhaps the year of beach pyjamas. Great Aunt Ada, born a reluctant woman in a family of soldierly men, would have looked severely splendid in trousers, but (as I understood her views c.1927) believed that being a man meant boldly having legs and taking the consequences (there was a great sense in the family that much harm came from male legs), and being a woman meant having legs only when there was no avoiding it. Impossible to imagine her here now. She would turn to black stone!

48

We thought of two old women who sat on a step at the edge of the pavement, day after day, near the *supermercado* in the village, wearing what had always been worn – black, of course. Full black dresses, straw hats with black bands. We wondered what they made of the world of casually exposed secrecies that made its endless way past them.

And we had a little disaster on the sea. The Reconquest went on Mondays, Tuesdays and Wednesdays to a neighbouring island. Aperitiv was provided, with lanch. It would be a good lanch, said the skipper – 'enor*mouse*'. A pity about the weather. Yesterday was so beautiful. Today the sea was rough. But we would go. It looked as if we might be on our own, until just before departure we were joined by a German couple with their little daughter.

'You like being private,' said Kate.

'I like being private against a jolly public background,' I said.

We lay at the front of the boat on the top deck. We were bounced rather, but it seemed a good-natured roughness. More interesting, we thought, than glassy calm. Rolls were brought, a *rosado*. And between one sip and the next the weather changed. The waves grew; we laughed. They grew mightily; we became thoughtful. The deck was not for a second at a single angle. The others were helped down; we crawled across that crazy dance of slopes, knowing that if there'd been a sudden lurch we'd not have escaped being flung against a seat, some outcrop of wood. We had to be helped down the bucking companion way to the lower deck. There we sat until soaked to the skin by the pouring sea. We were helped further below, but were sickened by the smell of the engine and crawled back to the lower deck. As we became menacingly chilled, were sick, shivered helplessly, clung together for such warmth as we had to give, we were shocked by the quick fading of strength in us. Since that abrupt change in the weather, the boat had been attempting an emergency return, taking us across to the nearest harbour; but we could tell it wasn't easy. We were trying to maintain a direction across a surface that ripped and reared at a tremendous grey angle to us. We ached with longing for the rise and fall to cease – the rearing of the little boat on a wave, its brutal crash into the trough. It was the nearest I'd come to those many tempests at sea I'd survived as a childhood reader, and what I'd not known was how the sea appeared to be engaged in some immense activity of inventing and re-inventing itself: how suddenly irrelevant a boat seemed; how profound and instant was the making of great valleys and stupendous hills of water; how it was all forever on the move, a hugeness of tearing movement; and how indifferent it was to any dangerously chilled human being.

When we were ashore at last the owner of the boat was waiting for us with his car; he bundled us in, drove us back fast to our apartment, raised his hands in apology, returned the money we'd paid for the trip. And we fell into bed shaking and shocked, and woke hours later, when the sunshine had become enormous (oh, enor*mouse*!) and the sea was pretending never to have had anything worse in mind than a very bright shaking.

# 7

I'd brought those 1940 diaries on holiday with me; able, at last, to read them continuously. The trouble had always been that there were these jungles of introspection that I dreaded to be lost in and those others in which I reformed the world, or expressed my failure to understand why a universal condition of noble earnestness did not set in this very evening. But if, here, there was an observer under handicap, he was still an observer and suddenly a cause of surprise; connected to me, of course, by our sharing the same essential envelope, but otherwise, pretty unfamiliar. Extraordinary estrangements could occur between an envelope in the late 1980s and the same envelope as it was in 1940.

I was reminded, now, how Jenny Lawrence had been mixed up in my imagination with a young woman called Pipit, who existed only on paper; and with whom, despite the quite spectacularly unencouraging fashion in which her creator wrote of her, I fell in love.

I can fix the year it happened. I wrote the date 1937 in T. S. Eliot's *Poems 1909-1925* – my handwriting having suddenly become decoratively furtive, as befitted a seventeen year old who'd saved up three shillings and sixpence for this medium-slim green volume.

If I'd hesitated about the purchase, old Jack, our French master, would have made up my mind for me. 'Queer lot, you young . . . *intellectuals*,' Jack said once: a sad, sour man who loved Maupassant for the calamities towards which he suggested all of us were heading. Jack himself, as he spoke, was on course for an ironical *coup de théâtre* in his own life that might have been devised by his favourite author. 'You all think a lot of this man T. S. Eliot, don't you? Taste for obscurity, eh? Crossword puzzle poetry, eh?' If Eliot was out on a limb, I was gratified by being placed alongside him by bitter, puzzled Jack. The only thing was that he'd made me uneasy, for I thought I understood Eliot, here and there, and now wasn't sure I should do so. If being an intellectual meant, by Jack's implied definition, being baffled by verse, I wanted to stay like that.

Pipit was the despised heroine of a poem called 'A Cooking Egg'. She sat upright, her knitting close at hand, among photographs of her family, and at some distance from the poet, with whom she might have been taken to be living. I thought in 1937, when this was a natural thought, that they must certainly be man and wife. I took it there was a suggestion that her reading was of the coffee-table kind ('*Views of the Oxford Colleges*/Lay on the table'), except that those were the days before it was specifically the coffee table that lowered the literary status of any book lodged on it. The phrase here made me, half a century ago, uneasy about placing a book on any table at all. In this opening there was, as I registered it, a rather noble atmosphere of disparagement, a sort of tapestried sneer. The poet went on to describe his, as I thought it, complacently ironic certainty that in Heaven he would not want Honour, or Capital, or Society. He would meet there famous persons who would offer him each of these things at its best; among them Lucretia Borgia, with whom he was already contemplating a sort of *post mortem* bigamy. (I thought at the time this might lead merely to a second *post mortem*.) She should be his bride, he said. Her anecdotes would be more amusing than any that Pipit had to offer.

There was, up to this point, not much reason for a seventeen year old with a lower middle-class background, a more or less self-made reader of verse, to think at all favourably of Pipit. I certainly didn't understand, entirely, the grounds of the poet's animus against her. Well, of course, she was not likely to have been as rich in first-hand Renaissance gossip as Lucretia Borgia; but then, was one's wife to be scorned because she had not moved among poisoners? I sniffed anxiously around the implication that there was something objectionable about her sitting *upright*. Great Aunt Ada was the most upright sitter I knew and something of her made its way into my view of Pipit – another reason why I should not have fallen in love with her. Great Aunt Ada's uprightness was punitive. 'You'd think the old girl had a broomstick up her back,' my father would say, admiringly. Remembering his account of the Roman-sounding discipline exerted among the family young in his generation, by Great Aunt Ada eminently (compensating for not having been born an instant sergeant-major), I imagined it might have been a cane that continued to prop her spine dramatically when she was in her eighties.

At this point, the poem ducked under a row of dots, separating the poet's assertion that he wouldn't want Pipit in Heaven from the following verse, and, to my young understanding, came out on the other side a different poem. First, there was the couplet that made me captive to Pipit, as I believe I may still be.

> But where is the penny world I bought
> To eat with Pipit behind the screen?

I saw well enough the connection there was between this couplet and the rest of the poem, and indeed that it was intended to be as disparaging as the earlier verses of Pipit and the establishment set up with her by her Borgia-preferring poet; yet in another sense it formed, for me, an entirely separate poem, complete in itself. I found I had a desperate desire to live frugally with this creature with the charming name, who now was not sitting upright, did not knit and would not dream of perusing such a book as *Views of the Oxford Colleges*. It was suddenly possible to see her as a lower middle-class Pipit of an aspiring kind. Such a marriage of passion and unpretentiousness ours would be! Our entire furniture, a screen!

The notion of being behind a screen with Pipit was more fascinating than that of being in bed with her. My sexual education had been so blank that I guess I could hardly have avoided some displacement from obviously erotic furniture to peripheral items: a sort of fetishism in the sphere of goods and chattels. I was clearly in danger of wishing to persuade young women not so much into bed as behind screens.

I was probably lucky, at this stage, not to be inflamed by a mention of chairs.

But now the poem, having begun in what I saw as an unhappy upper middle-class setting, became more and more a poem about me, and my kind, and our problems.

> The red-eyed scavengers are creeping [it continued]
>     From Kentish Town and Golder's Green;
> Where are the eagles and the trumpets?
>
> Buried beneath some snow-deep Alps.
>     Over buttered scones and crumpets
>     Weeping, weeping multitudes
> Droop in a hundred ABCs.

And there it was – out in the open – that pitting of a sonorous past against a thin-sounding present; Pipit being made a scapegoat for the existence of Kentish Town and Golder's Green (and only for metrical reasons, I thought, *not* for Monmouth Hill). It was her fault that, in their ignoble teashops, persons consuming unambitious food did so in a dispirited fashion.

I had personally, day after day with Jenny, drooped in the ABC in Monmouth Hill Broadway.

Oh, I think now, the contradictoriness of it all! There was I, loving Pipit for her imagined readiness to share with me the simplest sort of existence! (Tess Grayson and I had made a poetic fuss about living on little, or even nothing, in the spirit

54

in which my friend Ben Fletcher had declared in a sixth form discussion that he intended to take up residence, like Diogenes, in a tub – a design that did not survive his marriage.) It was all a dream of modesty! It was why I was drawn to Pipit's very name, so charmingly simple! It was birds and apples! I'd written once to Tess proposing we turn to the former for music (no radios, gramophones, a proud ban on orchestras and virtuoso pianists!) and to the latter (scrumped, as the best apples of my childhood had been) for nourishment! And here I was in Monmouth Hill, despising Jenny, who was truly a Pipit, because . . . Because she was not Lucretia Borgia! In fact, she had cheeks like apples, and was truly devoted to teashops. She loved to sit at their tables, the tops littered with the crumbs of buttered scones and crumpets, and droop in her own pleasant fashion, elastically despondent because of the war and the tedium of our round among the police stations and the presbyteries! 'The red-eyed scavengers are creeping,' I'd mutter, infamously, as harmless elderly persons gave themselves, amid the smell of tea-urns, a respite from the fatigues of shopping. I'd read the poem to Jenny. She was theoretically in favour of literature, and wrote short stories herself, a matter of tremendously secret manuscripts, but in practice was often irritated by what she saw as its habit of exaggeration.

'You're so intolerant, Blish,' she'd say.

'And T. S. Eliot?'

'You and T. S. Eliot!'

'And D. H. Lawrence?' When recently she'd insisted on some mild *double entendre* as we toiled from Crescent to Avenue to Drive in search of pastoral trivia, I'd quoted his phrase about 'tickling the dirty little secret'.

'You and T. S. Eliot and D. H. Lawrence!'

'You've missed out Henry James!'

'You and T. S. Eliot and D. H. Lawrence and Henry James!'

And I'd sit there, half way through my teacake, wishing she was Pipit and loving her for her apple cheeks, and despising her for her formal awe of literature and actual dislike of much that it said, and angry with T. S. Eliot for being beastly about teashops, and detesting teashops for the precise reasons for which T. S. Eliot appeared to detest them. I was arrogantly in favour of modesty, and modestly in favour of arrogance.

Eight years later, when Jenny was dying from tuberculosis, I was to marry Kate and with her, in our first lodgings, eat at a card-table; this separated from the rest of the room by a screen, which had belonged to Kate's great-grandmother and was covered with little coloured cut-outs from Victorian Christmas crackers, mostly of angels with apple cheeks.

# 8

'I don't know what we're going to do about the BBC,' I'd overheard someone say as he strolled past us in a little garden in the harbour – a black garden, the island being composed of volcanic filth. He was saying it to his wife, who in her turn we'd overheard in the supermarket explaining that the place wasn't as it had been; only ten years earlier it had 'begs of cherecter'. I thought no one made such a comment about the BBC, in such a voice (it was a match for his wife's), without having, personally, a firm and probably violent notion of what he'd do with it. Given the discovery that February afternoon that I worked for it, he might have begun by hanging me from a yardarm. There was no actual yardarm to be seen, yet this was a spot, glitteringly adjacent to the Atlantic, where you'd not be surprised to find one round any corner. When we sat in this garden, close to sunset, looking out across the water to the tiny distant floating hills that were other islands, I longed to set off on some desperate journey: and thought again how odd it was that we'd had a small taste of such a journey, and had been enormously relieved to have it aborted. My boy's imagination had filled up with yardarms and, in a literary sense, there were few as adept at clinging to shattered masts. (That, of course, was before the Fortunate Isles became winter holiday places for any old Englishman and Englishwoman.) But as Kate had commented on what had turned out to be a displeasure trip, our lives had been shown suddenly to be remarkably soft. In a corner of the world that might have been a model for the starting point of most of those desperate journeys, I'd made a late discovery of my undesperateness.

I thought of that enemy of the BBC when I was back in London. What was *I* going to do about the BBC? Mr Broom had gone, but the new, clipped order of things was always imminent. Interviewing as a sort of warm blundering about might be seriously threatened. It was difficult, returning from sunshine, not to feel fin-de-everything. The sky was an old dishcloth. The trees were bundles of twigs. There was a heavy wintry refusal by our local world to shrug itself out of this mood, its very blankest, into any other. This was the bottom of everything, untransformable.

Despatch riders should remove their helmets before entering the building, it said outside Bush House, the headquarters of the BBC's external services, and I'd feel for mine before realising I wasn't a despatch rider. Then, almost at once, I'd meet Jean.

She was an essentially decent, intolerable person who saw everyone in terms of their need to be winkled out. You were coiled deep in your shell, which did you no good at all, and here she was with her pin, determined within half an hour at most to have you wriggling on the end of it, all your shames healthily exposed. You said something tired and flat, and she seized upon it as the tip of something shadily significant. '*Why* do you say that?' You'd said it to keep the lunchtime conversation going. Eager to probe, she succeeded only in ruffling. Faces would redden. Food was hurried through, the table vibrated with apologies and departures; there was a sudden general need to be in studios.

One of the producers I'd been deeply happy to work with, and the one with the most devotion to making something pleasant and individual out of the untidy rags of an exchange, began to copy old interviews, as she put it, so that she could have something for her relatives to throw away without a second glance when her time came (as in this weather it soon must) for the old producers' home. Here, for example, was my interview with Rosamund Lehmann, in the course of which she signed my copy of her first novel, *Dusty Answer*, forty-seven years late.

In June 1937 (again a date in a book makes me certain: it was the year I met Pipit), Williams, our English master, had discerned that I was dismal. My father, having reluctantly agreed that I should stay on in the hope of a state scholarship, had eagerly changed his mind.

'I will have a word with your worthy parent,' said Williams, who was curiously given to using this adjective for those he disliked. He'd warn me against treading on the headmaster's toes: 'We may need our worthy leader's support, at some point, if we're to carry out our plans . . .' 'Meanwhile,' he said now, 'my driving licence is in need of renewal. So if you'd like to take the bus to County Hall and arrange this for me, I will present the worthy headmaster with a dignified and even plausible reason for your absence. It's a sunny day, I know from personal experience that the Castle grounds are pleasant to sit in, and if there is change from the money I shall give you, buy yourself a Penguin.'

There *was* change (sixpence), I *did* buy a Penguin (*Dusty Answer*), and I found my way to the Castle grounds and sat there, in the mid-afternoon sunshine, on a grassy bump that is for ever memorable to me; for there I fell absurdly and unsuitably in love with Rosamund Lehmann and her characters. The novel is about young upper middle-class persons of misty beauty tipped with tragedy, who love successfully but not often, and unsuccessfully very often indeed, along the banks of the Thames and in the university of Cambridge, for which our worthy headmaster thought I should not try on the grounds of my character needing screwing up tight, and Oxford being the better screwdriver. It's a recklessly warm, swooningly intelligent novel, socially as remote from the situation of the semi-official truant in the Castle grounds as if its characters lived on the moon. (I thought the Thames, and Cambridge, did sound most moon-like.) I came back to Barton by the latest possible bus ('I hope little Williams knows what he's doing,' said my father), intent on being a character out of Rosamund Lehmann when there wasn't a single detail of my life (apart from my passion for books) that made me fit for it. It was the beginning of a long period when the hopeless sense of being a stray from her novels, and those of Aldous Huxley and Elizabeth Bowen, was relieved only by the feeling of being a stray from the novels of D. H. Lawrence, who was, with equal splendour, just as distant from the lower middle-class world of Manor Road, Barton.

When I interviewed Rosamund Lehmann, I told her this story and produced that old Penguin. And under my signature in the telescoped baroque I went in for in 1937, and the name of the memorable place with the castle, she wrote: 'Edward from Rosamund Lehmann with love.'

'I wish I'd been able to ask you to do that forty-seven years ago,' I said, demonstrating that the thrall was still upon me.

'What's forty-seven years?' she said.

Then there was an interview with V. S. Pritchett (who'd given me my first literary guinea in a *New Statesman* weekend competition, forty years earlier), in which I said I'd never caught him separating himself from a character, however unsavoury, and he said, well, he thought a writer had the duty of an advocate; his purpose was to try to suggest why his characters were what they were. He knew what it would be like on Domesday, he said. He'd be hurrying from tribunal to tribunal, muttering, 'No, Lord, no, *it wasn't like that at all.*'

And Feliks Topolski. He was ill, then, had just published his autobiography and had given instructions for entering his flat, in the Adelphi. In this peerless tenement, he had a key, on a string, to be tugged out of his letterbox. We entered and were at once in an immense room; on all sides were bookshelves of a monumental nature, constructed out of the thickest wood I'd ever seen used for such a purpose, and soaring to a ceiling perhaps fifteen or eighteen feet above the floor. In the centre of the room, on a sort of catafalque, lay the artist.

'Please.' His first words. 'Cross the room. You see that door in the left-hand corner? Go out through it, and climb the steps. Do not look as you do so. Keep your eyes lowered. When you are at the top, then look. Please. Do that.' As if mesmerised, we crossed to the door to which he'd pointed, stepped outside, climbed the steps, were aware of reaching a balcony and looked. And behold, we had Monet's view of the surrounding world. We were jammed up against the river; and when we looked left, we were intimates of St Paul's, and when we looked right, we had Parliament at the end, as it were, of the garden. We had that immense celebrity of view at our fingertips: Westminster gold to our right, City silver to our left. We went back then and talked to Topolski, who was ill, he said, partly because he'd wanted complete command of the design of his autobiography and had not been allowed it. I'd thought it a work that verbally conducted itself as he'd always conducted himself when drawing; that famous setting down of all the lines necessary to establish the actual line of a face or figure or a scene of any kind, had been mirrored in prose by an offer of a word and some alternatives to it. ('This shaggy/bearded hulk of Augustus John.') At eighty he was ill, handsome and odd, on that theatrical bed in that amazing room with its barely believable view from the front window. What a setting, I thought, for an interview, and how it might have brought about the early death of Mr Broom; but he'd gone to current affairs, oddly thought of as the prime home of the simple and direct. Topolski said afterwards he'd expected we'd start at some obvious beginning and go on to some obvious end, but we'd opened instead with a pitch somewhere in the middle, and it had unfolded from there; and gone on, of course, far too long, and been generally circular. He asked me to stay, to keep him company through what was for him an aching afternoon, and I fetched drinks from a kitchen that was half an artist's stockroom, so you'd be in some danger of a dish of paint powder when you'd aimed for one of corn flakes. His young fame had been part of the world that had excited Ben Fletcher and me in the grammar school corridors in the

1930s, and I remembered Ben worrying over the judgement we should make about Topolski's manner: was it threatening a cult of carelessness, or did that excitement of lines say something about the excitement of observing the world? And here I was fifty years later being careful not to provide him, dying, by some confusion in his artist's backroom/kitchen/wine store, with a tumbler of yellow ochre, crumbled.

And oddly I was reminded of a moment when Tomlinson, science master, had ridiculed a drawing of Topolski's, I think of Bernard Shaw. It was an example of obscurity again, Tomlinson seemed to be saying, though his dislike of that clearly had to be distinguished from old Jack's; here was a man who couldn't draw, so he turned that failure to account by erasing none of the lines and strokes by which he'd missed the target. Tomlinson was the dryest man I've ever known, who I now think regarded art itself as an example of human incorrigibility; it was warm, imprecise and in general resembled any situation in which chemicals were encouraged to get out of balance. I see at this distance that the young Topolski was the simplest Aunt Sally he could lay hands on; but he'd not have scrupled about making one out of Michelangelo.

All those voices in one's head, after so many years of being alive, and all those many-layered ironies of juxtaposition! Here I sat talking to this young/old man, and remembering Tomlinson, who in the range of character provided by the grammar-school staff represented the idea that a powerful sort of person might draw his strength from a resolute colourlessness. He kept the vivid at bay with every shrug of his thin grey shoulders (it was the only colour I remember him wearing). As a boy I understood that he was widely admired for being, essentially and with a kind of deliberateness, unattractive. I'd dread his tongue for the cold distaste it seemed to express for one's condition of being a child. He found immaturity displeasing. A child tended to act, and speak, with anarchical vividness. Tomlinson shrugged us all greyly out of his way.

And . . . curiouser and curiouser! When in 1935 he came to Tomlinson's England, from what he thought of as the spreading monotone of the Continent, Topolski said England seemed *exotic*!

In so far as my memory was a grave for old Tomlinson, I felt him turn over in it.

And to Oxford, to interview Nirad Chaudhuri.

Here was a ninety-year-old Indian who'd just published an immense volume of autobiography, all but a thousand pages of it, under the thunderous title *Thy Hand, Great Anarch*. His publishers, I knew, had wanted it less alarmingly long, but he had refused any thought of reduction; and he was not the man to lose such an argument. He'd always thought in a fashion that lay athwart much of the mainstream of thinking in his time, about the fate of India especially, but there was something enormously grand as well as intelligent about whatever was most infuriating in him; and when he was penetrating, he penetrated with a vengeance. And he wrote beautifully.

His language had a vivacious clarity, and raised no question of its being of some other time. I thought of *that* quality in it often when I read him, for over his shoulder I saw an old acquaintance, an Indian who lived unhappily in London from the 1920s onwards, and also wrote beautifully, but in a manner that wasn't of the twentieth century; his education in India had prepared him to take by storm the literary London of 1860. He felt deeply the bitterness of rejection, and carried with him everywhere a pamphlet in which he'd assembled the opinions of distinguished writers, who'd attested to the fineness of his prose, but had not gone on to say what had to be said: that it gave to everything he wrote a disastrous air of parody or pastiche.

Some of Chaudhuri's opinions made me bristle with dissent. He held that pacifists were plain cowards; and that no one objected to the death penalty on true grounds of conscience, but because they had no wish to be reminded of their own mortality. He was not to be read, I thought, for opinions, but for his gifts as an historian, and as a portraitist. He wrote best (or perhaps the rarity of such passages in accounts of modern politics made one value them most) when, as in his account of Gandhi, he had to report perceptions that ran absolutely against the current of his thinking. He was deeply suspicious of Gandhi, not in the least willing to be swept along by him; his heels were firmly dug in when they first came face to face – and he was bowled over, and unforgettably explains why. He'd expected Gandhi to be insignificant of frame and plain of looks, and hadn't guessed that the expression on his face made the rest of him perfectly unimportant; it was one of extraordinary innocence and benignity. A plain man, Chaudhuri concluded, could hope only to look as attractive as a plain animal, and to him Gandhi suggested some kind of monkey: in fact, the tarsier. 'But a beatific unworldly look suffused with what was basically mere animal innocence.' With his profound dislike of Gandhi's ideas, Chaudhuri looked on at him, at that first encounter, spellbound.

I'd interviewed him once before, when he'd published a formidable life of a great scholar who'd specialised in Indian studies. So I knew he was physically a small man of buzzing energy, his own scholarly seriousness always mounted – as I'd think of it – on nimble and often dancing legs. He had a quality of mischief, which hung about his writing, too, reminding the reader that history might be a matter of grand thunders, but there were historical squibs and bangers, too, and history itself spent a lot of its time leaping nervously in the air as events exploded around its heels. He came to the door of his house in Oxford, the day I went for this second interview, tinier than I'd remembered, in his Indian jacket and white trousers, and put on an instant show. I mean nothing theatrical, or false; but he was quite unable to risk a dullness, even an ordinariness, on any occasion. So he had Handel on the gramophone as he went in – 'A new voice, Emma Kirkby . . .' There was talk of Handel, and of the books on his shelves, and of the binding of those books, carefully chosen ('I never buy paperbacks'), and of his collection of sterling silver, and the prints on the wall –

64

a long buzzing, which ought to have been difficult to endure, monomaniac, but wasn't at all, for he was like the owner of a dozen or so small and remarkable museums, and as he took you from one to another (I remember his curtains featured in one such collection), his vanity and possessiveness were so innocent, and his erudition so rich and odd, that there was no possibility of being affronted. It was as if you had, indeed, been lucky enough to qualify for entrance to a little panorama of exhibitions. When we got down to a recording, he kneaded my knee throughout – very Indian, said my producer, who'd been born on the sub-continent – and wasn't content that I should be the only one to ask questions; it was an interview, I thought, not totally unlike an exchange of paper darts . . . And it was barely done than he was talking about his latest study of the places mentioned in Jane Austen, the towns that had marked the stages of journeys – that arising, I remember, from my saying I came from Barton, and this nonagenarian quizmaster at once asking me in what journey in Jane Austen Barton was mentioned as a halt – and look! such and such a critic had made a foolish comment on that chapter of the novel from simple failure to look at a gazetteer and calculate how long they'd need to get to Barton from Hatfield. How long – he pounced! – now we were talking of it, did it take to complete the journey from Bath to Mansfield Park? He took us then downstairs to a scullery where Mrs Chaudhuri sat, a beautiful small lady, nearly as small as her husband, greatly arthritic, newly recovered from a heart attack; she sat smiling at a table, turning a script of Chaudhuri's into Bengali, a page like a painting. I thought how *Thy Hand, Great Anarch* was a great history of his time, and that set into it was a portrait of this buzzing inquirer himself, and that behind that portrait lay a grateful and tender portrait of his wife, to whom he'd been wed in an arranged marriage to which he'd come reluctantly and in the greatest possible fear that his bride, never before encountered, would not share his new love of Western classical music. So that on their first night he asked her nervously, as they lay on the bed, if she'd ever heard of Beethoven, and

65

waited with bated breath, and she had; and he felt bound to make a further test, and asked if she could spell Beethoven's name; and she could. And she reached over and laid a hand on his thin arm and said she would take good care of him. And here an immense time later they were, in this scullery in Oxford, and I said, 'You are the heroine of your husband's book,' and she said the man from the publisher's had said so, too; but she'd not yet read it all. It should, I said, be called *Mrs Chaudhuri*, or, at the least, *Thy Hand, Great Anarch: or, Mrs Chaudhuri*. While we were talking together he'd rushed upstairs again, and now called down to us to return at once, and when we re-entered the living room, with its fine books and prints and silver and those volumes of Jane Austen strewn about, open, a sort of methodical strewing, he'd drawn the curtains and was ready to demonstrate his system of lighting, based on the notion that you should use it to reduce, if wished, the size of the room; or, if you preferred, enlarge it. Asking, as we made our way to the front door, how long it had taken Elizabeth Bennet to fall in love with Darcy (answer: an hour and a half), and explaining that he'd learned about the treatment of ceilings from some Renaissance manual (intended to help the decorators of palaces in Florence or thereabouts, but adaptable to the needs of the owners of modest houses in Oxford), he opened the door to let us go, but was reminded that he'd meant to say how relieved he was that we weren't wearing jeans. Knowing we were coming from the BBC, he had had a calamitous expectation of jeans. My producer lost marks, a few, for wearing trousers; as she said afterwards, it was the most charming disgrace she'd undergone. On our way to the front gate, he explained his techniques of gardening, and why he'd placed this shrub next to that, and showed us a letter he'd had from another Indian scholar living in Oxford who deplored Chaudhuri's presence in the city and signed himself 'Wounded Soul'; and asked me to send him a note of other recordings of Emma Kirkby's that I'd quite forgotten mentioning to him, something like fifty topics back.

66

And as we moved away down the road and turned to wave to this brisk little man watching us go, I thought it was a good omen, somehow, for Kate's and my imminent visit to India, to celebrate a long marriage that was still sixteen years shorter than that between the Chaudhuris.

# 9

Before stepping out of a taxi at Nirad Chaudhuri's front gate, on our arrival, I'd taken a tape recorder from the floor and put it on the pavement; and once out myself, I bent down to pick it up. It was the equivalent of knifing myself in the back. I felt the stiletto enter . . . a wave of hot pain. It wasn't unfamiliar. I knew I must straighten up slowly, if I could straighten up at all; and just, with a shout or two, made it.

Not long after that, I was shown my spine in an X-ray. It wasn't as tilted as it felt, I thought, but perhaps like a tower of paper cups from the BBC canteen, one not quite securely on top of another. A mildly dithering tower of BBC cups.

Yes, said the specialist, that was it. Nearly seven decades of failing to take my father's advice. Ray Bolton's mum had been wrong. I couldn't have been standing straight enough, even then. Physiotherapy, said the specialist.

And *that* turned out to be a succession of steps by which you were soothed back to at least an illusion of suppleness. You started out rusting iron, and ended as a sort of thick, but distinct, rubber.

Her smile was always the first soother. She even smiled curatively. On your tummy, she'd say; and then, a more difficult instruction, relax. Tensely, I'd relax. She'd start on a shoulder, which would respond with a sulky twinge. The ache of it would rise to the roots of my head, and I'd groan; then

68

say, 'Sorry. It hurt. But so it should. You carry on.' She'd have carried on, anyway. 'You groan as much as you like,' she'd say; so I groaned. What helped as much as anything was the fact of her persistence, and the powerful suggestion she created of someone who knew what she was doing. This *thing* you'd lived in for over sixty years and been content to know very little about – the word *thing* expressing the ungrateful vagueness of your knowledge of it; it was a remarkable example of your acceptance of ignorance – was no puzzle to her. At times she'd name parts that she wanted me to activate thus, or thus, and I'd not be sure exactly where they were, not inconsiderable components of the body or the sites of major organs inside it. Now and then she'd say: 'Well, put your hand on me . . . *there* . . . that's what we're talking about.' We were talking about the hip, and it was a *glory*. Later I'd have had to struggle to keep the ladies of Khajuraho at the back of my mind, if not out of it altogether. This easing of bodies – how close to that unashamed carnality, which surely also rested on an understanding of this subtle parcel into which we were wrapped! I'd not be surprised to know that somewhere on those surfaces 6,000 miles away, a scene of physiotherapy was to be found.

For the rest, it was a process of causing, and then dissipating aches, especially the long one that made the spine a rusty spear thrust into the head. Left, then right: kneading, rocking, provoking, soothing. She'd make a pivot of my buttocks, resting the heels of her hands on them, and spread long arcs of curative pressure.

'Do you have many who fall asleep?' I'd ask.

'Some. I think it's a compliment.'

'I'm nearly asleep myself.'

'That's good.'

She'd tie the whole exercise together with a long seminar conducted along my spine. Some vertebrae were easy, some were not. When she'd done, all were easy.

'That's a different back now,' she'd say. And it was. I'd thank her for the diligence of it.

69

'You have to concentrate?'

'Absolutely necessary. Or it doesn't work.'

'I could feel that. Thanks. I think you should charge double. But don't.'

'I shan't,' she'd say. 'But thank you.'

I'd walk home, twenty again – *twenty*!

# 10

Lord, what a fuss I made when I *was* twenty, in that year 1940.

The sky that night, I find, was 'dish-cloth dark' – 'a splendid mauve light surrounded the house when the curtains were still open – earlier it was yellow, as if the air had jaundice.' I'd been talking that day to Jenny Lawrence about marriage. She was against it. I didn't care for this making up one's mind before there was any offer of such an event. 'Let it come!' I advised myself. 'The unknown is so much greater than the known. Be still and receptive at the bottom of the great unwieldy mountain of life.' Down there, in the lee of this mountain which in 1940 was about to declare itself not simply unwieldy, but volcanic, I swung at once into one of my blasts against my friends.

'They are afraid of age and marriage, not in themselves, but in the types of them they see in their fathers and mothers. They have never got over this childish "I won't be". "I won't be" is only the beginning: "I will be" is the important thing.'

I sat in my armchair at 10 Manor Road, speaking with a voice that owed a tone or two to D. H. Lawrence, making my daily parcel of wrath, irritation, admonition. I was alarmed by the brevity of spring blossom.

'There is nothing so sad as the white petals lying on the pavement, and the green deserted cups with their little hard sediments of next year's seed. It takes so long to prepare for this short beauty.'

It had taken long enough, I think I was implying, to prepare for the short beauty of myself, suddenly a twenty year old and, therefore, close to the end.

Jenny and I had talked that day about dress. She'd said she'd like a world in which everyone wore what they wished, and no one would turn round to jibe. As a little girl she'd take off her frock, and fasten her brother's belt round her grey petticoat with its rounded neck. Ah, I said eagerly, ever ready with a generalisation, especially an unsound one, the tunic was the basis of all dress, and it was bad for us to have forsaken it.

'Our modern clothes, which we wear through a complex dictatorship of unanalysed conformity, were disjointed and . . .' I could have thought of many other adjectives. I am certain I could have done so, and am surprised I did not provide them instantly. This theory of the basic nature of the tunic, of its return being an important step towards social regeneration (night after night I added to these steps), and of its being universally worn representing an avoidance of conformity, led Jenny to say (eagerly, I noted) that the editor of her newspaper would look wonderful in a toga.

'Serious as I am in this matter, I could hardly resist smiling. Bertie Brown has a resoundingly Roman face, but – a toga! I have somehow an affection for the awkward dress of our time, when it comes to him. Trousers are really a humorous invention, whilst as for their feminine counterpart – in their luminous invisibility!' (Oh poor twenty year old, for whom knickers, out of sight, failed in such a floodlit fashion to be out of mind!) 'DHL would say our uniformity of dress was a result of democracy; but I think it belongs to those things which oppose democracy.'

Here I have a round or two with Lawrence, asking him to reconsider his dislike of the notion of equality, without much regard for his being in no position to do so.

72

'It is funny to think of Brown in a toga, because Brown is so much a part of things as they are; you have to change people first, then you can change dress.'

At this distance, I understand myself as regarding tunics and togas as suitable garb for reformed human beings, those who'd headed in the direction proposed by those nocturnal adjurations of mine: *then*, 'there wouldn't be any more Bertie Browns, so a Roman-faced young man could wear a toga without incongruity.' (*That* was ruthless! Bertie was a kindly, modest and usefully prosaic man, who gently took the wind out of those grandiose sails of mine on a number of occasions; the world would be a poorer place if the flow of Bertie Browns ever dried up. I appear to have thought Jenny herself unworthy, as yet, of a tunic. My own qualifications for utopian sorts of dress are not canvassed.

And so to this matter of having, that day, become twenty. 'It is climbing onto an even higher ledge of that giddying cliff,' I wrote. My hunger for images had me, night after night, contradictorily situated; here, for example, being ten minutes before at the bottom of the unwieldy mountain of life, I was suddenly halfway up this giddying cliff. 'To look back on the abyss of actually twenty years! My poor mother, so little, who has produced an ageing giant!' And so on. Later, it was crossing from one ocean to another, from childhood to adulthood, and being able 'to explore some of the million islands with which this further sea is set . . . It is unfair that I should enter it in the midst of a fearful storm that has a particular grip on the narrow channel between the two seas.' Well, yes. Nothing less could be said of being twenty in 1940. However, I wished it to be known (I seemed to think of keeping a diary as a successful means of informing the world of my intentions) that my 'trembling small ship' would not 'slink with secret sails towards the further ocean of thirty'. And indeed, some of the most abominable twists and turns of human history were to make slinking difficult.

I was against twenty merely as a number. 'It is holding up all your fingers twice: a savage's arithmetic.' Being nineteen was older than being twenty. This was the cue for pages of expostulation against the entire idea of birthdays; soon I was adding 'the gloomy priggishness which is the essence of numbering' to the errors that prevented us from being suitable wearers of tunics or togas. Arithmetic had been a tremendous human mistake. The glory of Time was its 'enormous and splendid vagueness', in place of which we'd chosen the 'mean accountancy' that, among other things, insisted on my being twenty.

I'd woken that morning from a dream. 'Some fantasy of being followed, in the company of a girl. Fields, black mud, behind us the trailing Gestapo. We held hands, we were closer than any earthly bond could make us . . . Then she became – an actress? Partly Jenny. Tiptoeing across the room with a magazine, I was – partly me; partly a person of nauseatingly Grecian handsomeness; and looking at this face, I knew it was T. E. Lawrence in his early years . . .'

There were many difficulties for anyone entering his twenties in 1940; but I seem to have added to mine by having flooded my young life with Lawrences.

# 11

'For the same money we could have had . . . I can't work out
how many weekends in Brighton,' I said at a low point in our
preparations for India. That was when, as they unfolded, they
began to resemble those one might make for an almost certainly
tragic descent into a live volcano. You should never drink
anything, you should barely eat anything, you should beware
of picking up fearful diseases from mere surfaces, you should
expect unspeakable problems with passports and tickets
and visas, no part of the journey would go as planned,
there was vast uneasiness in Kashmir, you must accumulate
a portable pharmacy but were bound to discover, at some
life-and-death moment, that it was inadequate. What had we
done?

But forty years of marriage was a lot of marriage, and
could suitably be celebrated only by some kind of substantial
experience. Sneaking repetitively to Brighton wouldn't have
done. And we longed for India the more intensely as friends
spoke of their unwillingness to go there as if it had been a
virtue. Couldn't face the poverty. Would find it all too distress-
ing. Some made it sound as if, in electing to go, we were
demonstrating a positive appetite for the spectacle of beggary
and over-population. We were some dreadful kind of sociologi-
cal *voyeurs*. Arnold Pribble drowned my explanation of our
choice of the sub-continent with such a blast of 'right right

right right right' that people in the morning train looked round, alarmed, and then expounded the economic reasons why we shouldn't go. In essence it appeared that the XYZ was against us, and he need only tell me that Kartoffel himself was of that opinion.

That clinched it. We would go.

'Do you take this man/woman to be your lawful wedded scape-goat, to misunderstand, misrepresent and blame till death do you part?' At times, Kate and I had fondly to confess, that might have been the vow we'd subscribed to, in Barley Church on the day when a man called Dewey was amazingly defeated in the American presidential election by a man called Truman. My mother, who was to die an obstinate little skeleton, was then very round; and in a photograph, taken as we stepped out of the church, Kate in a yellow dress of her own making and with yellow roses in her hair, I seeming a presumptuous lad of roughly thirteen in an astonishing suit with vast turn-ups, my mother looks deedy, her own word for being preoccupied. With my sister intending to marry within a month, she was faced, I now understand, with my undiluted father for ever and ever. Kate's mother wears an unattractive hat of the kind she cultivated, in which parabolas of brown felt collapsed inwards; and Kate's father, a shy boy in his fifties, clutches a simulated horseshoe, clad in silver paper, that had been thrust at us by workmates of Kate's. My friend Ben Fletcher, best man, admirer of John Donne and Ben Jonson, smiles at the November sunshine, and his wife Marie, at his side, beautiful in a tunnel of an overcoat, is deep in thoughts caused by contemplation of Kate's shoulder. My own smile conceals a chaos of thoughts set in motion by Kate's shoulder, but by much more of her than that. It is 1948. Ben, a married veteran already, has bought on my behalf what he calls 'necessities'; but I have confessed, as we walked pre-maritally among the tombstones (including that of one of Anthony Trollope's sisters, dead at eighteen), that I have, by recourse to devious-nesses of purchase, equipped myself. I am astonished, reading

76

my diary account of all this, to discover that, reader of Aldous Huxley, D. H. Lawrence etcetera, I myself refer to 'necessities', and also to the anxieties felt by Kate and me as we approach 'the crowning experience'. (Which, in our case, involved a crown that fell lopsided over our eyes, partly because I was not content with being married, but felt moved to have flu, as well.)

Forty years is an even longer time than it seems. Sometimes, nowadays, I was surprised by my own surprise at discovering that Kate, that long-established confederate, who to me was still essentially young – age seeming an unconvincing disguise she'd assumed for no clear purpose – was herself oppressed by our having had so many years heaped upon us. It was hardly what we'd had in mind, that November morning so distant yet so close at hand that yesterday seemed more remote.

India seemed absolutely the country in which we should celebrate this experience of having hung around so long, so briefly.

We'd chosen October. September at home was beautiful. The field I faced when writing was crossed with the soft shadows of trees, and sunlit women trod it from time to time in the company of sunlit dogs.

Before we went to that Indian summer, an Indian summer.

# PART TWO

# 1

Kate stood in the doorway of our bedroom in this excessive hotel in New Delhi, round her neck a garland of marigold heads.

'Do you realise,' she said, 'that this extraordinary day began with Jim not being there?'

It had certainly not been the beginning you'd expect for a day that was to end with garlands of marigolds in an establishment surely intended for persons arriving by elephant. Entering, we'd been bowed to by men ten feet tall, one thought hurriedly, in scarlet turbans, their waists, clearly slender enough anyway, being narrowed by sashes, black and gold. Did they have swords? I couldn't remember now. I did recall the combined gleams of teeth and moustache. In the enormous vestibule, women who seemed to have been selected for their unlikely beauty floated to and fro in stunningly-coloured saris. I'd never become reconciled to these absurd transitions imposed by air travel. It might just have made sense to take weeks by ship edging slowly away from Jim, not present this morning in the ticket office in Barley Wood station, to this world of floating ladies, successfully feigning to be flowers, under a painted ceiling depicting events, one imagined, from Indian history; a general tangle of elephants, militant moustaches and lances, with a leaping tiger or two. To be catapulted across such a gap within hours was a dizzying nonsense.

Jim, we knew, was on mornings that week in the ticket office. He was from Jamaica, had grown accustomed to the dampness and dinginess of things in London, was politely rueful about it, never, I thought, quite managing to conceal his faintly disdainful pity for us, natives of a land so ludicrously ill-served by the sun. I'd had fantasies of Jim returning home and causing hysterical amusement throughout the island by his account of the wet, white men and women of Barley Wood, hurrying for their crowded trains or hurrying to escape from them. 'Goodnight, Jim,' we'd say, moved by the particular gratitude we felt for this pillar of the daily process, and the sympathetic tone of his response was never quite free of a suspicion of laughter.

We'd had to catch a train that morning too early for him to have arrived. A miserable rain was falling, made sidelong by wind. Barley Wood had the blankets drawn up over its head. So the world might end, I thought: no one in the ticket office, to give the arrangement of things a face or a voice; desolate rain, a fiddling small wind. You looked along the empty railway lines and realised that your trust had to be entirely in some automatic fidelity of the timetable. Why should there be a train, as promised in that small grey print?

This was no way to set off for India.

But average probability had prevailed, the train had come, connections had been made, the morning had rubbed its eyes and become half-awake; in Heathrow there was a tired Indian woman, more distant than the six thousand miles between them from those sisters of hers we were to see in the vestibule in New Delhi that night, pushing a mop round the floor of a buffet and pausing to pick her teeth with a groping finger.

And so to that near-forcible feeding, seven miles up in the air, and the curious sensation of exile that flying offers; you are not here, you are not there, you are in a state of suspended transfer from one set of conditions to another powerfully different. You are a chrysalis; metamorphosis is the name of what's happening. Beneath you, in the frigid bowels of the plane, your new guises travel with you, the garments you have chosen for a climate melodramatically different from that at home.

And so, down. I am in India, you think, failing to convince yourself. Passport control is as pedantic as you'd been led to expect. An immigration officer with moustache and turban of ferocious precision looks through metal-rimmed spectacles at every detail of every document proffered to him, demands further documents, waits frozen while they are sought or not found, unmoved by pleas, protestations, hysterics: has eternity to spare. Kate leans against me, asleep as she stands. The Worldwide party assembles. In the hotel, making so much of its Indianness, there is Viennese music. Our nerves groan at being made, however subliminally, to waltz. Garlands. The room, with what we guess are the clichés of Indian luxury, including cushions on a platform by the window. I want Kate to lounge there, perhaps in harem trousers, drinking sherbet. She turns the role down flat and falls into bed. I fall into bed. India, which has not yet made itself at all probable, easily swims away, and I am back in Barley Wood, which has multiplied in size since we left it this morning, and through which I hunt for a library book that should have been returned some time in December, 1943.

In the morning we went carefully down to breakfast. Ate with such frugality as was possible. Tried to avoid reading a card that stood on the table and recommended the delights of Dum Pukht. This was, said the card, the fine art of cooking food with the unhurried panache of aristocratic gentility. Or, to put it slightly differently, it was a secret of gourmet excellence, gleaned from the tables of Nawabs.

We went into the garden: bright bushes, rivers and lakes of spreading succulents, humped lawns. And, again, women both beautiful and graceful; but these were labourers' assistants. Work was being carried out high on the curved face of the hotel, and debris came snaking down in shallow baskets. These the women, with an effect of the most delicate disdain, picked up, placed on their heads and took to a place of disposal. I'd never seen a menial task performed so haughtily, with such a sense of remoteness as between the carrier and what was carried. A small child, his mother one of these elegantly fine-stepping women, came close to me, called: 'Papa!' When I continued to approach, he fled to his mother's side. I smiled, but this beautiful woman's gaze was fixed high above my head. They all seemed to be looking into some rather better distance.

Across the road was an immense wood. It was tight and curly with trees, and seemed a magnification of one of the carpets of succulents at our feet.

And then we went back to our room and slept on and on, I on that platform in front of the window. It was like sleeping on the stage of a little theatre. We woke at last and made our frail way down through all the marvels of landings and lifts to go out and look at New Delhi.

# 2

There we were, in immense heat, at the heart of that administrative fantasy created by Lutyens and Baker. I wished I could like it. It seemed a statement in terms of buildings and boulevards of a surely over-tidy notion of government. Should bureaucrats be housed grandly in an area given over solely to officialdom? Wasn't it better when a seat of government was nudged and kneed and breathed upon by shops and concert halls and railway stations and street stalls? All there was here of that sort was a cause of distress: monkeys heartlessly dressed in saris, little bears that leapt when their keepers clapped. Hands, as they would do everywhere, swarms of hands flying at our faces, proffered postcards, paper birds airborne at the end of strings, small brass animals. Oh, apart from these irritations it *was* elegant and spacious and . . . Emerald, our guide, was using these words, and more. I tried not to catch her large, sparkling eye, for it invited our admiration, and what I liked best was what we were being asked to deplore, the bungle that had ruined Lutyens' vista with Baker's hill.

But an hour later we were among the grand debris of an older city, and gazing up at the Qutb Minar, a tapering finger made of tight-packed columns and ringed with galleries as it rose, built like so much in India out of apparent solid sunlight. (Captain Birt gazing for the first time at the temples at Khajuraho in 1838 spoke of them as 'sunburnt', which is absurd, but

85

an idea difficult to resist.) That a minaret is to a minar as a cigarette is to a cigar, merely a junior, was something I felt I should have known, but certainly hadn't. The Qutb Minar grew out of what appeared to be a forest of small Acropolises. There was no understanding much of this on the confused ground. Even given a guide with the most perfect articulation, speaking directly into my ear whilst powerfully built assistants held me by the arms and perhaps also by the legs to prevent me from wandering off, I'd still come away with the muddled half-understanding of someone easily distracted by things seen, many of these of absolutely no historical weight. By the time I'd finished wondering at a rainbow of a family that was striding across this extraordinary site as if headed for an appointment in the topmost gallery of the Minar, seventy-two metres above us, I had lost several centuries as expounded by Emerald, who provided a distraction from her own discourse, teasing her sari as she talked, arranging and rearranging it. Perhaps, a day and a half out of Barley Wood, I should content myself with bemused appreciation, and happy bafflement. The late after-noon sun fell on carved columns, and here were chains . . . and snakes . . . and now, surely, petals . . . These seemed to be surfaces that broke daily into seasons according to the light, so that an entire springtime might occur between, roughly, four o'clock and half past, when the sinking sun plucked leaves and flowers out of the sandstone.

And there was this other pillar, far shorter than the Qutb Minar, much older, 1500 years old, and made of iron; and it had never rusted. I probably wouldn't get round to understand-ing this, either. In the midst of these glowing sandy marvels stood this modest anachronism, that might have been an early product of Britain's industrial revolution, in its man-made material confessing with restrained decoration that it was rooted in a world otherwise less given to plainness. Most of it was undecorated black iron, which had aged like velvet and at this moment had a sort of surrogate rustiness applied to it by the setting sun. The trick was to stand with your back to it and see if you could embrace it with your arms; if you could, you'd have a day's luck, though no more. Over there, other minars that had got nowhere, the great roots of towers-that-might-have-been, tumbled Babels.

We walked back through this historical litter, and, returned to the hotel, after some dazed bathing and a certain amount of falling down unconscious and having to be revived, went to sample what must have been a modified form of gourmet excellence. Miss Baker at Barley Road School had taught us to think of praise and blame in a very distinct gradation: Excellent, Very Good, Good, Satisfactory, Very Fair, Fair, Poor, Very Poor. This was a pleasant meal, but probably an instance of gourmet satisfactoriness rather than excellence, gleaned from the tables of persons who, discriminate enough, may not quite have been Nawabs.

# 3

Listening to Alec McCowen as St Mark (or St Mark as Alec
McCowen – sometimes for a confident disentanglement it was
necessary to check with the programme) I'd noticed what a
springboard the disciple had made out of the word 'and'. I'd
always loved this word for its spring, its projective quality,
and had had many moments of grief, attempting to teach
children who'd been led to think it despicable. If it was all that
was left of any account we might give of our lives, it would
still beautifully do: 'And . . . and . . . and . . .' I wasn't
expecting at the end to feel the need of a much more extensive
vocabulary. The actor had said that adding 'moreover' increased the bouncing-off effect, but I thought I'd stick largely
to 'and'. Learning his way into St Mark, and then engaged in
replication after replication of the matter learned, he'd found
the incredulous shape of the story St Mark had worked on
until he could do no more to ensure it expressed his final
desperate credulity. Arriving on the stage, with head bent,
holding it all in, waiting for the moment when it must begin
(not quite with an 'and'), it was as if the actor were about to
release some tremendous flow; which, once released, could not
be stemmed until its two hours' course was done. And at times
that flow reached a point, a ledge in the story, a foothold, a
place to stop and pant, or to stop frozen with a sense of climax

that amounted to the merest advance rumble of climaxes to come: and then it would start again with –

*And* . . .

I'd been struck by a moment when, having built up such reserves of suspense, such a tremendous right at certain moments to keep the audience waiting – in the audience, such a desire to be kept waiting – the actor had judged it possible to walk round the stage, examine the back wall, sip at a glass of water and fall into a trance, all between a full stop and the following capital letter.

'A full stop!' he cried, when I expressed my astonishment. 'It was a *comma*!'

To give any account of travelling through Northern India as an absurd member of an absurd party of visitors, gaping, gawping, and getting most of it wrong, there is great need for the word 'and', so helpful at closing a curtain over a bewilderment, and whisking one open over another.


And we took the road to Jaipur.


Whatever I'd thought India would look like as you travelled through it was effaced beyond recall by the reality, most of it unexpected. I'd known there'd be great crowdedness, and every sort of traffic, and bicycles galore, but I hadn't imagined . . . miles of moorland, accommodating enormous numbers of garbage heaps: a sort of Himalayas of mixed rubbish. Or, suddenly, a kingdom of poles; they stood in their thousands in the fields around us. How extraordinary other people's landscapes were! That entire town of rags and scrapwood had been set up by building labourers! Black shininesses everywhere were the rumps of buffalo. To the right, a signpost said: PATAUDI. In 1934, I'd opened for England with the Nawab of Pataudi; he'd scraped together an admiring supportive 99, hard luck, while I topped 300. (That was one of my busier years, when I also won the air race from England to Australia and wrote *My Man Jeeves*, until then falsely attributed to P. G. Wodehouse.) Outside tea houses, the frames of beds were waiting for lorry-drivers in need of rest. And in their thousands, an unbroken hooting stream, the lorry-drivers themselves, all their vehicles the same vehicle, but each made perfectly different by patterns painted on the bare metal, and by the assertions and appeals they made fore and aft: PRECIOUS CARGO: HORN PLEASE: TOURIST PERMIT VEHICAL: OK TA TA. Standards of driving, said Laura, had to be judged against the background of the local habit, when it came to a driving test, of sending a substitute to take it for you.

And here was Jaipur: the horizontal crowdedness of the road becoming the bustle added to bustle, spreading in all directions, upwards included, with more bustle thrown in, of this city, oleander pink, ragingly populous. And just before we reached the hotel, a shop that summed up the entire journey. On many wide-stepped shelves in front of it, a cascade of pots. Never in my life had I seen so many pots at once. The shop made me laugh with its pure extravagance of pots.

I wanted to go back and pass it again and again, for the sheer wild pleasure of having been made so lunatically aware of *pots*.

# 4

It had begun to strike me that one of the earliest and best-documented package tours was one that set out from Southwark for Canterbury in the late fourteenth century, with a Mr G. Chaucer in the passenger list. By the time we'd reached Jaipur, it was possible to make out the shape of this or that individual in the Worldwide party; much as, I suppose, ten miles out of London, Chaucer began to be aware of the Miller and the Carpenter and certainly the Wife of Bath. Mammoths, as I thought, compared to mice; this emerging as the first crude distinction between members of the party. The mammoths were the naturally dominant persons who from the beginning naturally dominated. There was Ted Drake, who was some sort of free-wheeling businessman, tall, handsome, travelling with a remarkable wardrobe and a handsome wife, who was travelling with a wardrobe even more remarkable. We were led into the Indian scene by the gleam of their expensively tended and cheerful teeth. I'd thought the worst of him at once, on the narrow grounds of his being, in his amiable and well-dressed way, so clearly at home in the world. In early discussion at breakfast he said he thought the best sort of government was a benign dictatorship; and, challenged, had no clear idea how you guaranteed the benignity of the dictator. A chance reference to Australia led him to reveal that he was opposed to that continent and its population, seen by him as roughnecks to a man. And woman? The women were crushed creatures, he believed, and never heard of. Germaine Greer? Joan Sutherland? He was unmoved by these names, as also by the names of several Australian writers I mentioned. He seemed to think of writers, in any case, as persons moved by a pitiably backward passion for words. He measured his success by his ability to dispense with these, from which, fortunately, modern technology had given us the opportunity of setting ourselves free.

'Words are the devil. Always getting you into trouble,' he assured me, briskly. 'I suppose it's a bit late to offer advice' – it never ceased to astonish me that people spotted my white hair – 'but I would say, whatever your occupation was' – a delicate pause for me to reveal it, but I abstained – 'if you could during your working life have limited your reliance on words, you'd have been quids in all down the line.'

'Thank you,' I said. I thought, Oh Lord, and avoided his company at breakfast.

But I began to see that his habit of careless generalisation and all those shaky certainties of opinion were balanced by considerable and true good-nature. He'd make jokes about the Indianness of Indians – out of their hearing, speaking of their 'dirty nightshirts' – but face to face was unfailingly courteous to them.

'A man out of a sitcom,' I fumed to Kate, after he'd strewn our early visits to tombs and temples with one-liners. But he was watchfully protective towards the more timid women in the group, to whom much in India was alarming. (I thought alarm was felt also by the more timid men, but they weren't covered by Ted Drake's philosophy.) He had a general habit of being careful towards people, as long as they were present in the flesh and weren't out of sight, like the population of Australia. I thought if we'd been a ship he'd have been our figurehead, boldly coloured; except that, for this, his wife would have been better.

The Drakes, with Michael Reemer, the historian, were the most prominent mammoths; you became aware of them long before you began to make individual sense of the mice, the quiet ones, shy or reserved or timid or simply dull. But among them was at least one pair who became prominent early on by virtue of, as it were, the colourful nature of their colourlessness. They appeared to have come to India to despise it. They'd been all over the world, it seemed, on similar missions, and had only recently returned from establishing that China was a washout, and, in terms of topography, architecture, population, the Great Wall and the excavated terracotta army, tremendously overrated. *He* spoke of her methodically in her presence as 'she'. 'She was sick most of the time,' he said, as if this clinched their notion of China as a territorially vast let-down. They had already seen through the pretensions of Delhi and she had a particularly petulant, though unexplained, response to the Red Fort. *'The Red Fort!'* she'd cry, as if she might have thought better of it had it been any other colour. Their actual names took a long time to register, someone early on having called them the Drearies. Some members of the party seemed convinced till the end that their names were, indeed, Mr and Mrs Dreary.

I had a particular liking for the gentleman from Leamington. A retired solicitor, he'd come without his wife, whose detestation of travel he referred to with resigned amusement.

'My lady has one serious objection to this planet,' he said. 'That's its size. She even thinks Leamington's a bit much.' It was she who, finding Richard wistful for great coarse voyagings, had persuaded him that he must set out alone. 'I think she's quite looking forward to my return with traveller's tales,' he said. 'She'll give little screams of horror as I tell them.' He was a man deeply persuaded of his own conventionality. 'If you want amusing opinions, don't come to me. I always say, part of me's dyed-in-the-wool, the other part's stick-in-the-mud.'

'What made a stick-in-the-mud come to India?'

'Wanted a change of mud, I suppose.'

He had struck up a friendship, drily warm, with Kate. She found some moments of explication by guides hard to bear, especially when they were made difficult to follow by oddities of accentuation. She was still puzzled by having seemed to hear that Buddha had done something or other whilst in third gear.

'I'd rather look around me and read about it before or after,' she said. Richard was sympathetic.

'Let's not listen,' he'd say; and they'd go as courteously as possible out of earshot of the guide and discuss this or that past season at the theatre in Stratford-upon-Avon. For a conventional man he had a lively interest in Shakespeare.

'Don't expect penetrating comments from me,' he'd say, and then provide them.

I'd discussed with him my growing conviction that my dreams were a sort of cauldron into which were thrown, nightly, a sample of the contents of my memory, in such a fashion as to remove from them any impression I might have been entertaining of their being harmless because familiar.

'At this end of life,' I said, 'don't you think our dreams are pointing out that this is hardly the place in which to suppose we're at home?'

'You sound surprisingly like my wife,' he said.

'Visiting India increases this sensation,' I said. 'Well, *here* is unfamiliarity, if you like.'

Richard had a way of indicating serious thought by his disposition of himself on his shooting stick. 'By George,' he said.

'Well,' I said, 'I think it must be the same for anyone of our age.'

'Never dream,' he said quickly. Then: 'Well, not if I can help it.'

We were looking, as we spoke, down at the dead city of Fatephur Sikri, which Shah Jehan had abandoned only four years after he'd had it built.

'Actually,' I said, 'that *does* look familiar.' It was extraordinarily like one of the empty towns in which, night after night, I went in search of a mislaid briefcase, mackintosh or camera.

'If we were in court, and you were in the witness box, this

is where I'd politely suggest you were getting confused,' said the gentleman from Leamington.

I thought that if I could choose a companion on those enforced nocturnal perambulations through the empty Indias in my head, I'd be quite glad if it was him.

# 5

I'd been told to look out for the cheese factory owned by the poet, Peter Levi. And there it was, suddenly, on the horizon; in fact, an immense cheese, the size of a block of flats, blazing with light inside its orange rind. I ran along the train to tell Kate, who said she couldn't see it; but I realised that that was because we were passing through a small wood. At once I'd joined her at the factory, which was more in the nature of a cheese farm. Or perhaps it was a town devoted to cheese. There was a hint of yesterday's landscape on the way from Delhi. A grove of cheese, delicate pale droplets of it, hung on poles in transparent bags so that the shapes were those of trees. There was everywhere a huge sense of crowdedness, but this was a bustling and jostling without people. We came to a farm door, gigantic; far above us, from the keyhole, the carved wooden shapes of men came tumbling. I said I must go back to the train and fetch my camera. At once the attempt to find the way I'd come led to every kind of doubt, not only that of direction; and in one place I found a river had begun running, greasily grey with pollution. I wondered now, panicking, about the train. It had been very short, a carriage or two. Only Kate and I had been aboard. How had we brought it to a stop? Did it matter that it was now standing untended on the line? Had it been sensible to leave our luggage unguarded?

'The trouble is it might run out of heat,' said a woman, suddenly appearing, who was not quite Laura. 'Or it might become so hot it will burn up.'

I woke, horrified at the thought of that immense illuminated cheese. And behind it, the more terrible for not quite declaring itself, I suspected, there'd been a cathedral, dwarfing the cheese, and itself flooded with blinding light. It was a typical scene as provided for me by the internal package tour company that arranged my dreams. The distance always swarmed with buildings of unspeakable size, cathedrals a hundred times as tall as any on Earth, palaces that consumed the horizon and beyond.

But daylight made things manageable. Amber Palace, to which we went that morning, was very large; but, being finite, bearably so.

Kate was sick, and added herself to those who'd gone back to bed. Sadly, I went to Amber without her. It had been the name, perhaps, and pictures in brochures of a golden hill wrapped in golden walls, doubled in the water of a great tank at its feet, but Amber had drawn us curiously. Now Laura was anxious we shouldn't delay, wanting, she said, to beat the tourists to the platform where elephants waited to take us on the climb to the palace gate. I thought how odd it was that Laura should not regard us, but only other people, as tourists. For some reason she wished to see us as whatever is slightly superior: some kind of disinterested and discriminate travellers. And I remembered how, on bank holidays in the twenties and thirties, the people of Barton, swarming into Barley Wood for picnics and games of French cricket, would disparage family parties coming from elsewhere. 'From the East End,' they'd say. As a child I thought of the East End as the source of all anarchy and outrage, and of a bawling tendency to occupy green spaces belonging to others. 'Trippers,' said my fellow-Bartonians.

And now Laura was rushing us to get to the elephants before trippers could arrive. It had seemed in prospect an absurd ritual, this being jolted up the hill on a huge beast with a painted trunk, and being passed by persons walking. Yet it was the right way to enter Amber. This was elephant-land! I liked the soft jolt and roll from side to side; the way one step took you sharply to the west, and the next headed you due east. It was a trudging observation post you were being transported on; and as the road turned and turned on itself, you saw now Jaipur on its level, now the long shoulder of a hill sporting some solitary cupola, a helmet-shape standing out above trees; now a great walled tank of water, and then a flank of the palace wall itself, thirty or forty feet high, the golden stone stained with centuries of furious weather. And so into the immense main courtyard, essentially now a garden for gathering in and for assemblies of elephants; an exhilarating sense of elevation resulting from the spectacle of hill-tops only just rising above the height of the walls. It was as if the whole palace were built and balanced on some vast elephant's back.

Oh, I wished Kate were there for the hall of audience, elephants everywhere alluded to in its red and grey marble, columns topped and roofs supported by strong curves of stone celebrating the curve of the elephant's trunk! In Amber it was like coming home at last to the true world of elephants. Sixty years before I'd watched them make their way, heaped with children, down paths in the London Zoo, where they were solitaries to be gaped at, exiles under a sky often greyer than themselves. *This* was their place: in the courtyard at Amber, surrounded by little shops that had once been their stables.

And now we were ordered into line by Mr Pram, a sort of glorious improvement on Sergeant Clinker, who set about whipping us with historical detail.

# 6

Our guide was too splendid for us, and far too splendid for his trade.

Mr Pram had a fine brow and flashing eyes, made much of being descended from Rajput warriors; and, standing at the front of the coach, a microphone in his hand, thundered, orated, philosophised, laughed ironically, was bitter, argued mockingly with himself, uttered tragic parentheses, made jokes and was amused by them; his audience being evasive, irregularly attentive, vaguely ashamed of being unworthy of him. He was well-known, said Laura, for enjoying the display of knowledge and opinion. We were to take it that he was perfectly happy, given this pulpit and making dramatic use of it. All the same, we did feel uncomfortable, his passion being so splendid and our interest so fickle.

Much of the time he seemed to be moved by political emotions of great ferocity, signalled by some storm of comment on 'the bad customs of my country.' 'My country' was a phrase again and again on Mr Pram's lips; one moment employed with what sounded like pride, the next with what was certainly scorn. 'One of the *bad* customs of my country,' he would cry; and clearly he was not addressing us, Mr and Mrs Dreary and friends, so momentarily and confusedly in India. Where we sat or stood, the Indian Parliament trembled; the Government threw in its hand. We barely heard him, were staring at the

Palace of the Winds, that high pink fan of windows behind which the women of the court had peeped out at a world that could not peep in. It was standing now in the thick grey soup of a stream that lined the street.

'The ladies . . .' he said. He was always jocular about women. In the presence of Ted Drake's wife, he became almost foolish. His moustache seemed to double in size and somehow to swagger across the finely judged space between his nose and his mouth. As we stood outside the Palace of the Winds she made it plain to him that if, like the ladies of the court, she'd been required to confine her participation in events to sly glimpses through the windows, physical violence would have had to be offered.

'You wouldn't have got me in there very easily!' she cried, looking up at all that averted fenestration; and you saw that an entire royal regiment might have been needed for the attempt.

Mr Pram instantly made it plain that he'd have been charmed to provide this violence, single-handed.

'You don't know what you're taking on, Mr Pram,' said Ted Drake, offering to show his bruises. Mr Pram's face became submerged in moustache, and he strutted up and down for a moment or so, eyes very bright – on patrol, I thought, along some thrilling sexual frontier.

'You will know,' was another cry of Mr Pram's, 'the national bird of my country?' A long, noble stare down the length of the coach – all whispering, unreadiness to be interrogated, guilt. Mr Pram persuaded himself that he'd heard a unanimous cry of 'Yes'.

'It is not for nothing the bird of my country . . .' There was a grand passage of ornithology. 'I come,' he cried, 'to what is called, in my country, the caste system . . .' The analysis was largely sardonic, and was interrupted by the need to stop the coach to allow photography.

'I know what you want,' Laura had said, in respect of such stops. 'Camels and waterwheels.' It seemed a dreadful reduction of the appetite of Worldwide parties as manifested

100

over the years. She had in any case omitted palaces in the middle of lakes. Here was one now. Mr Pram stood at the door of the coach and hurled his voice up and down the line of cameras. The palace had been far more splendid than its present appearance suggested. His country did not always exercise care for its buildings. We got back into the coach. 'As I was saying . . .' cried Mr Pram. The analysis deepened – here and there he laughed, brokenly . . .

Full of drugs, India, Dum Pukht, I began to hallucinate and saw Mr Pram distinctly in Sergeant Clinker's place, in that Indian playground at the grammar school so long ago, that pebbled surface, that sunshine, the Crimean cannon that stood in the shade of the mulberry tree . . .

Lined up in the Amber courtyard, we were lashed by Mr Pram with his explanation of the immaculate state of all that decoration in the Hall of Audience, which when Akbar's inspectors were known to be on their way had been hastily masked with plaster, for the emperor would have ordered the destruction of a splendour equalling if not exceeding that to be found in his own palaces. The unusual speed of action in applying the plaster was followed by a more typical delay of three hundred years in its removal.

Elephants and mirrors! Glass was everywhere, as the smell and shape of elephants was: green, orange, purple glass making outrageous richnesses of pattern on walls and ceilings. In one room, under a curved ceiling divided according to some extraordinary geometry, a marriage of square and round, and all a splendour of small inset shapes of dark green and white, sat a pigeon, in a niche framed with golden tiles; it was curious that, because the eye was already amazed by the beauty of all that artifice, the living beauty of the bird, its head and breast, were almost unbearably evident. And there was the king's bedroom into the ceiling of which hundreds of tiny convex mirrors had been set; so that as he lay there, the window open, the blowing air made the candles flicker, and the ceiling became a sky of winking stars. To make a dance of light seemed

101

to have been the intention everywhere in the palace; when air-conditioning was installed in an outer room, open to a small square garden, it took the form of water running down a ramp set in a wall, along a decorated runnel, and so into a pool among the flowers; convex mirrors being so placed that the sunlight already dancing in the water danced in them, too.

How Amber must have winked, until that day, precisely 17 November 1727, when Raja Jai Singh the II, the scholarly king who'd built a great open-air astronomical tool-kit in Jaipur, decided the time had come to move to a new palace, a new town, the date having been fixed of course, by measurements among the stars. I imagine he took his grass-tearers with him. They were at work now, in one of the Amber gardens, a man in white, a woman who'd enfolded herself tightly in mustard-yellow, trimming a lawn with their bare hands. Oh, how close I'd come to imagining myself a king, having a king's dreams (something about lost crowns or mislaid consorts?) under a ceiling of false stars! But clearly, in eighteenth-century Rajasthan, I'd have been lucky to be recruited for grass-tearing.

Mr Pram left us at this point for a guide of less seniority, for what we were now to do was something for which his moustaches made him too spectacular; we were to visit a textile factory followed by a carpet factory. Tied to the tail of every grand experience on the journey, a commercial tin can of the kind! But there was no such visit that didn't offer a joke, some modest amazement thoughtfully staged. At the textile factory, for example, we were ushered into a shed where blockprinting was done, and a small hoax was perpetrated, one honed on a thousand such occasions. The block was apparently inked, and offered to Ted Drake, as the largest man in the party, and he was shown how to bring it down hard on the cloth. Lifted, it had made barely any imprint. Such glee! This feeble strong man! And now, inked again, but this time properly, it was offered to the frailest woman in the party (having been refused by Mrs Dreary, who'd seen this sort of thing all over the world, and had known it to end in law-suits), who brought it down on the cloth with splendid results. Warmed by the comedy, people went off and bought skirt lengths, curtaining, bed covers, cushion covers. Already the purchases made by some exceeded any rational possibility of their being carried across India, and into and out of Nepal, and back to London. We'd think of certain members of the party being intimately searched and discovered to be not so much human beings as pantechnicons.

And when we came to the carpet factory, what astonishments there! Not just the carpets, many of which were beautiful, as a good carpet may be seen to be if you're required to give it your full attention. It was also the way that attention was enforced upon us, by sinewy men performing a feat I couldn't see too often repeated. Well, it was embarrassing, sitting there and being pressed to purchase carpets; and yet . . . One roll was brought in after another, seized by the athletes and unleashed. That's to say, they were startlingly flicked open; one minute there was a mere roll, the next an exposed surprise of pattern and colour. The exercise of this skill, surely resting on some phenomenal development of the wrist, would have given glamour to the most banal carpet. I found myself each time crying out with delight, and being plainly marked down as a customer on a grand scale (still thinking myself a king!), so that I had to follow every expression of my bewitchment with some cancelling shake of the head.

And I thought how, by adaptations of this technique, you could startle the world on almost every front. If only, in some such fashion, you could snappingly unroll a book that you'd written . . .

# 7

'*Worldwide!*' cried Mr Pram, a scoutmaster calling to his pack. This was the great palace in the town. We'd been sent off on assignments, to explore this courtyard, look into this armoury. Our twenty minutes up, we reassembled, drifting until in sight of Mr Pram, when we became subject to a strange obligation of obedience. We'd been astonished, perhaps, by the curious flowers that could be pinned to a wall or ceiling, composed of swords or rifles. Some little garden, seen through a stone screen, had been converted into a bewitching construction of coloured dots. On the roof of the palace the monkeys were scuttling silhouettes: an alternative gang in the air, much like the one we formed on the ground, given to the same impulse to dart about, freeze, nibble a tail. Mr Pram held us in a gaze like a noose.

'In this place you will have noticed . . .' He never doubted our having noticed things. 'You will have wondered . . .' Alas, we hadn't. We fell further and further behind Mr Pram's expectations of us as sightseers. But I *had* noticed a group of very young schoolgirls, in dark green skirts and pale blouses, an astonishingly prominent part of them consisting of knees, with their teacher, bearded, whose turban was the colour of those skirts; they looked like birds, sitting on the low edge of one of the halls of audience; behind them, on a sandy wall, yet another bristling circle of muskets. And *they* were noticing the monkeys, scampering from pose to pose, so that as the light faded and they became silhouettes, they appeared to be architectural features in constant motion. And I thought that once, of us all, those monkeys would have seemed the only acceptable (perhaps unpreventable) visitors to the courtyard. The Worldwide party, and those little girls, their touchingly comic knees akimbo as they stared up at the scuttling roof, would have been quite seriously unwelcome.

And children again caught my eye, incurably a teacher's, when we were taken to see that astronomical toolset, open to the sky, in which the tools were massive dials, great staircases, huge statements in stone and brick of measurements or means of obtaining them. Among all those handsome geometries went a party of older schoolgirls, in deep pink uniform. Squatting round a pit that demonstrated some vast solar fact, they made a garland. They rose and fell apart, and made their way as separate petals to a monumental triangle of brick, thirty feet high with its own stairway; and there they made a deep pink hypotenuse.

And everywhere a flickering of the bodies of small monkeys, suggesting a sort of anti-arithmetic, a retort to the solid assertions of that beautiful eighteenth-century classroom.

As we ate, a pianist played, appallingly, a medley of sentimental tunes from old British musicals, among them, 'Tea for Two'. Of this song my mother had given a virtually non-stop performance from about 1925, when she was taken to see *No, No, Nanette*, until the end of the decade. It was the one piece of theatre she saw during her early married life; and the endless repetition of the song was a celebration of that single bright, improbable evening. Because she sang it, my sister and I sang it, and the general effect, for none of us had well-managed voices, must have been abominable. Now, in this hotel dining room in Jaipur, it sounded even worse than when my mother gasped it out whilst turning the mangle, with the aid of inexpert and contradictory juvenile descants. When the medley came to an end, there was no applause, which prompted Kate to provide it. The pianist directed at her a look of deep gratitude, and played the medley again.

We talked of the problem with which we'd guessed being in India would present us – some of our friends had said the very idea of it made a visit impossible for them. It was that of being luxurious gawpers, borne from hotel to hotel and from one great historical crumb to another, in the midst of a scene bursting with such evidence of poverty as we'd never seen. Late that afternoon, returned from the observatory, we'd tried to walk into Jaipur. It had been like stepping into a scene in which most of the elements were perfectly familiar, yet did not add up. We knew about bicycles, cows, kerbside markets, and sewage. In these streets, they were mixed impenetrably. Every inch of the edge of the road was occupied by some valiant enterprise, an attempt to make *something* out of the sale of the most residual trash. There were the remnants of what might have been once, perhaps never were, sidewalks: broken stone, the rifts in which revealed a sluggishly flowing, grey, glue-ish effluent, revoltingly thick, bearing with it every kind of debris. The smells were complex – as of a mixture dominated by oil, rotting fruit and shit. As much as anything, it was the acute difficulty of navigation in this crowd of broken objects and buzzing people that drove us back (together with our having inadequate experience of cow-avoidance), but it was also a sense of the absurdity – and, essentially, the offence – of our dainty attempts to keep our shoes clean. At least, since we weren't where tourists were expected, we were spared all those begging hands, those postcards and puppets and little wooden boxes being thrust at us. Laura had said the only salvation of the besieged visitor was to look straight ahead, not even by a meeting of eyes acknowledging the existence of those swarming hands. To Kate, delighting in children, the need to cut them dead was a very serious pain, that never became easier during the whole journey. We clung to a sensible remark of Mr Pram's:

'If you feel bad,' he said, 'contribute to an organisation such as Save the Children.'

106

Now the pianist crossed the dining room to speak to us. He expressed dismay about his own playing, and said he was from Goa, as if this might have been an explanation. He seemed, however, to think it had all sounded rather better in Goa. When we left, he interrupted his fourth repetition of the medley and stood and bowed us out. Kate's heart, that had bled for so many small children touching her arm in hope of rupees, or climbing fences in the attempt to dominate their rivals and so establish the superiority of their pack of postcards over all other packs of postcards, now bled for this inept pianist, his soul possessed by chagrin and gratitude. I was simply glad my mother hadn't been there. In her last year or so before she died at 91, she'd become a shameless singer, likely to perform anywhere, and I had a wild vision of her standing at the piano, perhaps leaning against it on one of those mangler's elbows of hers, and aiding and abetting his inaccurate fingers with her inaccurate voice.

# 8

The desk clerk had used a pocket calculator to get our bill meticulously and rather awfully wrong, but I almost threw my hand in when the alternative turned out to be a good deal of very public mental arithmetic, engaged in on both sides with courteous puzzlement. *He* gave in, in the end, with a smiling sigh of resignation, which made me, though I knew I was right, feel dastardly. I had behind me, though he wasn't to know it, the tremendous authority of Miss Baker, who, at Barley Road School between 1928 and 1929, had made me secure for ever in that sort of calculation. That was when I was about to become the nearest to a perfect creature anyone could be: a scholarship boy. Thereafter the grammar school had taken over and I'd lost touch for ever with the idea of being academically incapable of error, and also with mathematical reality; but, made awesomely exact in the realm of pounds, shillings and pence (a graduate of the penny world), I couldn't avoid being accurate when it came to rupees. It was all that was left of the terrible little marvel I'd once been.

Kate had been as dreadful, she reminded me now, at her little school on the village green outside Barton, and cringed from the memory of being such a pert and insistent answerer of questions in that open-plan setting. You couldn't help hearing what was being asked in the next-door class, she said, and she'd been ticked off more than once for projecting an

108

answer across that large room. The vicar, after a visit in which any hesitation by a classmate had Kate dashing in with at least a proposal as to a reply, had called her 'a bright little candle'.

The butt-end of an arithmetical paragon, I reflected, was about to take the road to Agra with the stub-end of a bright little candle.

Almost at once, a whole republic of bricks. So large an area couldn't surely be given over to bricks and little else, in stacks squared off and spilling, or built up into arrangements of every kind of eccentric shape, including little mad tilting towers, with men and women walking among them of whose wrists I was suddenly aware, such a general gracefulness of wrists! There were tiny houses built of bricks, not cemented together. There were dwarf granaries, and suddenly, peacocks; and suddenly again, a hut like the idea of a witch's hat, and as black. Now the earth seemed to have been bitten into by giant teeth. Down the road came a single peacock, closely followed by a loose selection of camels. The camels, their bodies sandily dipping and shrugging with every step taken, the heads infinitely aloof, reminded me of any caravan of boys I'd attempted to lead through the streets of Hampstead or Islington. Like them, these suggested the complete absence of an intention of getting anywhere, ever. Now, in the centre of a huge field, a single woman, carrying an immense black umbrella; and then, on the roadside, as if a whole farm had been squeezed into a rectangle five yards by a hundred, a family winnowing. There were what looked roughly like grandparents, parents, uncles, aunts, sons, daughters and cousins, tossing grain into the air – Laura thought it was the sort of moment we'd wish to photograph. And I wondered what it was like to be winnowing and suddenly to be surrounded by strangers aiming cameras; specifically what it was like to be two little girls, as brown as the grain they stood in, wearing vivid scraps of cloth and grinning at the pale creatures disgorged by the coach. If it was taken that we were amazed by camels, it was clear they were amazed by tourists.

And so into Agra, through avenues of men and women squatting in battered boxes to sell everything under the sun, though so many boxes must have meant some of the goods needed another definition. One box cried BRAS FOR SALE but was selling metal pots. All the bicycles in the world were in simultaneous use. Back, then, to the unreal magnificence of a hotel, where we were insistently saluted by men in red turbans.

'I wish they wouldn't salute me,' Kate murmured. We had no gift, either of us, for being saluted. I braced myself for the moment when Kate might actually remonstrate, asking a man whose whole occupation lay in saluting to give her perhaps, instead, a democratic grin.

But Kate agreed it would not be tyrannical to ask someone to come up to our room from Housekeeping to show her how to use her international adapter so she could make her hairdryer work, and the neatest of men came and most neatly instructed her; and once he'd gone the hairdryer broke, and Kate had to be persuaded that it would not be a monstrous display of neo-imperialist arrogance to ask for the use of one of the hotel's own hairdryers. I'd not been eager, I said later as we walked in the hotel garden, to spend the holiday in the company of a woman tense from the effects of *coiffure interruptus*. We seemed to be alone in the garden, except that phantom gardeners emerged from bushes and instantly disappeared. There were little birds shaped like Concorde, totally ashen, feet included; and tiny squirrels, tails perpetually up, with three black lines dragged across their pale backs where, it was said, a god had once scratched their remotest ancestor. There were hibiscus and an entire rose garden, and an old howdah that Kate climbed into; and the garden walls were topped with broken glass, so that penurious India could be kept out of this expensive paradise.

And beyond one wall, a dab of white on the horizon was the Taj Mahal.

I'd remembered the feeling I had when I was married – that simply setting off for such a purpose amounted to a ridiculously mundane approach to it. There must be some more suitable form in which the act could be cast than merely going out and doing it. Now the day had come when the basic diary entry, which sixty years ago had been 'Went to school', had become 'Went to the Taj Mahal'. Even given the half century or so in between, this seemed a ludicrously sudden change from the banal to the sublime. Was one really in the position of getting up this morning and going out to see the Taj Mahal?

It should have helped that the everydayness around us was exotic. But that chattering and chirping flow of things, and general sense of a great colourful shabbiness of angels going in all directions on bicycles, only made its being everyday more marked. Here, within a quarter of a mile of the Taj, was a long stretch of wall topped with intermittent railings, outside one of those open spaces that in India seem in some disputable way to be parks; and along the wall men were perched. Some simply sat, legs hanging; some were squatting; some, narrow though the wall was, were loosely lying. At home the only living things you ever saw making such a line of perched creatures were birds. Here a man was fastidiously dusting the edge of the road with a short brush made of twigs; behind him came a tarring machine, supplied by a boy who appeared to be making, in a tin, a surprisingly small amount of tar. A man was climbing a lamp-post, heading for the comfort of a short bar projecting from under the lamp, on which he settled himself as if it had been an armchair. An entire family was squatting on the pavement: the father cutting his son's hair, while grandparents, mother and six or seven other children sat patiently, in what would have been a drawing room arrangement had they been sitting in a drawing room. Nothing whatever had anything about it but an everyday look. This seemed to be India's everlasting and invariable daylight occupied by its never-ending and unmomentous bustle. Even those lying on walls, or on pavements, gave out an impression of activity; there was a busy quality about the ingenious postures in which they rested. The sun itself was bicycling across the sky intent on some perfectly small routine purpose.

And here was the approach to the Taj.

Miss Hampshire, former schoolteacher, informed me that her eyes, for all but the coarsest needs of navigation, were now shut. Her dread was of disappointment. It could not be as beautiful as they said. She had looked forward to this moment for years, and now could not bear it. She was half-minded to return to the hotel. Would Kate, please, tell her, when at last it came into view, whether she could safely gaze, or should turn and run for it. I said I thought we were probably all in the same boat. The next time some of us – a very few of us – felt like this would be as we walked up the celestial drive to the last bend beyond which we'd catch sight of the Pearly Gates. My problem, I said, was that I'd never got over a scornful verdict committed to print sixty years ago by Aldous Huxley. He'd said a great quality of the Taj was that of expensiveness, and it was the money lavished on it that seemed to please most who praised it. He thought the minarets that stand at the corners of the platform (but were they not, I thought, remembering Delhi, minars?) were among the ugliest structures ever erected by human hands. This hideousness he ascribed to their being too thin, and feebly tapering. As for the Taj itself, it was negatively elegant, and dreadfully short on formal elements; St Paul's, for example, could wipe the architectural floor with it, having a great variety of elements, all those cylinders and square-faced pilasters and triangular pediments. The much-praised bas reliefs of flowers on the gateway of the Taj – how weakly laborious! They were neither good literal representations of flowers, nor good floral inventions. Oh dear, said Huxley, it is made of marble. 'Marble, I perceive, covers a multitude of sins.'

Huxley had been my hero. I'd adopted his opinions much as, about the same time exploring *Whitaker's Almanack*, I'd chosen an alternative name from the section on the peerage, signing myself 'Abergavenny', once absent-mindedly doing this at the top of a piece of maths homework. Percy Chew, our headmaster, had correctly, if unhelpfully, discerned in me a reach-me-down, threadbare suburban Huxley. There must have been hundreds of us in the grammar schools of the thirties, pretending to be wittily fastidious Old Etonians. It still seemed to me terribly possible that everyone but he, when they looked upon the Taj, had demonstrated their incapacity to see plain, or rather marbled, vulgarity when it was in front of them. One's own disappointment aside, there would arise the problem of breaking such ghastly cultural news to Miss Hampshire.

And here was a gateway, and there it was. It was an ordinary sort of light, there wasn't that early mist one had seen in some photographs, or moonlight. It was a blank plain light on a blank plain day. And the Taj Mahal was beautiful. It made a shape that . . . it stood on its platform and . . . It lay upside down in the basin of water in front of it. It had extraordinary loveliness, standing there. It stood there . . . Well, *of course* it stood there; but I'd rarely seen a building that so distinctly did so.

We froze, and not a person referred to the expense of erecting it. The gentleman from Leamington said 'Good Lord!'

And then we remembered to tell Miss Hampshire she could look. She did so, and wept.

For the next hour or so, I had poor Huxley's lapels in my grasp. *Of course*, the Taj was a central exhibit in the land of Cliché. *Of course*, anyone might be doubtful about the encounter with it, as with any other wonder that universal admiration had turned into a commonplace. One understood that Huxley had programmed himself not to yield easily to approval. But I wondered (and shook him a little, my hands on those lapels) if he'd not simply resolved to resist that universality of praise, for the sake of resisting it. Take those minarets, to begin with. Ugly? Too thin? Define, sir, the respect in which their taperingness is a feeble taperingness. And did the beauty of the Taj not result in part from an economy of formal elements? One formal element more, and would not that extraordinary pale simplicity have been ruined? It was surely like accusing a

113

rose of being formally elementary. And there were glories about it that nothing by way of photography or film had ever brought out. For example, the effect of standing on that tremendous marble platform. That was as splendid a table as any building ever stood on. The effect of shadow inside the great arched niches, in the doorway and to each side of it! *Because* it was marble (I shook my old hero a little) the shadows were massive yet delicate, strong yet soft. There was everywhere a shifting additional architecture of shadow! It had been so devised that shadowy Taj Mahals were everywhere emerging and vanishing as the light of your position altered! And then, when you walked *behind* the Taj, where cameras so rarely went – there was the broad river; and there, on its brown surface, lay one of the maligned minarets, as a most striking, slanted shadow.

When you went close, when you went inside, when you peered, the astonishment lay indeed in that richness of detail: those flowers inlaid or applied, marble, to the marble; that pervasive intricacy of arabesque and tendril and leaf. In the dusk of the interior, into which darkness seemed to have been crammed, so that you needed a torch to see much of the shining detail, I found myself standing next to Mr Rose, who was, at home, an undertaker and stonemason. That last was my family's old occupation, and talking to him I'd thought of the little cenotaphs of marble that had stood on the mantelpieces of my childhood. Now he said he did not know how to express his professional awe of what he saw, here. That inlay! Those fragments of colour, petal and leaf, would have had to be cut with perfect precision, and fitted into cut-out shapes in the marble also absolutely exact, for there were then no high impact glues! I asked him (giving Huxley a little last shake) how much his estimate would be if Shah Jehan had been *his* customer, and he said reprovingly it wasn't a place where he cared to think of cash. I shifted the burden of that reproof to my old hero – who, with sudden affection, I remembered had been tall, pale, slender, much like the minarets about which he'd been so abusive.

114

Across a sea of marble I caught sight of a worldwide couple, in conversation with an Indian who gave no impression of being indifferent to cash. I thought it was most likely that he was offering the Taj to them, and that after some brisk bargaining they might add it to their carpets and chess sets; and might very well manage to sneak with it through the green channel back at Heathrow.

# 9

'I am not a diplomat,' said Michael Reemer that evening at dinner. He was once more attempting to define himself for our
benefit, a major occupation, and was beginning with this auth-
oritative negative. It was as if a bull, pausing in his tour of a china
shop, had taken the trouble to declare: 'I am not a mouse.'

'He is,' said his wife, 'a *grand enfant.*' With that he was not
dissatisfied.

'I agree.' She rang the little bells of her laughter. 'Nobody
knows,' she said. He looked round the table, into one mild
face after another.

'*I absolutely agree.*'

'He likes a little –' said his wife '– struggle.'

'Conversational struggle,' he said.

'Without it he becomes . . .'

'. . . restless. I agree.'

My friend Richard from Leamington clearly felt obliged to
make some response, though the conversational sequence was
not of a type familiar to him. 'It takes all sorts –' he murmured,
but could not bring himself to complete the cliché, and returned to his curry. Reemer breathed heavily. He'd offered
himself as a person congenitally ferocious, but instead of
the abrasive discussion that ought to follow, these evasive
Anglo-Saxons were failing to react. Oh, if only they would
formulate their argument, such as it was, in favour of being

polite, unaggressive and uncontroversial, then – how he would . . . *controvert* it!

He turned on his chosen dish, instead.

'This is something I like?' he asked his wife.

'You have liked it when you've had it . . . here and there,' she said, guardedly.

'I may have liked it *there*,' he growled, 'but *here* I do not like it! *Here* I find it horrible!'

With Miss Hampshire I was trying to account for the effect of the Taj Mahal, which seemed not to be wholly covered by the obvious statements that were to be made about it. It had struck me that in part it might be a matter of that tremendous detailed delicacy of treatment that you might think could be brought to bear on, say, some fairly small box, being applied to a building of considerable size.

Kate was one of those saddened by the tale of Shah Jehan's last years, made a prisoner by his son in a little pavilion in the Fort, so rubicund a neighbour of the Taj, so pale. But at least he had those views of the Taj, everyone of them arched, of which imprisoned accustomedness could surely not have dimmed the impact! As one of the world's grass-tearers, I was careful about offering my sympathy to these men who'd left such bulkily exquisite evidence of their power.

Ted Drake, hearing Shah Jehan's story, said: 'I have relatives like that.'

Our guide said: 'That means you are very wealthy.'

Ted's wife said: 'I wish I knew where he kept it.'

Ted said: 'All right, I'll buy you another necklace.' This guide, too, had been bowled over by Mrs Drake.

'You will build her a tomb . . . like the Taj?'

'Wouldn't get planning permission in Sutton, Surrey, mate,' said Ted. We crossed to the emperor's bathing pool, overlooked by whispering balconies, and I imagined there were ghosts here that might be turning up their noses at this dialogue.


And we flew to Khajuraho . . .

117

# 10

But not as easily as all that. It was an early call, and we were at the airport at 6.30 a.m. It was our introduction to a fact about internal flights in India: the timetable is a work of fiction, but the carrier requires you to treat it seriously. You arrive very early for what quite certainly will depart very late. A great element of mystery is insisted upon by the airport staff. They move slowly in the distance from one door or desk to another, often with a vague appearance of intention, which is rarely genuine. Early on, these emergences inspire hope; later, they inspire a particularly desolate kind of despair. At some stage in our ordeal at Agra we were told by Laura that four officials had arrived unannounced, and had set in motion a plot to have four of us taken off the passenger list and sent to Khajuraho by car, a journey of ten hours or so. (The plane would take forty minutes.) At moments like this there seemed to be four or five Lauras, arguing energetically and subtly on our behalf. Several of us were beginning to have the feeling about her that might, I guess, easily arise when some splendid person takes fearsome burdens off your shoulders. Adoration, I suppose, was a word for it. In this cockpit of anxiety, she was all-enduring.

She was angry, she said, only when it was assumed that she too was on holiday.

And at last we were among Khajuraho's temples . . .

\*

118

It was one morning in 1838 that Captain T. S. Birt, roving engineer and archaeologist, arrived on the scene, having been tipped off about the temples, at that time lost in jungle. Noting his excited responses as he went – for he was another damned diarist – he described them as 'venerable and picturesque'. He then rested for a moment from such pathetic fallacies and made a rapid breakfast. Soon after that, ducking under branches, he discovered an inscription, the largest, finest, most legible of any he'd yet met with. He copied it, established a date, and continued to make his happy notes. He then decided to have a look round. *Si monumentum quaeris, circumspice*, he reminded himself, tucked his notebook, I suppose, into his backpocket, explored a little, and was soon scribbling again, enthusiastic about what he was able to make of this curious tangle of nature and art. He couldn't help, he said, 'expressing a feeling of wonder at these splendid monuments of antiquity having been erected by a people who have continued to live in such a state of barbarous ignorance.' It was an old story; basically, the one about Shakespeare having been unlikely to have written the works of Shakespeare.

'It is a proof,' Birt added, 'that some of these men must have been of a more superior caste of human beings than the rest.'

I imagine him sitting on some stone or other, or leaning against an intrusive tree, to record these banalities. If he was condescending, it was an awestruck condescension. Well, there appeared to have been a time when Hindu society was divided into a very great majority of uncouth persons, and a very small minority given to the building of immense and spectacular temples. It was enough to cause awe in any man. At this point he resolved to look more closely; and when he came back to his notebook, his mood had changed. He had found seven temples, 'most beautifully and exquisitely carved as to workmanship, but . . .'

It must be one of the most dashed and astonished 'buts' in the annals of aesthetic exploration.

119

*But* 'the sculptor had at times allowed his subject to grow a little warmer than there was any absolute necessity for his doing . . .'

Poor Captain Birt! Could disappointment have been expressed with a more moving effect of someone having been, at that moment, personally wounded by one he had trusted? It has the very tone that Herring at the grammar school would use, arriving late in the classroom to find us rioting. He'd relied on us to behave like saints, and we'd proved incapable of doing so. Captain Birt, for his part, had praised the creators of these temples most generously, and they had let him down.

How generally odd the terms are in which his censure is couched! By now he must surely have discovered that it was by rather more than some shade of warmth that the sculptors had exceeded his estimate of the amount of sensuous emotion an artist might devote to the decoration of a religious edifice? And that talk of there having been 'no absolute necessity' – it surely suggests that conditions can be imagined in which the artist might have been under some obligation (an absolute one) to offer a frank image of the gentleman of Khajuraho and his friend. Captain Birt can't have meant to imply as much. No, he is hurt, and is emphasising the fact by his sorrowful mildness; but that lasts only as far as a semi-colon. Beyond it he cries, 'Indeed, some of the sculptures were extremely indecent and offensive, which I was at first much surprised to find in temples that are professed to be erected for good purposes, and on account of religion.' There can't be many archaeologists who've had a more disturbing morning in the field, with such a drastic alternation of delight and disgust! For an hour or so he'd felt unexpected admiration for a few Hindus, and now he must unequivocally withdraw it. Their worship, he wrote, could not have been 'very chaste if it induced people under the cloak of religion to design the most disgraceful representations to desecrate their ecclesiastical erections.'

You feel ashamed of wondering if that last word might have tumbled from the captain's pen as a result of what he'd just seen, and recoiled from.

He notes that his palanquin bearers did not share his distaste. Indeed, 'they appeared to take great delight at those, to them, very agreeable novelties, which they took good care to point out to all present.' This last scene I imagine as an old school-master and father, recalling the sensation of moral isolation your solemn adult feels when an enormity to which he has pointed turns out to be, for the young, an occasion for glee. 'You will all be horrified by Hobday's behaviour'; but there they are, cheering him. But in fact I'm not sure that there isn't, under the captain's prose, an incipient naughtiness stirring, even something like a desire to be, at least for a moment, a palanquin bearer. At any rate, he did not leave the scene immediately, shaking off that libidinous dust, but stayed instead to measure a lingam, which he calls 'the representation of the vital principle'. (Wildly I imagine Birt, standing somewhere on the site, brooding on the bewildering events of the day, and with the help of his own representation of the vital principle, spraying leaf and stone alike.) The height of 'the gentleman' was eight feet, and the diameter four feet. Birt calculated that it weighed seven and a half tons, and was probably 'by far the biggest lingam in India'.

His notes remain under control; but I'm not sure that in these later ones he doesn't display some symptoms of an erotic equivalent of tipsiness.

At last Captain Birt took himself off, with his notebook and a head full of measurements and inscriptions and, I suspect, a fairly muddled sense of outrage. There was a pause of almost exactly 150 years, and then Kate and I and the rest of the Worldwide party arrived. The interval had been more than adequate for clearing the jungle. When E. M. Forster first saw the temples, they were still shrugging their great shoulders out of the trees; he did not care for the improvements he discovered on another visit, when the present parkland had been established. It was, though enormously hot, not wildly unlike being in the recreation ground in Barton, as to the implied politeness of the walks one was invited to take through it, the (as it were) rural urbanity of it all. But there was certainly nothing in Barton to compare with those joyous temples. Our Rec was not in the same world.

How could it have been? The Rec was only a brisk military step from the old grammar school playground, and Sergeant Clinker was often there, frowning at the flowers.

I try to imagine Sergeant Clinker in Khajuraho, but fail completely.

At the end of our journey, when some of us were in Kashmir, an excellent man splendidly worn out by headmastering said it had been generally noticed by the party that at Khajuraho I'd gone photographically frantic. Amused, he said they were, but I heard the Clinker-like sternness in that statement. Black mark. Inability to conceal indecent interest.

'You young fellows,' Percy Chew had said. 'Pick up indecencies from . . . so-called poetry! But' – I remember the occasion with a clarity it needs no diary entry to sharpen; Percy Chew looked round to make sure he was not overheard – 'don't often tell doubtful stories to boys, but all the same – fellow said of the eunuch: "But what does he *know*?" Eh, Blishen? Eh, eh, *eh*?'

Oh! At the end of this long journey – not through India, but from Queen's Grammar School, Barton, *c.* 1936, to this jubilant spot in the late 1980s – I was in possession of the retort perfect to my old headmaster.

Sir, Khajuraho to you!

# 11

We longed to walk to the village, about a kilometre away. Well, we simply longed to walk. There was a lane, and though it was in India, and astonishing temples peered above the trees, it was not unlike the lanes we walked in at home. We had such a desire to walk slowly, quietly, looking about us, talking of what we'd seen, perhaps convincing ourselves that we were really here! For all the resemblance of lane to lane, we'd have escaped for a moment from the European world we carried about with us.

But first we had to face the resistance offered by the rickshaw men who pedalled round and round in patient circles at the hotel gate. Our appearance brought them all, a flurry of voices, petitionary and then angry.

'We want to walk,' we said.

'But,' said one, cycling ahead of us, round us, ahead again, 'what of my job?' There was no decent reply to that, nothing but obstinacy.

We walked until they fell, furiously, behind. But at once, from everywhere, came children. They gathered, from no obvious source, out of hedges, out of the blue. ''Allo!' they cried. Following Laura's sensible advice we should say nothing, simply stare ahead; but neither of us knew how to cut dead Indian children crying ''Allo!'

'Where you from?' they cried. 'What your name?' They offered bits of French and Dutch. 'What your room number?'

'Please,' we said, 'we just want to walk quietly.'

'You want to be ha'lone?'

'Yes, *yes!*'

'They want to be ha'lone!'

This information, shouted in several directions, was productive of reinforcements. They demanded one, two, three rupees for services already mysteriously rendered by their mere presence. Attempting to send them packing was like trying to remove burrs by some process of shooing. But slowly from this steadily growing, ruthless little mob, asking again and again the same questions, offering and simultaneously withdrawing their sympathy, and hideously like the prep school children who in Hampstead long ago had made playground duty an agony for me, at the mercy of bombardment by questions that became increasingly and in the end hysterically absurd, two boys made themselves felt, and began to give an impression (not much more) of perhaps being able to bring about a precarious sort of order. There must have been collusion between their vague emergence as leaders and our sensing that some sort of half-way salvation might lie in accepting them as such; in the end, anyway, there was a hesitant and then rapid falling away of child after child. We were left with somehow contracted guides, their appointment arising from the exercise of juvenile politics at its most unfathomable. We were not going to be allowed to be ha'lone, but they'd be as discreet as was possible, given a natural tendency to officiousness, soon apparent. They nudged us into the village street past a broken plaster deity marking the entrance. Seated on a sludge-coloured monster, the goddess wore robes of duck-egg blue; her legs were broken off at the knee, her many arms shattered and pointing in unnatural directions. Our guides said nothing of her, but began at once drawing our attention to this and that, in what might have been a staccato parody of Mr Pram. It was difficult to know why we must look *here*, and then – if not simultaneously – *there*, for they scrambled for

124

words and were often at odds; and when there was a choice of roads, they conducted little wars as to the way forward. We found it possible in the end to ignore them; they were content to have us in their rather bored power. But we were not to tread in puddles; at the sight of one, they'd come to life, grab an elbow, cry 'Mama!' or 'Papa!'

Someone in the Worldwide party had said the temples appeared to have escaped being broken up for village use. But now everywhere we saw marvellous fragments. Fantastic beasts guarded the entrance to a garden; and, above a simple doorway, lions, fit to scare the besiegers of any Red Fort, wasted their growls. Whole carved lengths had been cut into walls. ''Ospital, 'ospital!' our guides clamoured, and we looked ridiculously for some institutional building of size; but it was a dispensary, a small part of a small house. Suddenly, on an embankment, there were four children sitting with their teacher. They abandoned their books to stare frankly at us, bright-eyed. As an old hand I felt the teacher's pleasure in having, drifting up the street, such visual aids as we were. He spoke about us to the children; smiling at us as he did so, being polite to us as visitors while, I felt sure, he was, speaking to the children, candid about us as teaching material. I picked up a book. 'Twinkle twinkle little star' was where they'd got to. In an intoxication of what must have been some kind of conceit, though it was also an old teacher's absurd pleasure in finding a classroom by the roadside, I read it aloud, and there was applause.

Then, in a doorway, a woman as beautiful as any I'd seen, in her lap a child as beautiful as herself; and wishing never to forget them I lost my diffidence, pointed to my camera and mimed a question, and she held up her hand, as I thought, in refusal, and I smiled and turned away; and as we walked up the street our guides made it scornfully clear to me that she'd held up three fingers, for three rupees. And as they pointed out the house of the Brahmin, we passed a tiny child dragging her knickers down as she went, and she looked as if she might have been some apprentice figure in the corner of a carving.

The last few yards, before we left the village, were taken up by our guides in an anxious discussion of the idea that they were our friends. It was clearly important that we should accept this description, which had a contractual force. A friend was someone who was confident of being paid for services, and so we paid for them; and immediate rivals for rupees, a dozen furious claimants to the title of friend, ran up to clamour for their dole. Their angers followed us up the lane, along which, under a huge setting sun, men and women were returning with their cattle from the fields. In the end one bitter child hung on, violently snarling his view of us as among the most unjust of human beings. He constantly plucked at my arm in his anger, ran ahead of Kate and blazed at her:

'I am your friend! I am your friend!' Kate, enraged, and unable to endure the sore meaning given to this word, cried:

'You are not my friend!'

*'Why not?'*

Kate said later it was not a question she'd quickly forget. If she'd not been so busy being angry Kate, Kate tormented, she would surely have found it easy to imagine what it was like to be this little, bitter boy, who now fell back, muttering.

The cattle, as they made their bony way past us – so beautiful, their knees and haunches emphasised by black lines in the skin! There was a solitary cow, with a pinkish-brown belly and a black propellor of a tail. Their colours were enriched by the light, at this end of the day so intense; the sun falling, as much as setting, a great glowing thing dropping towards the distant tips of temples. It must surely land, you thought, and shake us all with the bump of it.

Near the hotel gate we met a young Belgian on a bicycle. He'd been in India a fortnight – had come from Gujerat, where there was no tourism; he'd been struck by the natural friendliness of the people. He'd been invited home for meals. The contrast, by way of the corruption of relationships, became horribly marked, he said, once you entered the tourist belt. He'd come to see the temples, but was glad to have his bike, so he could cycle back to where he'd not be seen as a mere source of rupees.

# 12

I picked up the *Times of India*. In its 'Encounters' column, Rajev Jain was asking Supriya to remember him as a break in the wall of her heart; while Jehan, having assured Piya that he would love her always – day and night – when birds and lovers were asleep, when golden dawn was sweeping high and waking birds betuned the sky, had appeared to tire of aiming so loftily, and had aimed low instead: *I luv you*. I began to read a report that had about it a quality of dejected apoplexy. 'It is more than four days since the loaded service revolver of a sub-inspector of police, Mr Bibhuti Panday, was snatched away by some hardened criminals,' it spluttered, 'but nothing has been done to recover the weapon. The incident took place on September 27 at Bijapur village, where the sub-inspector had gone to arrest some criminals of Bihar. While the sub-inspector has been transferred to the police lines, no action has been taken against the culprits, named in a report lodged by the sub-inspector.' I tried to imagine the actual snatching of the revolver: it seemed a bold thing to do, given the fact that the gun was loaded; but then, Mr Panday sounded an unimpressive officer, submitting to such contemptuous assault when everything appeared to be in his favour. If they were hardened criminals, this was surely a softened sub-inspector.

As I thought over the gunfights I'd read of or seen on film – had there ever been, among them, an occasion when the baddies triumphed by simple confiscation of the armaments of the goodies? – Kate nudged me. A messenger was passing among us. By a singular misfortune, an aeroplane had crash-landed on the only runway at the airport. But . . . *no problem*! Cranes in plenty were on their way. He could assure us confidently that the runway would be free within hours. He disappeared; to return after no interval at all to assure us, confidently, that the problem was insuperable, one should not imagine that cranes were easily found, how could that be supposed? We should make ourselves happy with the thought of a long stay in Khajuraho. At once it was stated firmly that we should leave within the hour by bus. News that the runway was now free produced a little surge towards the door, reversed by the instant news that it was not.

I continued to think of sub-inspector Panday and his shame. What would be thought by his colleagues in the police lines of an officer who had been unable to retain possession of a loaded service revolver? A party of Italians appeared and made their passionate way to the door of the hotel, discussing the two buses they had been informed were definitely waiting for them. They returned at once, discussing the absence of these buses. There was now one of the sensations with which we were growing familiar – of enormous agitation, bordering on frenzy, being followed by enormous and unnerving calm. The place had boiled with messengers – suddenly there was not one to be seen. There appeared to have been a simultaneous with-drawal of hotel staff. No one had ever stood at the reception desk. The absence of the least hint of drama was complete.

At once Laura emerged from some unimaginable conference. It was her belief, she said, that the crashed aeroplane was unlikely to be moved in time for us to fly to Varanasi and keep our appointment with dawn on the Ganges. It was going to be a bus journey. She was afraid there would be no air-conditioning, and the journey would take at least ten hours. It would be uncomfortable, but we *would* get there. She smiled, to cover a great gap between reassurance and the reverse. We settled down to wait. Kate took over the *Times of India*, and became, as I thought, quite Indian in respect of sub-inspector Panday. He had clearly suffered, she said, a Hamlet-like failure of will, faced with criminals prepared to act with brutal decisiveness. A tendency to be overwhelmed by a vision of alternative actions had probably, when it came to the snatching of the revolver, deprived the sub-inspector of the kind of reflexes that I, perhaps, associated with gunplay. In India, a high noon might easily become a low sort of midnight. Much nicer, much nicer, said Kate.

I thought she was setting this value on sub-inspector Panday because she set very small value on John Wayne.

At this moment Laura reappeared to say the bus had arrived. We did not believe her for one moment, but went out; and there it was. Even in the context of the shabbiness of machines that filled the Indian roads, it gave the impression of having been a luckless bus. In several places its sides were deeply dented; and nothing about it was quite square. It was a sagging bus. At the wheel sat a man of apparent antiquity, his eyes closed. The hotel staff came out of hiding and began to load our luggage onto the roof. There, it looked as unsafe as it could be. So much by way of baggage could never be supported by the roof of so frail a bus; once seated, we'd be flattened by the descent of X's accumulating carpets, and Y's marble table tops. Two other buses, as battered, joined it; they were for the Italians and a French party, also needing to get to Varanesi. Members of a Dutch group, bound for the same destination but not yet, strolled about or sat in deckchairs on the hotel lawns, looking unforgiveably comfortable.

Now we were seated. The seats were made for persons relying on their own bodies for upholstery. Our luggage was not tied on, and attempts were made to represent that it should be. Laura spoke to the driver's assistant, who nodded warmly but took no action whatever.

Shortly afterwards, we jolted down the hotel drive. It was 1 p.m. The great journey had begun.

130

It *was*, Kate and I thought when it ended sixteen hours later, a very great journey.

India was an endless ragged ribbon of tarmacadam. This was wide enough for a single vehicle. Along it came, in both directions, a stream of, mostly, gallant ramshackle lorries, the usual silver in colour, with painted foreheads: their tails cried OK TA TA. Their technique was to drive head-on at each other until within a split second of collision, when they'd take evasive action of an extreme kind, ensuring that neither was doomed to travel for more than a few seconds along the badly bitten edge of the track. Though dreadfully visible to each other, they guarded against absent-mindedness on the part of the other driver, as he sat behind his bobbing fringe of dolls and votive objects, by sounding their horns, ferociously.

For a long afternoon and much of a night, with a break or two, our bodies were required to accustom themselves to a profoundly bruising pattern of sensation. A moment's clatter-ing advance on the remnants of the road, followed by as atrocious a concert of horns as could be imagined; then a sudden nerve-racking swerve outwards, a tremendous jolting, and a sudden nerve-racking swerve inwards. Clatter; massed honking; sickening swerve; the testing close to destruction of the springs of all our bodies; sickening swerve; clatter . . .

After one hour, we had covered fifteen kilometres, and were beginning to adjust to the curious general effect of our progress – which was that whilst we seemed to be charging along the road with desperate boldness, we were clearly getting nowhere, very much. We had also stopped, rather often. At every stop the driver, white-bearded, taciturn, climbed down and, together with his assistant, vanished. Laura, expert on India whom it still baffled, would run after them. 'They *must* get on! They must *get on!*' she'd cry. It seemed to be discovered (nothing was certain) that the driver was thinking in terms of finding somewhere that would serve him a meal, or of spending time with a relative. Unspeaking, he'd return in Laura's sigh-ing, nervously triumphant wake. 'We must *get on!* We *must* get on!' she'd urge. Once or twice it turned out that we were

131

about to cross a state boundary, and could not do so until a permit was granted. This involved a great deal of writing in roadside offices, and an astonishing amount of labour devoted to the lifting of barriers; undertaken as if these were the first barriers ever to be lifted in human history, and so a matter of completely doubtful experiment. Once it seemed we were doomed to wait for a permit to arrive from the nearest office, rumoured to be thirty miles away. Picking up such rumours, like someone receiving scrambled messages from outer space, Laura hurried here and there, being agitated as calmly as she could. An appropriate form must have been found closer at hand, for we drove on.

I thought no stop I could ever remember was quite so tremendously a stop as any of these. Everything ceased. I wasn't convinced that the disappearance of driver and assistant had to do with eating, or socialising. A stop was a stop, and they were off; and, but for Laura, might not have returned. At work here was surely some deep-rooted objection to one event leading to another. All of us in the bus had been conditioned to proceed busily from act to act. Here, the sense of an obligation to behave continuously seemed much smaller. An act tended to be followed by some distinct lapse of action. I thought back to subinspector Panday, and wondered if his stock of willingness to *do something* had been used up merely by going to that village; perhaps he simply did not wish to proceed to the further action of preventing the removal of his revolver.

The impatience inside the bus was great. And I felt uneasy about it. What a tremendous sense we had of the need to get on! How we twiddled our thumbs, how we bit our nails! How we murmured! Oh, these people, these Indians! How lacking in energy they were! How undisciplined! I wondered how *we* looked to, say, the driver, with his apparently blank face that was, perhaps, simply a face we did not know how to read. What did he think of all that nervous urgency, that glancing at watches; those groans as, again, the bus drew aside, perhaps at one of the great heaps of tyres with which every village abounded?

132

'Oh good, we're stopping beside another great heap of tyres,' Ted Drake cried. The bus was full of irritable irony.

The long bruised afternoon began to merge into what promised to be a very long bruised night. We stopped at a shrine, and driver and assistant were gone before Laura could stop them – to offer up, it seemed, prayers of a protracted kind for a safe journey. Just here, the road had run into a little forest of teakwood. Leaves hung huge, limp and brown. There were shaven heads, holy robes the colour of the sinking sun, the bright red caps of acolytes. Suddenly we were as far from the familiar as most of us had ever been. Then we drove on again, a lurching ant intent on evading, every thirty seconds or so, a silver ant going lurchingly in the other direction.

And then, in mid-evening, came a stop of a different kind. In the smoking dusk, we drew up in a village, alongside what was clearly the garage. Not that it looked much like any garage familiar to us. There was the inevitable stack of tyres; there was an air pump worked by a generator roofed with tin slung from a branch of a huge tree. And there was a wiry boy, perhaps fourteen years old, who turned out to be the genius of the place. All three buses had flat tyres. From the broken lip of the road on which they'd halted there was a steep tumble down to the bare earth where the work of the garage was carried out. Behind was an eating place, in front of it a long counter on which half a dozen immense saucepans boiled perpetually. There were explosions, here and there, of unshielded light. The darkening air seemed edible, somehow; it was denser and more odorous than the air we were accustomed to. There was a smell as though a cloud of garlic hovered above us. And the wiry boy stepped forward, and began work on removing the faulty tyres.

I can't say why the occasion was enchanting, as it certainly was. There was the element of sheer accident. By chance these English, these French, these Italians had provided, for what turned out to be a couple of hours, a weird addition to the population of this busily idle, battered village. Wildly different worlds occupied, for the moment, a single orbit, and there

133

seemed to be delight, in that, on both sides. Centre stage, the boy with his assistants, men who plainly left all major achievement to him. He beat the big tyres off the wheels with blows from a huge hammer. His apparently unwearying litheness glistening with sweat, he detected punctures, carried out repairs, used for inflations the air pump, which under its tutelary tree was like some gasping animal, beat the tyres back into place. Admiringly we watched this performance, shifted with him as the centre of his activities changed, spread back to give him room for some of his more Vulcan-like attacks on those large, often-repaired and profoundly weary tyres. And I had a sudden memory of standing, sixty years earlier, in Wood Street, Barton, part of an intent circle of small boys, looking down into a hole in the road in which men were working with pick-axes. Now all these sophisticated tourists from Europe had become small creatures again, absorbed in the details of someone else's labour, he looking young enough to need, if the Barley Road bell had had any authority in northern India, to run for the school gates as we'd have done, c.1928. At one point the Italians sang. We ate the packed dinners we'd been given, and out of those warm, appetising shadows came dogs, slinking, rushing at a crumb and fleeing from what they clearly thought must be an angry foot. One dog was a desperate cringer, and begged our mercy every creeping inch of his advance towards the tiniest fragment of a boiled egg. Behind the counter with its bubbling saucepans was a boy with teeth made to grin with; he reminded me of someone I'd taught at Stonehill Street, round about 1950, and I grinned out of old habit; and this echo of an Islingtonian did what Ronnie Smith would have done, bared those teeth in the boniest expression of amusement reciprocated. Throughout our stay we were trapped in a need to grin at each other. To one side in a sweet stall, the usual open box with a platform and short-legged table, sat the shopman, legs crossed; not a grinner, at all, a man with the grave face of a philosopher, but whose trade was in the very sweetest and most cloyingly foolish of sweets. They looked, displayed around him, like jewels of brash-coloured

134

jelly. The heat was still great. Behind another tree so tall that one could only say it became part of the night sky stretched a row of tiny houses. Open doors revealed the utmost minimum of furnishing; if a table, then no chair; if a chair, no table. One house seemed to be occupied exclusively by a large bright bicycle.

There was groaning when we took to the road again; but Kate and I thought we'd rarely had such luck. If that plane hadn't pancaked on the runway at Khajuraho, we'd have flown this distance in forty minutes, and never seen that village, never stood in it, never watched that juvenile Vulcan at work, never been, however briefly, part of a scene that had some remote and magic familiarity to us all. I thought I was back among my dreams. They, surely, offered assemblages of old landscapes, old habitations, that the profoundest sort of memory, and the imagination, agreed in recognising.

And as we clattered and bumped and vibrated our way forward, we witnessed the wayside Indian night as we'd never otherwise have seen it. How else would we have discovered that India appeared to sleep roughly between four and half-past in the morning? At any other moment we were likely to find an entire village sitting inside some square of blowing drapes and coloured lights, watching a single television set. At two o'clock in the morning, a whole town had turned itself into a musical instrument; the houses seemed to be drums, the air itself a flute. Somewhere out of the dark came figures carrying blazing torches, from some unimaginable seminar for which the only convenient timetabling was during the small hours. Half of India clearly waited till the middle of the night to ride about on unlit bicycles, relying for their security on the extravagant headlights of buses and lorries, which turned them into pedalling brilliances. And as the night wore on, the driver and his assistant accumulated acquaintances, relatives, picked up off the road, until the cab was full of uncles and nephews (if that's what they were) using each other's shoulders as pillows. It was as if we were preceded through the night by a gaudy sort of mobile bedroom.

135

Such a journey! Each lap of it seemed of infinite and hopeless length. For much of the way we had the torment of not knowing how far we'd come, or how far we had to go; and then a pair of French eyes detected a milestone – we'd missed these because they seemed to have been designed to look as unlike milestones as possible – and we then had the torment of knowing precisely how many miles we'd done, and how many were left to do.

But, weary far beyond weariness, we came at last, amid a sallow lifting of darkness, into the back streets of the ancient city of Varanasi, that used to be written Benares; and so to Clark's Hotel, old and famous, where we'd have been glad (quite apart from our now ungovernable lust for beds, sheets and pillows) to have spent the night.

But we were not to sleep yet. We were just in time for dawn on the Ganges.

# 13

The Dutch party from our hotel in Khajuraho was already there, had arrived the previous evening, the runway having been cleared soon after our departure: so they'd come in a flash by plane, and were as fresh as tulips. It was impossible not to despise them for their air of being well-organised and having slept. And then we were in a coach being taken to the Ganges; and although we knew about dawn in this city, there was no way of understanding the crammed, flowing, enormously murmuring, boiling, wide-awake nature of the streets. How, at five a.m., could there be so many bicycle bells? The whole world was up and about and, as it made its way to the river, hooting and bell-ringing and talking at the top of its voice. We left the coach and joined a stream with the breadth of a hundred pairs of shoulders . . . but there were many streams, in fact *everything* was plural, there was an amazing multiplicity of flow, with human snags everywhere, and every variety of collision; and among cataracts and cascades of people we were being swept down huge steps to the river. Here *was* the river, made gold in a hundred different ways by the rising sun; and over there, above the other bank, was the sun itself, a clumsy immensity of fire, and if you had eyes to spare you could have studied the many kinds of gold there were, all the golds of water and stone and the gold of flesh.

And we were in a boat, and two men, perhaps father and son, were taking us with thrusts of thick oars through the gilded water. It was the most enormous bathroom in the world. Every kind of ablution was occurring, accompanied by every kind of physical exercise, though what appeared to be gymnastics were perhaps devotions; and in niches, and on steps, and on coloured rafts and fragments of rafts, there were great towellings and the wrapping and unwrapping of robes: and everywhere, men and women stood in or out of the water, as still as statues. There was an immense watery hubbub. And we were intruders, we were prying; we stared but this dipping, dressing, undressing, surging, praying, meditatively roaring riverside world was too absorbed to stare back. At every other sweep of the oars we collided with floating salesmen, offering metal jugs and pots to carry Ganges water in. And so we moved through the glowing new day, through the live bustling water, with the generous warmth of the sun on our shoulders, towards the burning ghats, bonfires of the dead.

Here were those black biscuits, smoking, flaming, composed of logs and limbs. Strange, strange, from a world where the dead are burned out of sight, to come to these public cremations! A distant figure used a long pole to let air into a pyre, and among the disturbed faggots falling back again was a black smoking leg.

And I thought of the necessary fascination that was, for Kate and me. Nearing seventy, you returned from time to time to an exercise that no human being can avoid, though some allege they do so, saying it's morbid – as if being able to define it were in itself some kind of avoidance.

When that blackened limb rose and fell, I caught Kate's eye, and we smiled, ruefully. The sun, having raised itself at first slowly above the horizon, was now hurrying to take up its general morning position. Everywhere we looked there was that astonishing vigour, that constant shift of light, that elaboration of human movement, that marvellous living agitation, which prevents us, watching the public disposal of someone who was alive yesterday, from ever putting ourselves in his

138

ashy place; though the intellectual outline of the case is perfectly clear to us, and we have no difficulty in acknowledging that, perhaps on some morning when the sun is as impatient as now to punch its way towards the zenith, we shall be reduced to blackened bits and pieces, and, with professionally adept raking and pounding, to ash.

The guide pointed to the grandest of the riverside mansions: its filigreed stone brow sprouting plaster tigers, crows wheeling in the air above it. The sumptuous abode, he said, of one of Varanasi's most successful men – mortician and undertaker.

Heavens, I thought, catching the eye of one of our oarsmen, who gave a little duck of his head as if he were following my thoughts perfectly, and was much of my mind, heavens, how extraordinary, considering the myriads of the dead, is our capacity to believe ourselves to be alive till the very last moment! Well, of course, we *are* alive, but against the background of history, as they say, it's the rarest and briefest of attributes – and not to be made too much of. This huge beautiful Earth has been everyone's husband or wife, and everyone's widow or widower! If you looked for an adjective for the sun, the river, those steps, those ghats, those banyan trees it was the custom for builders to respect, so they'd intricately shape a house round the equally intricate agedness of a tree – if you looked for a word for all that, it was 'fickle'. The Earth loves us all, and has no difficulty whatever in letting us all go.

We turned at the burning ghats, and were rowed back to the steps where we'd come aboard. And so into the city, where, fresh from thoughts of death, I was struck by amazed thoughts about life.

The fact was that until I came to India I had not known what a crowd was.

We were borne back towards our coach by massive human swarms, and all that brief experience, of Jaipur and Agra especially, came to a head: and I began to understand the discovery I'd made in India, of a human circumstance unlike any I'd previously appreciated. Once before, reading Salman Rushdie's *Midnight's Children*, I'd begun to feel it, for that's a book that swarms and adds multitude to multitude. I thought it might have told me more about India than anything else I'd read. The word was Shakespeare's: multitudinousness. Now, in Varanasi on that extraordinary morning, I saw what that meant. It was as if, in every street in India, a score of theatrical companies were to stage, simultaneously, their most ambitious productions. Towards that kerb, though there's unlikely to be a kerb, *Peer Gynt* and *Hamlet* and *The Sound of Music*; on the other side, the *Mahabharata*, of course, and various low farces and high tragedies – though almost certainly there are also low tragedies and high farces.

Barton High Street on a Saturday morning was secret, silent, meagrely peopled, compared to these Indian streets, every one of them a congested theatre.

And above our heads as we reached the coach, the telephonic equivalent of the crowds below: an astonishing junction of wires, knotted, lashed together, darting in every direction from a chaos of junction boxes, a midair banyan tree of communications, through which at this moment I imagined hundreds of indecisions and prevarications making their baffled way.

140

# 14

We were the victims of a game being played in a tiny hot elbow of corridor leading to Emigration. Hints of a readiness to deal with us were randomly combined with hints of a total disinclination to do so. An official would open a door, peep out, make an appearance on our side, remain there for a moment while we began to form a file to pass through, and then return, shutting and noisily locking the door against us. Laura said it was impossible to tell if on this occasion they'd accept all our passports in a heap from her hands, or would require us to present them individually. I was shocked by the rapidity with which, in such circumstances, angers swell. Fury with the Indian game became fury with the game it turned out to be easy to imagine a group of Italians were playing, as they spilled into the corridor behind us. They exerted, or seemed to be exerting, pressures on us, and we exerted, or seemed to be exerting, counter-pressures. It was as if those involved in a scrum at Twickenham had pretended not to be playing Rugby at all. We were irritated by their national style, as it emerged in relation to the problems of being dreadfully squeezed together and threatened with asphyxiation whilst being boiled. They were musically exclamatory in their protest, made arias of it; we were laconic, deeply annoyed to have to express ourselves strongly in public. A Dutch group arrived to exert pressure on the Italians: and we deplored their style, too.

Uppish, we thought. Uppish in some sort of . . . *Dutch* way. There were unkind comments on Italian and Dutch as languages: one too playful to be appropriate to everyday affairs, the other held to have some sort of inbuilt impoliteness. Such nonsense spread among us, as the various official desks remained unmanned and doors opened hopefully only hopelessly to close. Kept waiting by India, surely stirred by long memories of being kept waiting by us, Europe began to behave very badly indeed.

At last an official appeared and remained; but he turned out to have a startling demand to make. All batteries should be removed from cameras. There was a puzzled, irritated move in this direction by most; I couldn't remember how the battery chamber on my camera should be opened, and was horribly certain I'd forced it fatally. But meanwhile Richard from Leamington required the official to say why this demand was being made. 'We weren't asked to do this in Delhi,' he said. Ah well, then, said the official, in the form of an abdicatory shrug. 'Don't bother!' called Richard, but too late for me and others.

There followed enormous disobligingness, a cine-camera was thrown from desk to desk. Rubber stamps were brought down on the pages of documents with grimacing violence. On the other side of this ordeal we assembled, shaken. I was surprised to hear myself say, so Mr Growserish you could almost see the brandished umbrella, that I was sure India, in some diplomatic embodiment or other, would not wish such resentment to be roused, by such ungracious treatment of a party of persons who had, after all, chosen India as a country they were eager to visit. There was a general statement of the intention of writing letters to the Indian Ambassador in London. Michael Reemer savaged one of the mildest members of the party with his view that the ending of the Raj had been a tragedy, and almost certainly a consequence of the British being averse to aggressive argument. 'This scene could have been predicted in every detail,' he cried. 'I am sure you agree with me in that.' The other man made as assenting a face as

142

he could, given that he clearly would never have presumed to predict anything. If anyone had lost us the Raj according to Michael Reemer's scenario, it was he. 'One is tired of being proved to be right,' Reemer groaned. 'It happens again and again to my husband,' Mrs Reemer explained.

Exhaustedly and absurdly fuming (and some of us fuming because the experience had so easily brought out the absurd in us), we boarded the plane to Kathmandu, which offered during the short flight small, delicious drinks. The plane was small, the air hostesses were small, there was a widespread inclination to think of Nepal as a deeply modest and attractive *small* country populated by modestly *small* persons, obviously preferable to the ridiculously vast and ill-natured country we had left.

Oh Lord, this was going too far, I thought, as we passed relaxedly through an absent-minded sort of official reception at the airport in Kathmandu, and stepped into a coach pointed out smilingly. How much easier to be good-humoured if you were a tiny mountain kingdom than if you were the stupendous bulk of a sub-continent! And as to size, not far behind that soft darkness surrounding the coach was Everest, to name but one item in a mountain range not famed for modesty. At the hotel a Gurkha doorman saluted, grinned enormously, and we were received into the eager embrace of the Everest Sheraton. To our rooms we were taken by a process close to wafting.

But no doubt about it, the door of the battery chamber on my camera would never shut again by the method intended. It struck me that I might mend it with Elastoplast, and I found that a strip of this indeed held the door in place.

I had, I thought ridiculously as we fell into a bruised sleep, the only camera in Nepal that had cut itself whilst shaving.

# 15

I don't see how you could not love Nepal.

Only a year or so after our visit, it was to make violently clear its wish to speak with more than the voice of king and courtiers. In the past it has suffered seriously from Western idealisations, and I wouldn't care to add to those. But being there was almost complete delight. I don't know how to account for it, except by way of a scene or two. It's as if being there was to be in the audience at a little theatre, specialising in marvellous tableaux. We didn't begin with the most tremendous of those, but it gives a measure of the depth of this playhouse, the smallness of which is that of a telescope when closed. Short journeys in Nepal revealed great distances, and not only geographical ones: not only, let's say, that represented by the Himalayas.

A mystery. What is it that makes the Himalayas, for which you are perfectly prepared – you know they are extremely large, and occupy a great deal of space horizontally as well as vertically – still so simply astonishing? I hadn't imagined that we'd be *taken to see them*, one afternoon, travelling for the purpose in cars. How could they, so huge, be nevertheless capable of being, in this sense, *seen*? We left the cars near the top of a winding hill road, and walked on, and turned a corner . . . and it was as if the world had stepped back, immensely.

Never before had I turned a corner and seen the world instantly step back such a shocking distance: a coloured gulf, beyond which, surely the most remote backcloth in the world's theatre, were mountains on the ground, and mountains in the sky. Somehow, you knew at once which were the stupendous Himalayas and which were stupendous clouds; ice and rock, in some fashion, declared themselves, as did colossal constructions of vapour. They seemed silent, which appeared an absurd thing to feel about them until you saw it was their necessary freedom from habitation you were aware of. It was part of the amazement that suddenly you were faced with a view that was not only one you didn't believe could be offered, but presented the largest area of rigorously uninhabited land you'd ever seen or were likely to see. Across there, beyond the immediate scene which was one of the greenest bushes, the most startlingly orange flowers, silently spread those vastnesses − creatures defining themselves by pure, cool, improbable size. I suppose, in the end, that was it: you were face to face with the greatest of all possible manifestations of immensity. Only the Pacific Ocean, if you could have seen it entire, would be more amazing.

We walked back down the hill to the cars as the night fell rapidly. On a bend, a family were making hives of drying corncobs: clearly visible as we passed them, within a few steps they'd become ghosts in the gathering dusk, tending what looked like small phantom pyramids. And the moon appeared; though it was so large, composed so purely of gleaming pale light, that we thought it must be a replacement for the familiar one. I said to Kate how odd it was to be trying hard to say Himalaya, house of snow, instead of that false plural we're accustomed to − odd because the correct form, correctly pronounced, had been one of a series of such exactnesses that our headmaster Percy Chew had insisted we adopt, with the result that we'd resisted doing so. Gentlemen, he declared, pronounced Trafalgar in the Spanish fashion. As for Rheims, another of these names by which your social status was established, he made so horrid a sound of it that the worst snob might have hesitated to adopt it.

145

I think it was one of the earliest things Kate ever said to me: that she longed to see the Himalayas. That was in 1946, when we were trying to sort out, and if possible authenticate, longings nearer home. I think of the talk there is between you at this early stage of a love affair. Almost everything you report of yourself to the other has alarming resonance: merely hinting at your tastes – in music, perhaps – suddenly fills the world with what seems astonishing information. Good Lord, here was Kate declaring herself a lover of *Little Women* (she'd wanted to be Jo – and for some time, before I began to work out who she was, I believed she *was* Jo); an admirer of the youngish Laurence Olivier, and a little more hesitantly an admirer of the youngish John Gielgud . . . with a guilty greed for chocolate.

And, of course, a necessarily patient greed for the Himlayas. She'd always wanted to see them, and I'd always wanted to see her seeing them; and so it was as suitable a celebration of forty years of marriage as I can imagine, going with her round that corner in Nepal. Forty-two years the journey had actually taken, and it was like that from Khajuraho to Varanasi – often deeply uncomfortable, with a strong tendency to flat tyres – but we'd not have taken any other route.

And Buddhism.

Here's a temple courtyard: at one side, four boys playing a form of football, with two rearing brass elephants as goal posts. The elephants have breasts, long eyes and trunks curved like French horns, and their elbows and shoulders are elaborately armoured. I try to imagine such a scene in Westminster Abbey. At a brass kiosk, its roof of copper, with prayer wheels hung in a workmanlike manner from rails, a priest leans on matter-of-fact elbows and talks to a friend; at their feet a brass tortoise. That is, I think it's brass till suddenly out of the corner of an eye I'm aware of the tiniest disturbance of the metal, a little gaping of a mouth. The tortoise is alive, and its mouth has opened in what must have been the slightest yawn ever. And I think, here is eternity, and here is the perfect expression of the tedium of it, a tortoise yawning . . .

146

And elsewhere, the most stupendous stupa in the world. You walked through a gateway most cheerfully decorated, between grinning white and green monsters baring phenomenal teeth, and there it was, a white bubble that took your breath away. It seemed at once to make a tremendous offer of religious jollity. From above the brightly painted blue eyes and the winding figure 1 representing the unity of things, lines of bunting flew to the distant edges of the platform as if elements of the maypole were added to all the other marks of delight, including two plaster statues that would have been equestrian except that they were elephantine, one beast mounted by a lavishly-moustached hero out of a mummer's play, brandishing a child's idea of a sword. I stood up there and looked at the crescents of small bright shops with which the dome and platform were enclosed, and at two stout women walking round the skirts of the stupa making one prayerwheel after another revolve in the great circle of them that was the circle of the place itself. Beyond the town, the plain; beyond the plain, the immense mountains, circle beyond circle. The spinning of the prayerwheels made you think these other wheels were spinning, too. I suppose if you come new to the spire-and-tower-thrusting religious buildings of Europe, you may be made to feel dizzy by a perception of how thrilling it is to aspire so candidly upwards. Here, on the platform of the stupa, I was made dizzy by a sense of the world, and time, as a system of spinning globes and rings.

Above us, the clouds seemed to stream at an acute angle, mimicking the lines of holy bunting. And, said Kate, those little girls over there, squealing as they ran to hide behind a grove of miniature white temples of the dead, had been enjoying mimicry of their own: of my elderly European's gait.

# 16

Mrs Dreary said you wouldn't catch her flying over Everest in the early morning or at any other time of day. Other people could do what they liked, of course. But she'd flown over the Grand Canyon once, on some similar tour, and been bitterly disappointed. Kate and I were alarmed, finding we were of her party. Not out of fear of disappointment, but because Laura said the price of a ticket had increased horribly since she was last here, but nobody would tell her by how much. You had to pay in sterling, and having put your name down you were committed to whatever price prevailed. It seemed alarmingly vague. Most of our lives we'd been easily capable of being sunk, financially, and we hadn't brought a large amount of sterling with us. Still, it was awkward, being grounded with Mrs Dreary.

In any case, she said, she might if pressed admit to feeling better than yesterday, but it was five per cent compared to nought per cent.

'There's no point in eating,' she said, daintily snickering, 'when you put it in one end and it goes straight through you.' I raised a glass of mango juice to my lips and had her husband's attention.

'Cured of having anything to do with mangoes during the war,' he said. 'Nasty greasy fruit.'

'I think I know what caused it but I'm not going to say,' she said. She looked round for someone to apply pressure, but instead there was a general rising from the table. We'd all grown accustomed to walking round with huge quantities of unused salt tablets, water-purifying tablets, mosquito repellent, lip salve and (more often in use) aperients and counter-aperients. For Mrs Dreary, this forbidding pharmacopoeia was an element in the landscape looming larger than the Himalayas. Her husband, who was given to speaking of her as if she were some absent paragon, said, 'She has to be careful what she eats.' On an earlier occasion he'd said, 'She has moods,' and they'd laughed together in a muffled fashion, as if there might be a meaning for the word one hadn't previously encountered.

'Brash about her bowels,' murmured the gentleman from Leamington as we fled.

My own bowels had behaved badly the day before. For lunch I'd had a glass of mineral water in our room, and Kate had gone to one of the little restaurants in the hotel in search of all I wished for when it came to eating: a perfectly plain, distinctly small piece of toast. There was toast-this and toast-that available in this oddly-named eatery, *Reputations*, and having made it plain that she wanted no this and no that, but toast only, Kate was handed her order packed in a charming small pale-blue box, tied with coloured string. Still smiling, for the waitress's own smile as she handed the box over had been one of those that make you feel pleasant for some time after being its object, Kate joined me and I unwrapped her offering. Inside the box was a distinctly small piece of plain bread.

I had come all this way, I thought, *not* to fly over Everest, and to lunch on bread and water.

But as I looked out of the window with a sense of fragile hunger comically thwarted, I saw on a flat roof opposite a child turning a great golden spread of rice to dry it. She did this by shuffling it with her feet, an accustomed shuffling that produced an effect of tides having receded from sand. What lovely things people did with rice!

149

Yesterday we'd been in Bharaktpur. I'd never be nearer than that, I thought, to the sensation of walking through a medieval town. There were narrow streets between high brown houses, most of them quite sensationally cracked. The lower rooms of a house seemed to be holding veils and curtains in front of themselves, a deeply shadowy shyness. They felt as if they were densely lived in, not in some commonplace sense of overcrowding, but as of complicated use. You glimpsed children with exquisite faces, women whose skins seemed pale in the dusk, though in fact they were warmly brown. And then, suddenly, a square, leading into another, a whole jigsaw of squares, and in all of them, women winnowing rice. There were hills of it, and as some made it dance in shallow round trays, others tidied and re-tidied the hills with little brooms. It was all a casting of grains in the air, clouds of pale dust, and sweeping and heaping. The women wore bodices, red, blue, silvery grey, and dark wrap-around skirts, hemmed always with red. Beyond them, armies of pots, hardening in the sun, many hundreds over here, many hundreds over there, made of a dark brownish-grey clay. The town was an open-air pottery, a farm, suddenly a market, the hills of rice replaced by rainbow heaps of cloth; and, somehow, street ran into square, square narrowed to street, mysteriously. There was a sense of unfamiliar sequences. In some dimension beyond the geographical, I had not been here before, was wonderfully astray.

It made me think of the story that first convinced me that history wasn't invented by schoolteachers: Hans Andersen's *The Magic Goloshes*. Having put the goloshes on by mistake, the old historian is subject to their power, which is that of granting any wish framed by the wearer. He thinks how much he'd like actually to tread the streets of fourteenth-century Copenhagen, which he knows so well from his studies, and from documents and old maps. And at once he is there, the night as murky as the one he's left, but he takes time to fathom what has happened: all the academic understanding in the world not enabling you to make sense of some actual

150

scene from the historic past. To be at home you must also have a grasp of the historic present. It's no use going there with 'then' in your mind, for the people you encounter will have made themselves unfamiliar to you by their obstinacy in thinking 'now'.

Here, a shrine: a fabulous animal baring its curved teeth, standing on a plinth on which a cat was curled that looked like some quiet commentary on the creature above it. Compare, it seemed to say, animal fantasy, and animal fact. But again . . . what did I know about fantasy? The steps of a temple were guarded by a hierarchy of creatures: sternly bland kings or officials at the bottom; then elephants, ten times more powerful than the men below; then appalling apotheoses of the griffin, each mouth a torture-chamber of teeth, necks garlanded with chains and bells, these being ten times more powerful than the elephants.

Fantasy, certainly, but fantasy in broad daylight: fantasy for common use.

And at a last crook of a street before it swelled into a square, a low shop, six foot high, crammed with creatures of clay: beasts snarling, tiny fat-bellied men smiling behind enormous moustaches, elephants amiable and elephants dyspeptic. And in the doorway, cross-legged, a girl, perhaps twelve or thirteen, shy-faced, I thought, such shy handsomeness! Well, it must be shyness, surely a modesty of some sort? And beside her, a very small brother, who might have been of clay, much the size of many of the ceramic fantasies around him. And I thought of Miss Baker, at Barley Road School, who'd first made me aware that I'd spend my life trying to find words for what was in front of me – Miss Baker, with her unrolling in the classroom of cracked pictures on some sort of oilcloth: a farmyard, a street, a beach. 'Describe what is in the picture' was the way the task was expressed. 'In the picture,' you responded, 'I see . . .' Now sixty years on and six thousand miles from Barley Road I looked at this sweet-faced child cross-legged in the doorway of that shop full of pottery, blue-grey and russet, and thought how profoundly I did *not* know

151

how to say what, in the picture, I saw. What I saw was beautiful, but there was the deepest sort of unfamiliarity about it.

And so into another square, and again rice being floated, fanned, thrown again and again, golden clouds in the air, golden heaps on the ground.

On the way home, we passed the Shangri-La Bakery. And alongside a copper fountain, from which a god raised his arm in a wave, his chest and belly like shields, knock-kneed, his tongue protruding, there was a knocked-together sort of box advertising jeans and tennis shorts, two white youths pictured lolling under a cry of WHAM!

We ourselves now had the habit of waving to children from the coach, feeling a safety and sad relief in it: they could not demand rupees from us for doing it.

# 17

Mrs Dreary's breakfast intake dropped to a single biscuit, ill-spoken of when she'd eaten it.

'I have to think about her health,' said Mr Dreary, adding his own weight to the attack upon the biscuit. 'We shall have to wait and see what the effect is on her.' Michael Reemer's intake of small green bananas, always remarkable, reached a new record of thirteen at a sitting. He became absent-mindedly good-natured when eating, but was soon ready again to cut down any remark made by anybody about anything.

'I think we have to look *twice* at that!' The remark had been made out of the generally pleasant and vapid wellbeing that resulted from being on holiday, and its maker didn't want to look at it once, let alone twice. But for Michael Reemer, debate appeared to be another sort of eating. He needed immense intakes of urgent dispute if he was not to pine away. Hearing his voice coming from a safe distance, triumphantly dissatisfied and challenging, members of the party made little effort to conceal their relief.

At times it was difficult to tell which form of hunger was gnawing at him at a particular moment. I had this problem when we'd been taken to see the Hindu temple where the remains of the kings of Nepal were burned. It was on the bank of a river, coming down steep steps busily to the water. We walked to it along the facing bank, past yet more winnowing of rice. In those shallow round trays they shook the rice and then used the trays to make draughts with, to blow the rice over and over – it looked as though they were making music that happened to be inaudible. And winnowing seemed like dance and music and semaphore together. Spread on the path, the rice was given the patterns made in sand by a retreating tide. Husbandry, the transport of the grain by water, and worship seemed such close and easy neighbours that the whole stretch was like some sort of religious wharf.

On steps outside the temple, a burning ghat and a lingam being devoutly tended by two women. On our side, a regiment of lingams, each in its stone house pierced with curved arches, so you looked through house after house at a sort of stammer of dark stone erections. I found myself, looking through an arch, staring at a staring monkey, also looking through an arch four or five lingams further down. His expression was one of such doleful recognition that I believed we must have met before. I mentioned this to Michael Reemer, who thought it was *glorious*, his usual term for a remark he liked (though it didn't guarantee you against attack for that very remark), but I could see he was made uneasy. 'You're not going Indian, are you?' he asked. I think he meant I might be allowing myself to frame unlikelihoods for the sake of it. Throughout the journey he'd launched assault after assault on what he took to be the Indian (and now the Nepalese) liking for mystical assertions, which he argued were devices to give a philosophical justification for their inability to run their aircraft on time. At this moment, I suspected, it was hunger of the belly rather than the brain that was bothering him. His appetite had been stimulated by the monkeys, who were given so much to the mimicry of mastication.

'I suspect they have secret sources of food,' I said, to test this idea of mine. He jumped.

'I'd like to know of those,' he said. Then he must have decided I'd not meant it seriously. 'That was *glorious*,' he said.

*

In Kathmandu we experienced some of the best, and one of the worst, moments of the whole journey.

The best arose out of the marvellous confusions of the city itself. Those white buildings with heavy, dark-framed doors and windows – I'd never seen such an assertiveness of these features – the pediments extended on each side of door or window to give an effect as of massive arms outstretched! The elaborations of carving, amounting in some cases to a kind of dementia of writhings, serpents and gods and goddesses with many arms, and labyrinths of worms. Some of the eye-windows, out of which you could see while no one could see in, were clotted with marvels of this sort. One, I observed, was a prodigious bouquet of symmetrical snakes ending in a tight posy of heads and fangs. A house itself was a god; and, cheerfully risking Michael Reemer's accusation of irrationality, I thought you could feel the truth of that. It was as in Bharaktpur: there was that sense of the house as a dusky box of secrets, a power. And in the streets, a pure clamour of colour, and so much hooting, so many bells, such movement – more like that movement of wooden carved snakes than anything I'd seen in a Western city, though I'd known in Africa a similar sense of streets being swarmed over. It was a city of puppets, too – puppets for sale, hanging outside shops, displayed on trees. I longed to take home an untransportable villain with moustaches galore, arms beyond counting, and each of all those hands holding a sword that the smallest movement made him seem to be sharpening, a Carborundum forest.

And there was Kumari Devi, the house of the living goddess. A chosen child, she lived there for the period of her divinity, a strange prisoner. We followed our guide into the courtyard and he clapped his hands and called her name, and at one of those windows so emphasised – so carved that I suppose part of the astonishment they caused us lay in the oddity of the frame being a work of art – there was suddenly a deep view of the child herself, in the dusk of a room, wearing a chaplet of flowers, appearing and raising a hand and vanishing, and round

155

her, the flitting whiteness of other little girls, her court and company. I thought inconsequently of Lady Jane Grey and Elizabeth I and all those captives in fairy tales, who coloured my amorous ambition at Barley Road so that I dreamed nightly of rescuing Jean Rawlins from cruel incarceration in a battle-mented version of Barton Council Offices, though I knew well enough that she was accommodated in the kindest fashion in a semi-detached in Barley Road itself.

We went off then to buy a Nepalese hat for a grandson from the meadows of Nepalese hats spread out in a square through which flute sellers strolled, their flutes made into a sort of portable palm-tree. A tiny child was curled asleep under the white belly, striped with red, of a venerated monster with a tremendous orange penis.

The bad moment came not long after that, when a young man drew up alongside us and produced a carving of a god, a king – perhaps it was both.

'Twenty dollars,' he said.

Kate forgot the need to be totally unresponsive, allowed some kind of eye contact, and said: 'No, thank you.'

He thrust it at her again. 'Only twenty dollars.'

'No, thank you.' We left him behind, but a few yards down the street there he was, ahead of us. He turned.

'It is twenty dollars only!'

'No, thank you.'

'But it is only twenty dollars!' – as if he suspected Kate of deafness in addition to stupidity.

'No, *thank you*!' He walked alongside us.

'In travellers' cheques! As you like!'

'Look,' said Kate. 'I don't want it.'

'American Express,' he said. He had a bitter face, made for the bitter game he now played with us, for perhaps half an hour. After the first ten minutes we'd concluded he wasn't going to be persuaded to leave us alone, ever – till the end of time, he'd drill away at us with this demand of his, fractionally altering by terribly slow degrees, and with his unbearable indifference to our distress. Kate was close to tears, I to fisticuffs. But then, we thought (in all the wretchedness of it, as the coloured streets became simply the setting for useless rage), our presence here, in this role, had brought about *his* presence, in the role of the bitter gadfly, whose technique was trade by torment. He was stinging us again and again with those faintly reducing proposals. Kate's frantic pleas for mercy clearly made it easier for him to be merciless. There was no escape. He was everywhere, bitter, beside us, ahead of us, round every corner. And then, suddenly, when we were sick from a hundred stings, he gave up.

'Ten dollars!' it had been; and then '*Fucking tourists!*' he hissed, and was gone.

And of course, as we shakenly thought – having found somewhere to sit and recover, and hardly able to believe that he'd accepted defeat – of course, it *was* what we were. No crawling out from under that. If you had no appetite for beating about the bush, we were certainly fucking tourists. It was not what we'd come to Nepal to discover; but there it was. I thought of one of those long marble characterisations on the walls of a cathedral, turning a life into round phrases. AMIABLE, it might say of us, giving us the benefit of every doubt: PUBLIC-SPIRITED, HONEST and the rest of it. But if it were itself to be HONEST, it would have to admit to its noble lettering this final truth about us: FUCKING TOURISTS.

# 18

If Miss Baker were to appear before me now, raised from that heavenly rest she deeply deserved to offer me a final teacherly service, I think I'd consult her on the problem of having found so many women, encountered on this journey, beautiful. The problem, that is, of avoiding monotony of description, and perhaps also the impression that I am given, in this field, to easy enthusiasms. I believe Miss Baker thought of the word 'beautiful' largely in terms of the agony that many had in spelling it at Barley Road in the late 1920s. Considering that the problem lay in that opening burst of vowels, and that there are only three of them, Jean Rawlins, as an example, was capable of misspelling the word in an extraordinary number of ways. I suspect it was because of my unnatural ease with such words, and not because of those nocturnal acts of rescue (of which I'd never, anyway, found a means of informing her), that she held out the occasional hope that my adoration was returned. But I think Miss Baker would understand the difficulty the word 'beautiful' represents even if you can spell it: that it may convince if used sparingly, perhaps once in a book, but that it risks becoming rapidly meaningless with repetition.

We went to see the carpet factory in the little Tibetan colony just outside Kathmandu. It was a long shed, full of dusk, and along each wall, and down the middle, the weavers sat, a beautiful sort of sitting. (There goes the word, once.) They wore broad skirts and sleeveless bodices, and their arms, stretched towards the loom, were busy brown tendrils. Their hair was, of course, uniformly and brightly black, and shone wherever it was in some patch of light. Each team of six had a delightful individuality that was an effect of difference of colour in their costumes, and of age. They were of many ages and all were beautiful.

There was a general beauty in these long busy lines of weavers with the wide fans of colour their skirts made, as if they were sitting on blossoms, and from the activity of their slim arms. There was also the particular beauty of individual faces. The colours they worked in were cool, mostly: cool greys, cool pinks, cool browns. Outside, a man in red shorts trod wool in a dyeing pool, smiling at us as he did so. Close by was a square plaster shrine, white and brightly red, draped with holy and patriotic rags and flags.

All these people had been insufferably in exile for thirty years. Their homes were a few hundred miles up the road.

I am certain that the right word is 'beautiful', and that I am not using it through a feeling of sorrow for these people driven from their homes, because I have the photographs I took that afternoon against which I can verify this.

There was a member of the party who was deeply hostile to photography. To her mind, it was a substitute for truly looking at things; it also provided those things with ludicrous understudies.

'So that tiny white triangle is Everest?' She was constantly, passionately begging me to throw my camera away. Her evangelism was so intense that I couldn't help responding with affectionate giggles, and naturally this made her more fervent, and more inclined to think of me as a lost soul.

'But,' I said, 'the practice of looking at a scene in terms of what record might be made of it, within a rectangle, might be a way of intensifying vision, not of avoiding it. And that tiny white triangle *is* Everest. It is true that, if you were being literal, Everest is an immense affair of rock and other ingredients, 29,000 feet high. But can you deny that from where we'd been standing one late afternoon in the neighbourhood of Kathmandu, it had been . . . a tiny white triangle?'

'Oh heavens,' she said, 'but when you remember this journey, you will remember your photographs, not the scenes of which they are unsatisfactory representations.'

'You mean,' I said, 'for the words are not strong enough for what you are saying, representations of a sordidly mendacious kind! But memory, to which we are both devoted, relies on a battery of imperfect instruments. The unaided eye, the mind, the imagination, we carry these slung round ourselves like cameras: and the camera itself may be among them a welcome accomplice, truly an *aide memoire*? The memory surely needs as many assistants as it can recruit, and film is one of them?'

'You are hopeless,' she said.

'My dear,' I said, '*you* are hopeless.' And I half-believed it, for she'd also become agitated about goats. They were, she'd understood, used for sacrificial purposes – and so any goat we met was seen as an imminent victim. My prosaic suggestion that, for most goat-owners, they had a value that resided in their continuing to live rather than having their throats cut, led her to characterise me as one of those who were supervising the process by which the world went down the drain.

'My God, look at that!' she cried on some occasion, pointing to a string of goats being led home from pasture, and clearly as likely to see their centenaries as any of us. 'Poor things! Aren't any of you going to stop it?'

It was one of the moments when I valued Ted Drake. 'Oh for God's sake, my dear,' he said, with his capacity to use such language with a general effect of good humour. 'Bloody well stop! – give us a chance! – you're chattering like a bloody monkey!' And though she was naturally inclined to despise such a loose characterisation of the monkey, she smiled and, for the moment, surrendered.

I look now at the photographs taken in that shed full of weavers and am glad my dazzled memory is confirmed by dazzled film.

160

# 19

On the plane returning to Delhi was a Sikh with his young wife. I looked desperately in Miss Baker's direction, but there's no way of describing the wife except as beautiful. Her arms were phenomenally loaded with bracelets, and throughout the journey he toyed with them. At first I thought he was counting them, and one certainly might have been drawn to doing that, out of incredulity at their number. But what he was doing was taking hold of each and letting it slip back on her arm. It was erotically mesmerising. Somewhere among the carvings at Khajuraho there was bound to be an enaction of love involving the gentle seizing, and then the gentle letting go, of bracelets. He was beautiful, too . . . but by now Miss Baker must have thrown up her 1928-ish hands in despair. Our work on streetscenes, even on farmyards, had never raised this sort of issue.

It had been the usual wait, at the airport, among the usual rumours. The space in which we sat, the walls nastily brown, was full of jabber. Jabbering arrest, I thought: the character of much in life. I had an unexpected understanding of those London clubs that enforced complete silence. An engineer from Bangladesh addressed me at length. He was travelling with a wrapped silent wife and five unwrapped unsilent children, had taken a degree at Swansea and then another at UMIST, and was clearly a charming and intelligent man, but

I could not hear him. It was a voice that offered music at the pitch of a recorder; he hopped across a sentence by way of unfamiliar stresses . . . and it was torment by way of *almost* knowing what he was saying. I felt a smiling ass.

Were the delights of travel worth the despairs of it?

Laura, pausing in her dash from desk to desk, was challenged by Michael Reemer to say whether Nepal was dirtier than India. She said the Nepalese towns, especially parts of Kathmandu and Bharaktpur, were the only places in the subcontinent that caused her actual nausea. I thought what an odd thing it was, this comparison of disgusts. Michael Reemer's view was that an innate regard for hygiene was a sure test of national quality. He was obviously ready to build upon this statement, nothing he said as an opening remark being intended as other than the foundations of some towering edifice of opinion. But Laura, whose seasoned nerves were clearly as stretched as they could endure, asked him if he'd been walking lately through London with his eyes shut, and hurried off to pursue a shadowy official. Michael Reemer said loudly he thought Leicester Square might not be irreproachable, but it was hardly Durbar Square, Kathmandu. There were times when I expected him to be taken away and shot, and wondered if I would be moved to beg for his life.

And then we were suddenly aloft, and an hour and a quarter later Delhi was as kind as it was ever going to be, slow but not inventively obstructive in its usual fashion, and by midnight we were back among the gliding women in reception at the Maurya Sheraton.

And in the morning, before we took off for Kashmir, we found ourselves in a shop that from a narrow front broadened backwards into a warehouse of *objets d'art*. There I looked for the first time keenly at examples of the copies of courtly paintings that were, some said, now and then better than the originals. I didn't know about that, but was captivated by these enchantments, painted with brushes that were single hairs, the colours iridescent. Within minutes I was the possessor of the image of a tiny encounter, three inches by four, between a

162

young lordly fellow, wearing a transparent shift enlivened with rubies, and a young woman semaphoring her complacence with unlikely positionings of the arms, and a charming positioning of, especially, the right leg which lay elastically across his lap, so that she managed with her heel to caress his elbow. She had been interrupted in her dressing at the moment when she'd donned her lilac-striped silk tights. There were rubies between her breasts, and her nipples were additional rubies. Exchanging these prefatory contortions, they sat on a carpet very like one Michael Reemer had bought in Jaipur, turquoise stripes alternating with gold. Behind the marble verandah where they had, as it were, run into each other, a delicate hedge of leaves of a green most delicate, and then a stretch of sea, on which remarkably formal ships (like red-tipped ants' wings) sailed at remarkably formal intervals, amid islands that were twists of green, geographical sweetmeats. The sun was setting, an episode occupying an inch and a half one way and a couple of millimetres the other, and above this the sky turned from paler to darker blue, accommodating at the same time a number of extremely tiny, extremely formal clouds, like heavenly pillows. Everything tended to promote the idea of going to bed, perhaps with some delay of sleep.

Made alert by this purchase, Kate and I gave our attention to other paintings of the kind in a shop in an arcade in the hotel. The shopkeeper spotted us being amazed by what we saw in the window, and invited us in. We really could afford none of this, we said: but he insisted that whether or not we were able to was neither here nor there. Our simple enjoyment was enjoyable to him. He clearly meant it. We'd have bought, if we'd been able to, a sort of (as it seemed to us) Indian Samuel Palmer. That's to say, there was a moonlight feeling about the painting, and a delight in flowering trees; and their floweringness was formalised as a round exuberance of blossom. Instead of Palmer's slumbrous shepherds, however, here was the prince (that may not have been his rank, but his lifestyle was clearly not that of a freelance writer and broadcaster), who was standing under a tree, encircled by ladies; and all were animated by an appetite for pleasure so great that one of the ladies, made impatient by the tiny interval between the moment of the painting and the moment when they'd move from expectation to performance, was embracing the tree. It was, we could see, a picture that equated the pleasure of a single man with that of a dozen women, and was in this sense disgraceful, and perhaps indefensible, and so on. And what sprang from it was a sense of moonlit delight, on all sides, of the happiest suppleness of limbs, and of music: for, though there were no musicians, no one could look into the small bright world of this painting without hearing music. Its presence was unmistakeable.

It was not a penny world, I thought, the difference in coinage aside; but its improvidence was not vulgar. These were people who may not have cared much about the difference between a lakh of rupees and three quarters of a lakh: but they'd have known what the difference was.

# 20

For as long as I could remember, I'd dreamed of visiting the Vale of Kashmir. It was the name that first drew me. You could smell it: a name that brought its own geography with it. Enormous, wonderfully green, spiced, a prodigious orchard, a soft thunder of ponies' hoofs; and everywhere, blowing, coloured scarves. As the visit came nearer, I'd added lakes, of course, and houseboats, but couldn't quite fit them into that original image.

And here it was, a rough road from the airport; in the late afternoon light, with small mists assembling, things looked as though they'd been nibbled. This tremendous scene turned out to be . . . moth-eaten. And the lake in our imaginations had been a spread of water almost without horizons, occupying the visible world, and us in the middle of it. Round the corner, we'd find, it was like that; but here, where our taxis had stopped, and we'd been met by the agent, it was a couple of hundred yards wide, our houseboat among those lined up over there, looked at from the promenade on which we stood, and from which embarkation would occur in the little boats called shikharas that served the houseboats.

And the embarkation did occur, all dropped jaws.

Sixteen of us had come as far as this, enough to fill two houseboats. The rest had stayed in Delhi, or gone, exotically, further East. There'd been anxiety about the division of the sixteen between the boats. Roughly, there were the smokers and the non-smokers; the exuberant and the quieter-natured; those for whom the swarming presence of vendors and the possibility of non-stop haggling was bliss, and those for whom it was hell. On one hand, those who might be described as *forte*, with some tendency to *fortissimo*, and others whose nature was *piano*. It was the latter who'd spoken anxiously to Laura, perceiving that there was an almost perfect division possible, and she'd sent instructions to the agent accordingly.

But things had gone astray. Her advice had been misread. There was *The Queen of Sheba* – that was for the mild ones – and there was *Old Edinburgh Castle* for the rest. We were to be on *The Queen*, together with the gentleman from Leamington, that late developer in the matter of globe-trotting who was beginning to ache a little (though the word would have seemed to him embarrassingly emotional) for the lady from Leamington. There'd also be a former schoolteacher from Suffolk, a pleasant man who made notes interminably. He said he'd hoped it might be a feature of retirement that he'd find it possible to live without this dutiful toil, a teacher's compulsion, but the moment hadn't yet come. He'd share a room with the gentleman from Leamington. And there were Philip and Meg, who divided their time, I judged, pretty exactly between the world of the books they were reading, and the world through which we were travelling. Philip was determinedly old-fashioned (his own word). He must, I thought, have been one of the last Englishmen to use the word 'bounder' – 'The man's a bounder,' he'd said of one or two of our party, and once of an aggressive vendor of postcards – but he was mild about it, and rather amused, you felt, by himself. He'd been in the Royal Navy, but had no obvious warlike qualities at all, unless a sort of unassuming briskness was one. Meg was old, but only arithmetically, looking like an intelligent young woman who'd powdered her hair and painted wrinkles on her skin. She had a way of being made breathless by unexpected events or turns of behaviour that, I had to confess to Kate, made me wish, from time to time, that we could (wearing some minimum of rubies) meet for an exploratory late-night picnic at the foot of a painted tree.

Three bedrooms-full. The fourth bedroom was to be taken by the Reemers. They smoked heavily, and *forte* hardly expressed the degree of their social energy.

Their distaste for incompatibilities was to be as great as ours when the time came; meanwhile, they were engrossed by their despair at what they discovered a houseboat to be. To us, it was enchanting. That sense of things being moth-eaten vanished almost at once. *The Queen of Sheba* was a marvel of fretwork. Behind its verandah, although there must be another name for this on a boat – even one so tethered – was a big living room, fretwork from ceiling to floor, with sofas (their frames of reinforced fretwork) and small (fretwork) tables. Behind that, a dining room; and then a fretwork corridor off which opened fretwork bedrooms. The light, we observed, was very dim – Philip and Meg sighed and laid down their books. On the boat, Laura had said (she'd flown home to have her nerves repaired), you'd get what you asked for, and no more. It was an accepted rule of the game played between staff and holiday-makers that, if there could be savings from failing to work the electricity generator as it should be worked, or from omitting to instal the stoves that could be installed in cold bedrooms, those savings would be made. But say 'We would like more light,' or 'We would like to be warm in bed,' and the generator would be properly worked, the stoves would be provided. It was a matter of insisting, and continuing to insist. 'Rascals, all of them,' Laura had said, 'but charmers.' Now it was clear that we needed to make a demand in respect of increased electricity supplies, and we did so. We were ready quietly and patiently to play the local game. The Reemers were not. They were scandalised by the low light. They shuddered in anticipation of cold beds. They deplored all this floating fretwork. The descent, as they saw it, from the splendours of various Sheratons and Oberois to such discomforts, and absences of expected services, was intolerable. They stormed. *The Queen of*

167

*Sheba* echoed with their furies. Tremendous disinclinations to stay were voiced.

'But don't you find this charming?' I asked.

'Anyone who could call this . . .' – Michael Reemer looked round at what obviously was not fretwork to him, but a monstrous amount of tortured matchwood – '. . . anyone who could call this . . .' – he fought for control of his feelings – '. . . *charming* needs his . . .'

'Head examining?'

'I didn't say it! *I didn't say it*! But yes, you read my thoughts! I have never known . . .' He stared out through the entrance to the living room to where, beyond the verandah (must be another word) the lake was a blackness splashed with light across which intenser canopied blacknesses, shikharas, idled. 'Isn't there some *door* we could shut?'

'Pleasant scene,' Philip murmured.

'My husband has reasons to avoid draughts,' said Mrs Reemer.

'Doctor Chasuble,' I said, reminded of the moment in *The Importance of Being Earnest* when that solemn prelate announced 'I myself am peculiarly susceptible to draughts.'

'At other times,' said Michael Reemer, 'I would be delighted to pick up such allusions; but at the moment I am interested only in the totally unacceptable nature of our accommodation here.'

'Oh, I say,' said Philip. 'We're rather inclined ourselves to make the best of things.'

Michael Reemer cackled furiously. 'If I may say so, that is the sort of outlook that brought Britain to its knees,' he said.

Meg became breathless. 'I think we should prepare for dinner,' she said.

'*Dinner*!' said Reemer. 'You expect *dinner*? The optimism of some people is extraordinary!'

'It's a bit much,' said the gentleman from Leamington a little later. 'One doesn't really want, on holiday, to be as close as this to other people's apoplexy.'

'Tiresome bounder,' said Philip. 'Perhaps he'll spend a lot of time next door,' said Meg. The *fortes*, with two misplaced *pianos* aboard, were along the wooden walkway, in the neighbouring triumph of fretwork. But Reemer, groaningly re-entering the living room, made it clear that, if comfort were not to be had, he'd not abandoned hope of enjoying a specific form of discomfort in which, as I'd become aware, he delighted.

What he loved was a desperate clash of opinion.

As the next half hour was to make evident, this meant that between most of us in *The Queen of Sheba* and him there was a quite catastrophic difference in style. For he loved to throw down the conversational gauntlet.

It was no ordinary gauntlet; it was certainly of *metal*, extremely large, and was flung down with a nerve-racking clatter. He'd then mount his intellectual horse, level the lance of some outrageous proposition, and ride straight at his interlocutors.

Never in their lives had our mild friends thought it proper to turn social intercourse into a sequence of tournaments. They were amazed. But they didn't run away; instead, our appeal for more light having succeeded, they elected to continue to read, knit or gaze at the darkling fretwork with intensified serenity. 'Ah!' someone would murmur. For Reemer it was as if he'd been Galileo, crying *'E pur si muove!'*, and the entire Florentine establishment, the faintest show of interest barely concealing their view that the statement was over-boisterous, had replied, *'Ah!'* Meeting with no resistance, he'd go thundering past his placid opponents, and the effect of tugging his passionate horse to a halt would make him turn purple.

It was I who, on this occasion and later, let my comrades down. Alas, I had the tournament habit. Hearing those provocative hoofs, I had my own lance levelled before I could remember that this was no occasion for it. The Indians were congenitally incapable of managing a corner store, let alone a continent, he cried. He trusted we were not misled by the actual obvious capacity of many Indians to run stores of every

169

kind. What he was anxious we should give our painful attention to was the idea that behind this appearance of efficiency lay a profound habit of disorder. He had no doubt the paperwork in the offices of Indian Airways was highly impressive, but consider the *actual* performance of *actual* aeroplanes, purporting to serve the needs of *actual* travellers! He beat his knees at every repetition of that accented word (his habit of beating his knees was regarded on the houseboat as a particularly ruffianly practice) and looked round for jostling approval, clamorous disagreement.

'*Ha!*' he cried, catching Philip's eye, that of a man who was finding it difficult to read. 'One throws out ideas!' he growled. I was struggling not to run, pick up those ideas and return them to him, with interest. Philip felt reluctantly obliged to mutter a protest.

'Bit hard on them!'

'*You* are satisfied with Indian Airways?' Reemer cried.

'Well, not quite! Difficult topic!' Philip resumed the appearance of a man for whom reading was an activity he could interrupt only at considerable risk to his health.

'Difficult topics are *glorious*!' Reemer cried, 'I *glory* in difficult topics!' Meg, knitting, gave a little helpless snort. It was clear that if she had to define a scoundrel it would be as a man who gloried in difficult topics.

And here, alas, my self-control failed, and I dashed in with the urgent suggestion that none of us could conceive what it was to be a native of an enormous sub-continent that had not yet had fifty years of modern independence. It was the answering lance that Reemer had looked for.

'So much better,' he cried, 'if the Raj had continued, offering British calmness and political composure as a restraint on the local taste for chaos!' There were twitches of annoyance from the actual and genuine exponents of British calmness present. I became terribly cross on behalf of India, and for some minutes there was an awful clatter of dispute. 'This I find *very* interesting!' Reemer cried. He leaned forward and beat not only his own knees but those of his wife.

'My husband likes the cut and thrust of debate,' she volunteered. At which point, our *major domo*, Mohammed, emerged, to announce the imminence of the only experience that Reemer valued above that of debate: that of eating.

# 21

It was a cold night. There were no stoves.

We had been warned that conversation in bedrooms, and all nocturnal noises, must be kept to a minimum; the walls were thin, and the boat was something of a soundbox. The Reemers were next door to us; our beds abutted on the same wall. Their anguish as the chill night wore on was transmitted to us, much as if we'd been sharing pillows. Even with his wife, Reemer's habits in respect of any dialogue prevailed. That's to say, on his side there was the stinging rebuke, the ironical snub, the intonation that amounted to a vocal raising of the eyebrows. It was like quarter-hearing a Socratic dialogue, given a caustic Socrates. A flight of sarcasm, deftly damped. A long flourish of irony, fielded with a laugh. A deadly insinuation, smothered swiftly with a light retort. Fatigue made itself master, if rather hesitantly, somewhere in the middle of the night. 'I hate going to bed early,' Reemer had said in Delhi, when there'd been a seditious attempt among his companions to retire at midnight. One of his reasons for being dissatisfied with his mild fellow-travellers, even the best of the *fortes*, lay in his passionate sense that, of all detestable quietudes, sleep was the worst. He genuinely needed to be aggressively present, *awake*, making his influence felt, for all but a despicable hour or two as late at night, or early in the morning, as possible. For a while now, beyond the fretwork against which our beds rested, he struggled with unconsciousness. There were immense yawns, as if some huge beast were trumpeting, unrestrained. The entire idea of the yawn was explored, from beginning to end, which, in this case, was some two minutes later. At last we all fell, on our involuntarily shared pillows, into an exhausted sleep.

And woke to complete delight.

Morning on Dal lake. Mist. We faced the full sun. The shikharas moved silently in all directions, black silhouettes. It was quickly warm. The barber called, the case he carried being so labelled, BARBER. Vendors of postcards came, and of jewellery. As advised, we confined them to the lawn in front of the boat. At worst they might be allowed to put a foot, perhaps not two, on the verandah. We discovered that we faced, across the water, a lumpy sort of hill, topped by a temple and a television tower. It was marvellous, sitting on the verandah – well, that advanced viewpoint, from which you looked down into water as it became thickly, exhilaratingly green with weed – and . . .

And doing nothing.

Enormous dissatisfaction expressed by the Reemers. They were in touch with everybody with whom one could, in a dissatisfied way, be in touch. They were prepared to give it a final try that evening, after the installation of stoves.

'But we will see what my husband has to say,' said Mrs Reemer. 'He will make the final decision.' He was . . . who knew where, furiously negotiating. I had a sympathy for him that the gentleman from Leamington deplored. He was driven by a need of self-assertion, I thought, as we were driven by a need of self-effacement. 'Oh, come on!' said the gentleman from Leamington, wishing himself to be reassessed, I suddenly saw, as someone unable to endure less than total limelight. 'Oh well,' he said.

And the shikharas took us across the water, and we were borne off to the Shalimar Gardens.

Pale hands, and so on. Some ancestor of Rosamund Lehmann's had written that song. Hearing it on the wireless as a boy, I'd imagined a vastly improved form of our back garden. The Blishen Gardens, in their military way (my father liked paths to be straight, flowers to dress by the right and vegetables to occupy the rear as a sort of horticultural Pioneer Corps) offered colour and scent in a fashion I didn't think could be substantially improved upon. I'd not at all understood how different these Indian gardens were, in their arrangement of water tumbling from a high point, by way of ponds, down towards the lake. Water was the beautiful dress worn by a sort of armature of machinery, pumps and other means of driving the water downwards, making suitable sprays and founts of it. Alas, water was now short, indeed absent, so the ponds were dry and the pumps and other machines were revealed in their plain ugliness. But between the ponds intended for water were floral ponds, and these thrived, oblongs of red and orange; and there were great trees, and from the top of the gardens you looked down at the lake, and across its surface at those pretty insects crawling, the shikharas. It wasn't at all like the Blishen Gardens, however much you enlarged them; but I thought how my father would have delighted in those regiments of marigolds. For so many years he'd spent his days essentially ill-at-ease in government offices, thinking of the evenings, the weekends, and marigolds.

It was in the neighbourhood of an institution ignored by Liza Lehmann, the Shalimar Cafeteria (given the wonderful shamelessness with which the shikharas were named by their owners, it might have been the Pale Hands Pizzeria), that a vendor badgering us was himself badgered.

'Do not press!' a passer-by paused to cry. 'Do you not see that they do not want to buy?' The vendor looked sullen, and continued to enjoin us to purchase Kashmiri gloves. 'It gives a bad impression,' said the other. 'They will go home and say this is how it is. That we will not leave them alone. It is bad for us.' They walked away, the argument no longer in English. Suddenly the vendor was sketching out a blow. They were joined by others and became a receding scuffle of voices. We felt absurd, the starting point of an argument that had no wish to hear from us. Not that we could have contributed to it, beyond a shrug and a sigh. Earlier, when the hundredth voice had cried 'Buy Kashmiri leather bag!' I'd absently confused this with some proposal Kate might have made, and murmured: 'No, thank you, darling.' Kate had laughed heartlessly, as was natural when the marital relationship displayed itself as being on automatic pilot; and I'd said when it next happened I'd reply: 'No, but will *you* buy an old English bag?' It would be odd to be home, I thought, supposing ourselves free of a specifically Indian annoyance, and to settle back into a world of billboards, television commercials, all the increasingly noisy, elbowing, insistent forms of advertising. 'Buy lager? Buy insurance policy? Buy Victorian-type conservatory extension?'

I imagined the glove vendor might have been fairly free of junk mail.

The stoves were of tin, and turned the bedrooms from ice-wells into infernos. But they were enough to persuade the Reemers to stay.

And so we settled into the world of the lake. Part of it was dominated by houseboats, shikharas, floating salesmen. All that, I thought, was enchanting in its absurdity – the names of houseboats and shikharas speaking for them. Walking beside the lake, you enjoyed an improbable succession of these. NEIL ARMSTRONG; MICHAEL JACKSON; ALEXANDRA PALACE, said the fretwork brows, or ACROPOLIS; PANSY; SAN SOUCI; NEW CHERRYSTONE; HIGH LUCKY FLOWER; KING OF KASHMIR; ROLEX; MISS ENGLAND; ROXANA; FAIRY LAND. You looked closer at hand to the shikharas jostling at landing stages. LOVER BOY; LOVELY HA HA; BROWN PALACE SUPPER DE LUXE; HOLIWOOD; THE LONELY HALLICOPTER PURE SEATS. An anxious emphasis was laid on the freedom of seats from unspecified contaminations.

FORGET ME NOT DE LUX TOUCH PURE SEATS. There were shikharas hung with beads and tinsel, with curtains meant to enclose some gaudy kind of naughtiness; these tended to insist not only on the purity of the seating, but also on its springiness. You enclosed yourself within those bright and jingling hangings and, in circumstances of guaranteed touch-purity, indulged in touch-impurity.

But beyond all that lay the native life of the lake, and it was beautiful beyond anything we'd imagined. Everybody here got about by water, in simple, usually uncanopied forms of the shikhara, from the plainest slip of a boat occupied by a small child on her knees in the prow, paddling, to heavy boats heaped with vegetables from the floating market gardens. Like the shikharas they moved silently, as if in a dream. Lovely, in some alleyway of water, to see a boat approaching, its woodwork turned to gold by the sun, and to hear nothing beyond, perhaps a murmured word, some faint rhythmic splash, to see the paddles rise and fall, to go silently past its smoothly advancing silence. There were villages, little towns, rough-and-ready and tumbledown Venices, watery high streets and back-doubles, and you drifted past living rooms open to the water, which made wriggling reflections of the bold dark limbs of trees against which the house at times appeared to lean. On the edge of some tiny grove with its roots in the lake, a man would have halted his boat; sunk into silver greenness, it accommodated a little mountain of flashing tin, pots and pans. People slept in boats, washed themselves in them; whole families reflectively drifted in them, keeping direction with the faintest, occasional use of a paddle. I thought if I lived here I'd plainly scribble in a boat, type in one. And everywhere, scenes that might have been assembled under the supervision of Monet: spreads of lily, strong greens and blues – you looked across the many-coloured flat face of the water and there they were, lying on and under its skin. A branch ended in a flower, but the flower was a kingfisher . . .

Kate and I could think of no objection to drifting here for

ever, waiting without impatience for some moment when a waterway merged into the general lake and across the great stretch of it you saw the low ring of mountains that most beautifully tied the scene together.

# 22

We stepped off at a honey factory. The proprietress (no other word would do for so positive a person) shooed us into her tasting room, where honeys of various origins were to be sipped from the variety of containers in which they'd ended up – largely, old gin and whisky half- or quarter-bottles. Her patter was powerful. I was reminded of gypsies at Barton Fair, who'd briskly prescribed improbable remedies to persons who, their health perfect, later found themselves leaving the fairground in possession of entire pharmacies. Prodding my stomach, and somehow contriving to suggest that it was dangerously distended, so that I felt an actual unease, she brought me back from the brink with a recommendation of lotus honey. It had my name on it. She pointed to a patch on Kate's shin that marked an old accident, and, laughing hugely at the thought of such a happy coincidence of blemish and cure, produced rose-apple honey, unfailingly effective in such cases. (She mimed a lightning account of the thousands of shins that, so treated, had become rather better than new). The odd thing was that she offered tastes of the different honeys in spoons that were then hastily plunged into water before being offered again, and this was a melodramatic breach of every hygienic rule impressed upon us since we'd decided to come to India – but Kate and I seemed lost to prudence, tasting this and tasting that, while our companions, shaking their heads when a spoon was proffered, directed at us looks of useless and thunderous admonition. Kate and I left with one or two wonderfully pleasant honeys in sordid containers, and back again in the dying light on the lake were only half-heartedly able to agree with our friends that we'd been crazy. Meg was breathless, so I knew that crazy was what we had been.

The proprietress accompanied us to our shikhara. With the air of someone who'd done well, but might have done better, she prodded at me with a shameless diagnostic finger and murmured of other honeys – other problems, other solutions.

'Old man!' she said happily – as we stood in what it seemed silly to think of as her front garden, an untidy brightness of plants sloping to the water (busy with medically-minded bees) – 'needs strong honey!' I smiled at her in genuine confusion as to the ailment hinted at, and then suffered a revelation by way of gusts of laughter and a great wickedness of eyes, while Kate was made the target of a volley of sketched-out nudges from the honey-maker's elbow. Good Lord, it was amazingly different from our Dr Smith's surgery on some dourly crowded Thursday evening!

And so, torn between a mysterious hilarity and a sense of probably being doomed (how odd it would be to die of honey!), we found ourselves afloat again.

# 23

'The worst thing a human being can do to another,' said Michael Reemer one evening, 'is to bore him.' He looked down the table and gave each of us an ironical nod. 'The worst thing, the very worst thing,' he said. To the rest of the table it was not clear how this followed from the preceding conversation, which had amounted to a leisurely exchange of news about the day's extremely leisurely experiences. The gentleman from Leamington had described, in some detail (rehearsing for the task lying ahead of him at home, I thought), a walk up the hill on the bank opposite. This had led to a temperate debate on the question of whether it is more tiring to walk uphill than downhill. Meg had volunteered interesting facts about the ankles. She'd been in some department during the war which had brought one face to face with problems about bones, and the ankles had featured prominently. Philip said, my word that was a good curry! I said I shouldn't be long out of bed. We'd needed relaxation, and the chance to do nothing of the slightest importance in some marvellous setting, said the schoolmaster, and we'd found it; and *all* the curries we'd tasted on *The Queen of Sheba* had been good. It was then that Michael Reemer, out of the quiet blue of things, had launched this idea that worse than physical assault, or gross misrepresentation, or murder, was the infliction of boredom. There was a little polite blinking round the table, but not much more, for it had come to be

180

taken that our companion was inclined to voice huge sentiments that rose out of him and sank back again, and had nothing much to do with life as one knew it.

And again I felt a sort of unsympathetic sorrow for him, understanding that he longed to clash shields with someone or other on some preferably sore topic. If Meg had only cried 'Can anyone deny that throughout history ankles have done more harm than any other joint?' or Philip had solicited ideas as to how the curry we'd been eating might be set against some eternal landscape of curries, how happy Michael Reemer would have been. His desire for dispute and raging discussion was bottomless.

And I thought how absurd and odd it was that intellectual wakefulness in, alas, a tiresome form had clashed, in the midst of this charming fretwork, with a sensible variety of intellectual sleepiness which consisted not so much of a dislike of argument, as a belief that (as practised by some, as a form of polemical gymnastics) it led to dispensable dismay, and that that wasn't what one had come to Kashmir for.

The usual head of *The Queen of Sheba's* staff, Mohammed, had gone off for a sister's wedding, deep in the hills. We'd seen him the first night only and the visitors' book made it clear that this was, for us, a small misfortune. Mohammed plainly had the gift of making any houseboat-load, however mixed, feel they were at one. 'He is', said a typical entry, 'a good lucky.' Gulam, who'd taken his place, was an agreeable young man, quietly effective; but he was not 'a good lucky'. He could not tame Michael Reemer, who said now, imperious in defeat:

'I *detest* boredom!'

We'd been, that day, into the outskirts of Srinigar, a district made up of things that tilted and tottered. There were buildings that one guessed had had for centuries their present appearance of near-collapse. For a time I stood trying to make an inventory of such a building, set at an angle as it marked the turn from one rough and deeply-rutted street to another. The bottom floor was a shop – as everywhere, an open space, a foot or so above the ground, in which the shopkeeper squatted or sat leaning against a wall, surrounded usually, by family or friends, or sometimes, it appeared from the furious look of it, business rivals or political or philosophical enemies. In this case, everyone was cheerful, in the midst of an enormous cheerfulness of fruit. The floors above were clearly to live in, though you'd think it must be precarious living, as in a construction of orange boxes at some late stage of dismantlement. There was a verandah made of patches of rough wood – with gaps through which, you suspected, small children and even larger ones must have fallen with fair frequency – to the side of which was simply an immense incoherent stack of wood, pieces of carpeting, rusty fragments of corrugated iron. And above that, the last breathtaking addition to a house of cards, a crazy cabin, the window space partly covered by shutters that had perhaps never been square, and were certainly not square now. Across this evidently durable wreck of a frontage, several lines of washing were stretched. On the verandah – wearing a brilliant red dress, her black hair parted in the centre – sat a young woman. If she was looking anywhere, it was up the street in the direction from which we'd come; but something about her suggested she had her eye, indeed, on nothing. For as long as I watched, trying to impress it all on my memory, she did not move, nothing about her moved, she was simply a thrilling coloured shape in the shadowy midst of that shattered woodwork. Then, between one blink of my eye and another, she'd gone.

I'd taken, with their permission, a photograph of a shopful of tailors: four men, stitching under a line of hanging gowns. They'd said they'd like a copy of the photo, and gave me their address. We were, I discovered, in *Chest Diseases Hospital Road*. And everywhere you read of sickness, and of proffered cures. Near at hand, three powerful words jammed together, the *Scientific Clinical Laboratory*, which professed to be able to grapple with a long and gruesome list of disorders. 'We are here to serve you at a democratic price,' the shopfront asserted. As in our encounter on the lake, the purchase of honey was urged as a counter to many frailties. 'Eat HONEY,' said a particularly breathless sign, 'and live longer in Autumn Winter Spring and Summer with Milk Tea and Cold Water One teaspoonful daily To keep you fit and healthy HONEY Natures Best Nourishing Food Collected from various Herbs and Plants RICH IN CURATIVE PROPERTIES of Various Diseases and Rajunevation Food of Oriental Apiary.' Oh such a desperate general search for health was declared! Among the words that accompanied you as you walked were SPUTUM, STOOL, URINE. If the *Scientific Clinical Laboratory* could not inspect specimens of these for you, then the *Cure All Dispensary* might help,

All three were elements in the contents of the open and stagnant channel that edged the street.

And here, a sudden cheerfulness after that, a tiny girl wielding a cricket bat. She wore a plaid skirt over pink trousers, was very little larger than the bat, and, as she failed splendidly to hit the ball, was awash with joy. I bent down to add her picture to others I'd taken of small cricketers in India (performing behind billboards, once on an amazing pitch on a hillside, with one wicket many feet higher than the other, so that bowling from either direction was a form of bombardment) and she caught sight of me, and delight became horror. Her whole small brown face collapsed, her tears were terrible. I murmured, lowered my camera, smiled with a horror almost as great as hers; and a man strode forward, her father clearly, lifted her in his arms and, with unanswerable enthusiasm, urged me to take the photo. I could not please her without displeasing him. It is why I have this picture of the tiny Kashmiri I terrified, still clutching her bat, weeping for ever. Behind her, I observe, a notice: STATE TUBERCULOSIS CENTRE OF JAMMU AND KASHMIR.

# 24

. . . the vegetable market. What this amounted to was that boats heaped with cauliflowers, turnips, lotus leaves and roots, gathered to make a sort of bartering whirlpool somewhere near the floating gardens: they eddied round one another, locked into slowly spinning disputes and sudden agreements. In the spreading morning light such a lovely watery clamour, the early sun making gold out of the old wood of a boat, catching half a face, a knitted skull cap, the snowy tip of a mountain of cauliflowers, and now and then, whole cargoes of flowers, and once, white lettering on green, an offer of DELICIOUS CONFECTIONARY. Here we were again, the voyeurs, Gulam taking care to make us eddy with the rest, and because we were there, the vendors were out too, offering knives, hats, jackets, bangles. On all sides dark robes, largely dark faces, dark boats. We were on the brink of buying a packet of the seeds of a tall mauve flower we'd all fallen for, without having a name for it – it probably wouldn't grow at home, even if we broke the law and took the seeds in – but in any case, the gentleman from Leamington chose the occasion for a venture at bargaining, and made a mess of it.

'Fifteen rupees,' said the vendor.

'Five,' said the gentleman from Leamington. The vendor paddled away in a state of high indignation, if his boat had been armed we'd have been sunk within seconds; and the call of 'Ten,' which might have saved the day, was left fractionally too late. The seedsman had by then vanished into the general blur of morning sunshine.

We returned for breakfast to *The Queen of Sheba* along lanes of water becoming familiar, now in this early light a denser blue than they would be later. And I felt a tremendous intimacy with these floating salesmen, making their way home in their emptied boats – the ridiculous intimacy you are able to feel in circumstances like these: and at the same time the melancholy that follows when you're admitted to a world unlike your own and, for an illusory moment, feel you might belong here, although so transparently you do not.

Deep roots for that feeling. I remembered how it sprang again and again out of childhood reading. I'd seen *The Cossacks* at the Barton Cinema, John Gilbert pretending to be a Slav; and then read the novel in the sixpenny Readers' Library, with photogravure illustrations from the film. (Oh, *photogravure*! What a word that was to me then!) And being a small boy of quiet disposition living on the edge of London and thinking of horses timorously in terms of their having unpredictable hoofs – what kickings out and flashings of metal at the annual horse fair in Barton! – didn't prevent me from feeling a displaced Cossack; yearning, when the book was closed, to resume the life of a Cossack villager. No whimsical emotion, but a profound notion of the possibility of it! Returning from this present journey I'd have, at the bottom of my soul, a small nagging sense of being a Kashmiri in exile. Gulam, paddling, was certainly thinking of ways of avoiding the use of the generator, or how to satisfy Michael Reemer's appetite, and he might have been looking forward to further raids on our whisky; meanwhile, he was a figure edged with the curious and not unpleasant sadness caused by these ventures into other people's worlds. By some genetic twist or turn I might have been Gulam, might have the secret of this minimal paddling of his, might be at home on this marvellous lake!

*

185

I thought of the old horse fair again when in two cars we climbed to Gulmarg, one of the hill stations where once Britons had hidden from the summer heat. A journey of extraordinary enchantment, at first along straight roads lined with poplars, their tall pallor giving way here and there to the broad blaze of a chinar, the local plane tree. Women crossing the road, at angles, coloured lines of them, baskets on heads. Shops selling winter wives, the pots men filled with burning coals to keep themselves warm when the temperature fell. Seen from a bridge over a river, an amazingly long sandbar: at this end, patches of blood-red carpet that in fact were squares of peppers, drying; at the further end, boys playing cricket, very small, like ants who'd taken to sport. Straw hung to dry in trees. Then open country with ricefields, lip below lip. And last, a long climb, through forest, one bend leading more and more quickly into the next, and mountains spinning round us, Nanga Parbat among them. (Another name I'd long loved!) And so to the flat top of it all, Gulmarg, which for me was an even more exotic version of what I'd thought exotic enough as a child, the horse fair. For a week or two, horses and ponies had made their way into the town by every road. From the beginning to the middle of September the lane that our road led into was one long jingle, one long clatter of hoofs, one long splendid sound of disgraceful cries and curses. People locked their doors, shuddering delightedly. And here again was a world of ponies, the strong smell of them, sudden gallopings, now a jostling bunch, now a single rider leaning forward like a jockey and having some intent difficult to make out amid this general sense of no one having much of a purpose. That was as Barton Fair had been, too: a sensation of horses being used as an expression of sudden and arbitrary impulse, a gallop, a trot, something made necessary by the fact of being a horse joined to the fact of being a horseman. Here men and boys were leaping on, leaping off, riding side-saddle, or riding whilst barely seeming to be mounted at all. An enormous restlessness of ponies and men; and drifting among them, the visitors, surely only one visitor to a dozen ponies, and most

186

content to walk. There must have been profit in it for someone, I thought, doubtfully.

We sat on a hotel lawn drinking beer and looking over the highest golf course in the world, and watched men attempting to lift, from the back of a lorry to the height of the lawn, an immense oil container. The operation was conducted in an atmosphere of perfectly cheerful and maximum risk, perilous possibilities being tried out at someone's merest suggestion, and a tremendous airing of ideas about what might follow if you tried this or that going on concurrently with trying this or that. It was brought up onto the lawn at last, and prevented from rolling back again and crushing half a dozen men as it did so by someone's laughing athleticism in the matter of spotting, and making lightning use of, an improvised wedge or two. Between the English party, on the one hand, and the men who'd done the work on the other – who seemed to be the driver of the lorry and his mate, with a couple of dozen self-recruited and madly happy assistants – there appeared to be a bond of shared horror and exhilaration for which there was no real outlet, except laughter, a shaking of heads, and gestures with the hands, but which might have led to huggings and even some rough sort of dancing if they hadn't remembered they must go on their way, leaving us with the problem of resuming our half-forgotten role of elderly tourists.

And down to the lake again, that beautiful journey backwards, corkscrewing through the forest, leaving the silent hubbub of mountains for the plain. And somewhere along the road, the sight of a bus halted beside a pond and a young man dashing bucketfuls of water over it, whether to clean or cool it wasn't clear; the pond copying this odd spectacle, with wonderful clarity, upside down.

The discovery that our supply of whisky, carefully judged to last till the very last night in Delhi, had suffered catastrophic reductions had been made by all of us who drank it.

'Well,' said the gentleman from Leamington sensibly, 'it's our fault, leaving it about.'

'We're all in the same boat,' said Meg, and then became breathless at having made that joke without meaning to. Philip had tried mineral water, and claimed to find it dizzying. I'd thought, lowering myself to mineral water, that the mere sound of liquid poured at the right moment in the day for someone robbed of true drink, was a small but distinct consolation.

At breakfast the morning after the discovery there was talk of childhood, and before he could prevent himself Philip had asked Michael Reemer what his earliest years had been like in Vienna. For a fatal moment he'd forgotten that Reemer didn't reply lightly and quickly to any question. And indeed the answer began with a heavy exordium on the issue of one's ever having been a child at all.

I thought how his response to a question was like . . . an army entering conquered territory. Everywhere, suddenly, billets were being arranged, communications established, bunting taken down, and other bunting put up. There was a tremendous movement of traffic, and a great anticipation of the issue of regulations and edicts. Philip's question had been asked as breakfast was coming to an end – it looked now as if breakfast might not end at all. Gulam, who'd been hovering with the intention of removing plates and seeing us out, looked appalled and sulky.

'You see . . .' Reemer was saying. By the roadside the conquered people stared dully as he passed, standing in his triumphal car. 'You see . . .' he said again, and paused. And smiled. This was not going to be rushed. 'Let me . . . place what I have to say in answer to that *very* interesting question . . . against the background of a view of childhood quite different from the one that was *prevalent* when I was a child in Austria . . . the view that doesn't mind handing children over to the . . . *cold* . . . care, if one can call it care, of your *nanny* – your *English* nanny.' He looked round the table. '*Your* English nanny,' he said, and smiled affably. The very term had made his point for him. Everyone knew about the frigid English nanny. She was responsible for the frigid Englishman

188

and Englishwoman, so averse to the splendid bullying uproar of disputation and controversy.

But three people at the table, it turned out, had had English nannies, and had known a wide range of other people's nannies, and not one of those but was outstandingly warm.

'I say, I think you're speaking without experience there,' said Philip.

'My goodness, how untrue that is,' said Meg, and became breathless. The gentleman from Leamington said it was an interesting case of someone being deceived by a stereotype. Suddenly the population of the occupied country had risen and was bundling the invader briskly back over the border.

'No, no, no, no, *no*,' said Philip. 'You really can't say that!'

'Astonishing to think that people actually believe it!' said Meg.

'*But* . . .' said Reemer.

'I expect you were pulling our legs,' said Philip, rising from the table. Gulam rushed forward and began to remove plates. The first vendor was already to be heard on the lawn, calling his wares, which seemed simultaneously to be of leather and chocolate.

And out there, such a morning!

Your bowels were never perfectly safe; the whisky wasn't going to last out; and, before we'd got to breakfast, there'd been a small sourness when it was discovered there was no electricity, and so no morning cup of tea prepared. The generator had been allowed not to start. I never knew how Gulam and his friends expected to get away with such boldnesses; it was like their raids on the whisky, as obvious as if they'd left signed confessions. It was all on the scale of hoping guests in a hotel wouldn't notice that they'd slily omitted to put beds in the bedrooms. Suddenly, this morning, there'd been a little outburst of colonial-sounding petulance. Hands were clapped. Someone cried: 'Tea, boy, *at once!*' Someone else: 'Damned cheek!' Well, it *was*: but Kate was rueful, thinking how difficult she'd have found it to be a memsahib.

189

Yet it was a morning of mornings. As we'd sat before breakfast on the verandah, the floor had been carpeted with sunshine, and not ordinary sunshine. Added to the pervasive fretwork had been another strong fretwork of shadows. The hillside across the lake bloomed with haze. There was a traffic of shikharas that seemed more thrillingly silent than ever. Sideways on, reduced to morning silhouettes, their fineness of shape was startling, that of the shallowest clipping from a fingernail: the canopy tilted down towards the front, raised sharply out of the water. The lolling passengers were tiny black shapes, and so were the paddle and the paddler's arm, engaged in everlasting plunges and returns. Beyond the lawns were catwalks, means of access to the boats; and between catwalk and lawn, that patch of water that had become another lawn, of floating weed: in the full light of the sun, bright green, but in this morning light, bronze. In Kashmir there was much work in metal, from the simple jugs offered by floating vendors on the lake to the elaborations of brass and bronze Kate and I had seen in the dusky cave of a jeweller's shop in Srinigar. *There*, there'd been a brass horseman on a brass horse with wheels, big, clumsy in some wonderfully attractive way, the man having huge brass moustaches and protuberant brass eyeballs. And this seemed a metal morning – the light making, of everything, such solid intensities of shape and colour.

I imagined there were people everywhere who'd sat on this spot, on such a morning, and had returned to the agitated flimsiness of their usual lives, but had never forgotten being here, fixed solid in a solid metal morning.

Not so much a journey as a love affair with places, inset with social comedy. Michael Reemer made his position plain to a jeweller with whom he might, or might not, do business.

'I am not ready now. I think you can see I am not ready now. (I think even he sees that I am not ready now). You could come back at two o'clock. Of course, I may not be ready then. There might still be no water. There might still be no electricity. I might still feel unwashed.' Kate said that

Christopher Marlowe would have written better lines for him, but still she heard the accents of Tamburlaine. But then, I said, coming both from the leafless ends of Barton, we'd find almost any imperiousness . . . imperious.

'Bought so much already, don't quite know what to do with it,' someone said. Another:

'And he's going to do the setting I want. And in the end I bought a trickle garnet and an emerald.' 'In the end' was a phrase covering the best part of a day's haggling.

'A boatful of Kashmiri sweaters. He's coming back this afternoon. They're between twenty and thirty pounds.' I thought there was such a thing as being purchase-crazy. And perhaps there was a sport involved. You pitted yourself against this master of the subtly shifting offer, and you set out to shift more subtly than him. Between some members of the party and some vendors there was a relationship for which a cool description was unsuitable. They recognised each other, the born salesman and the born customer, and their intercourse was sultry; they sought each other out in corners of lawn or verandah, as near to secret places as these sunlit sites provided. Kate was distressed, having long ago taken against the acquisition of *things*, a natural unloader: not quite convinced that we should have made ourselves possessors even of that tiny painting of love on a carpet. I thought that other members of my family, truer Blishens than myself, at home in the street markets of West London, would have felt enormously comfortable here, would have made massive purchases of gloves and garnets (for resale in Westbourne Grove), and would have been baffled by our abstentions. Almost everything in the homes of my uncles and aunts was claimed to be a bargain, the fruits of victory over old him, old her – who'd almost certainly thought of the transaction as a moment of triumph over some gullible Blishen.

But of course you could be acquisitive for things seen, and come home with your baggage disgracefully bulging with memories.

Kate and I had ourselves taken across the water by a speechless Gulam. We'd thought him shy, but decided his silence was a condition of his knowing little English: in fact we now seemed on positively talkative terms with him, for he had brightenings and dullings of the eye, a whole language of shoulders lifted and depressed, hands separated and brought together and mischievous shapings of the mouth, that amounted to substantial discussion about the passing scene. He was clearly in close league with the vendors who paddled up to us as we went, offering the usual range of goods and the usual pretence of terminal shock at our not wishing to buy them. I suspected that Gulam's skill was to suggest to them that he was surrendering us to their mercy, and to us that he was giving them short shrift.

What we'd wished to do since we'd arrived was simply to walk away from the bustle that spread between our landing place and the outskirts of Srinigar. In the other direction, towards the low mountains that fringed the lake, there was relative peace, increasing as we walked. In the afternoon light there were the softest subtleties of reflection, mists and blooms in the water; it was stretched as if it had been an immense grape skin, and another set of mountains, another hem of lakeside trees, were painted unmoving on it. The trees were mostly tall and pale, with the habit of poplars and the bark of the silver birch, but where the lake turned there was a single chinar, brilliantly red. That was our goal: and we walked, at last believing we were here – in Kashmir – in India. A curious square of black poles protruding for a foot or two above the water seemed, with their faintly wavering reflections in that silvery greyness, to have been inked there for the abstract fun of it. A boat slowly drifted, with a squatting man at the prow poling it along, and a tiny girl standing knee deep in sacks who was cheerful in some quite immoderate fashion. She was madly in love with the world, madly in love with being poled across the water by this old man, perhaps her grandfather, madly in love with having us peering down at her, and with the possibility of smiling up at us. They both smiled up, and when they'd passed, continued to look back and smile; and we knew

192

we'd never forget them. We knew, indeed, we'd never forget this simple, unimportant afternoon walk, down at the unbusiness end of the lake, past golden sheep curled up against a wall, their backs smeared with red paint: a kingfisher or two, extravagant amplifications of the idea of a kingfisher: hopping mynah birds, a hooded crow with one claw turned under. A boat, an inch long, set out from the trees, making as it went a long slow mark on the water such as you'd make if you laddered a piece of silk. Tied up and mysterious at an otherwise boatless stretch of the wall was one of those shikharas that seemed to be made for lolling wickedness, with drapes of tinsel and cushions lasciviously red: KISS KISS SHIKHARA SUPER DE LUXE it proclaimed itself. FUN SPRUNG SEATS.

# 25

The absurd reversed: here we were, being rushed from sub-continent to suburb. *Bum's-rushed* might be the word. In such journeys, for all the polite rituals of air travel, there was always an element of being taken by the scruff of your neck and thrown out. Within twelve hours we'd be deafened by the precipitate closure of those three weeks of being deafened. It would become, suddenly, very silent: and accustomed to making an effort to hear, we'd have difficulty in hearing.

LITTLE SUNFLOWER: CROWN OF INDIA: NOAHS ARK. That had been the road back to the airport at Srinigar. DERBYSHIRE: DULCE DOMUM: QUEEN OF HEAVEN: HMS PINAFORE: NEW CHERRY RIPE.

Where was OLD CHERRY RIPE? There was a relentless integrity of descent as from any abandoned title to its successor. At the tag-end of the lake, mostly mud, the skeletal remains of worn-out houseboats, let for a rupee a night to otherwise homeless families. Perhaps OLD CHERRY RIPE had become a sad momentary home of this kind?

At the airport, persons passing teasingly to and fro behind the check-in counter, but nothing happening; for three hours nothing happening at all. Then we were quite suddenly on the tarmac, and boarding a plane ringed with soldiers . . .

It seemed a pity that so many in the party were returning home thinking ill of India. That was partly a consequence of experiences with Indian Airlines, especially at the airport at Varanasi. But beyond that were grievances outlined for me as we waited for the plane to London by one of those who at home would spread a largely negative report. Indians, he said, wouldn't put themselves out, were indifferent to questions of time and convenience, and said one thing whilst meaning another. He'd been a headmaster, as it happened – as I guessed, most sober and able – and his comments were headmasterly. I felt that irritation I'd known when teaching at Stonehill Street: a boy or a class being scrupulously defined in terms of reasons for just rebuke – Oh very fair, very fair! – and, somehow, the whole life of it being left out. There was, of course, everything to be said for people making an effort for others, being sensitive to the needs of others in respect of time and convenience, and making a direct confession of difficulties. But tempestuous boys tend to fail these tests of agreeableness, and so clearly did a tempestuous nation. That it *was* tempestuous, subject to storms of history and population and size, was evident to all of us who, in those three weeks, had made its acquaintance. Well, one's head was crammed with India! The scale of its problems was beyond our experience, and certainly beyond our imagination; and a schoolmasterly frown seemed hardly to cover the case.

We didn't have to be married all that time to justify the visit, said Kate; but it seemed, so swarming, a suitable place in which to have celebrated forty swarming years.

London was still there. The flying palace sloped down, began to hiss, hugely wobbled. It was an elephant, aloft among the winking scraps of glass that had helped the king to sleep in Jaipur: and at the last moment it discovered it had wheels.

'Where've you been?' asked Jim, obviously aware, suddenly, of a gap in our encounters.

'We've been to India,' we said.

Jim laughed. He knew we'd been no further than Finsbury Park.

# PART THREE

# 1

'How far is it, then,' he asked, 'from Delhi to Kathmandu?'

I cursed my luck in running into James. Basing his presentation of himself as a blunt man on having come to Barton from a northern county in his thirties (when he'd married an old schoolfriend of Kate's), he was in fact absolutely the man in some whispering corner of a Renaissance court. He had an alarming need to seize you by a sleeve and draw you ever closer as he spoke.

'Heard you on the radio the other day.' Your arm captured. 'Tell me. How do you do it?' You were being reeled in. 'What's the trick, then?' He'd release you a little, narrow his eyes and begin to wind you in again. He seemed to believe that any unimportant appearance on radio could be brought about only through complex intrigue, probably involving substantial acts of corruption. He wanted names, dates, all the seedy details.

Or rather, he didn't want them. He was simply keen on your knowing that he was wise to you. The hand he wasn't using to give you the rope and take it back hovered at his waist. In the shopping precinct it was odd to think of poniards, but difficult not to. And certainly these courts and alleys planted on the bones of Sergeant Clinker's domestic life might have been a travesty of some Florentine quarter, *c.* 1440.

But what I'd been stabbed by was a thought never far away, and thrust home by James's inquiry. His question had sprung from the belief that nothing anyone actually said was even intended to be true. It was a move in a game. You challenged it, meanwhile carrying out an act of arrest but giving the other the intermittent illusion of escape. You were a mobile dungeon and interrogation chamber. ('Met the Not-so-very-grand Inquisitor today,' I'd tell Kate.) So he'd checked on the story he'd heard, that we'd been to India and Nepal, getting me to make the assertion in person – and then called my bluff. How many miles from one capital to the other?

It worked, of course. I simply didn't know. The poniard slipped successfully between my ribs, because what had always worried me, and at this end of life worried me tormentingly, were the gaps between hard fact and hard fact in my apprehension of any experience whatever.

Already I wasn't quite sure where Fatehpur Sikri was, and though I'd commanded myself sternly to refresh my memory, I hadn't done so; and in any case I was uncertain that there was a memory to refresh. Even when there, had I known where Fatehpur Sikri was?

But worse than being aware of my ignorance was not being aware of it. How many statements would I now be making about that northern wedge of the sub-continent that were assured, even impassioned . . . and essentially inaccurate?

Such hope as I had that I might get India right was undermined by a recent occasion when I'd got London, on the doorstep of which I'd lived for nearly seventy years, remarkably wrong. London in the nineteenth century, it's true: but even so . . . Someone had been looking at early photographs and had been struck by the tremendous dominance of St Paul's – not simply the dome, now so hemmed-in a splendour in that raggedness of a skyline, all boxes of depressingly unrelated height, but the immense shoulders of the building. It was a holy fortress, a squareness that made the dome floating upon it more astonishing than ever. Well, a very different London, I said. There was that figure I'd read and was always quoting for the number of horses that on any working day at the end of the century could have been counted in its streets. Good

200

Lord, I said, think of that pandemonium of hoofs, and the snorting and the jingle of harness and the cries of the drivers of carts and carriages and horse-buses and drays and . . . Imagine the effect, at times surely choral, of so many cries of 'Whoa!', 'Geeup!' 'Giddup!' Well, when I was small, horses were on their way out, but still they were almost as common as dogs, and I remembered the subdued but distinct hubbub of their presence. It was part of one's casual general awareness. I could still take you today to the spots in Barton where the horse troughs had been. My perambulations round the town, I said, warming to all this, were haunted by the ghosts of old horse troughs! As a very small boy, I'd taken an ambiguous view of something I found ambiguous about horses themselves: that they had a confusingly fire-engineish capacity to produce a hosepipe from nowhere, or nowhere that I knew of, and flood the gutter with prodigious amounts of urine. I seemed to remember having to skip out of the way, at times, as the torrent approached me at a bubbling, foaming pace . . . Yes, yes, someone said: but what *is* that figure, that figure for the number of horses you'd find in central London any working day of the week in, let's say, 1888? Oh yes, of course, I said: it was 1,500,000.

This inquiry came from a neighbour whose resistance to romance I'd often found phenomenal. She was one of those valuable people who keep their heads in the most tumultuous and ecstatic circumstances. I'd sometimes thought that, if the end of the story turned out to bear any resemblance to a scenario widely promoted during my childhood, I'd do well to keep close to her during the approach to the Pearly Gates or the downward plunge: in the midst of all that hosannaing, or those screams of terminal displeasure and dismay, she'd watch points, propose steps that might make felicity less exhausting, in one direction, or incineration faintly more bearable, in the other. Now she said, quietly, that she couldn't, of course, do the sum in her head; the necessary elements of the calculation were not at her fingertips. But instinct told her that one and a half million horses in the streets of central London would need

201

to be head to tail, a city-wide horse-jam, making the passage of any other conveyance, and perhaps that of pedestrians, impossible. No, she said, *no!* – not 1,500,000! And with the indignation of someone whose reliability in this matter rested securely on his having adduced the figure so often in discussions of this kind, I said I knew where the original reference was to be found – and I went to a shelf, and took down the book, and found the page. 'On any working day at the end of the nineteenth century,' it said, 'something like 150,000 horses could be counted in the streets of central London.'

To what extent had my stay on earth been dotted with daftnesses of this kind? How often had I multiplied the truth, or divided it, by ten? Beyond some general remark proposing that India was a sub-continent, in an area bounded on one side by . . . Africa, on the other by . . . South-east Asia, perhaps it would be better if I said nothing much about our visit, and certainly very little of an arithmetical nature.

'Ah. Yes,' I said now, in James's grasp. 'I suppose . . .'

'*You don't know!*' said James: and then, 'Some other time.' I was suddenly free, and he had become a figure, not actually cloaked but appearing to be so, scurrying in the direction of Muscles, the new and already doomed shop offering male dress of astonishing baggy abandon. My puzzlement eased as I saw that James had taken some other acquaintance into custody and was fast reeling him in. It was, presumably, someone whose pretensions were even more worth exposing than mine.

# 2

Sarah was my producer now. She was so much in favour of an interview, in the raw, amounting more or less to the interview, when edited, that she wanted me (though not with Mr Broom's peremptoriness of wanting) to 'talk her through' a book when I'd read it so that she could tell me what questions to ask. I was fascinated by the vileness of that phrase. It was like . . . proposing that a lover should *talk* a friend *through* a girl he'd wooed, so the friend could make love to her. 'Talk me through it!' – ugh, that brisk jargon! (Was that the voice of Mr Growser? But surely the phrase belonged to the order of latterday slick imperatives that sought to mask difficulty with an easy image?) I smiled and she smiled and nothing happened. But she was remorseless with the trailers I wrote and recorded, a sort of contents page to accompany a tape to its destination in Sydney or San Francisco. A snatch of the signature tune, sixteen seconds of trail (as it got itself called), and back to the signature tune. I enjoyed the exercise involved, being as it were pithy with a kind of flourish, and could now, most weeks, hit sixteen seconds dead. Sarah brought that to an end – took *that* smile off my face. Her aim was for an effect she defined as 'sexy'. She'd worked in local radio, and said sexy trails were the essence of the local broadcaster's skill.

'"A new life of Thomas Hardy . . ."' I might propose.

203

'Oh dear, oh dear, oh dear, *oh dear*!' Sarah would say. 'Now, *come on*! What does Thomas Hardy suggest to you? What's the first thing that comes into your head. Don't think! The first thing that comes.'

I struggled helplessly against my habit of thinking. 'Poetry. Novels. Wessex,' I said. I was letting her off lightly.

She'd sigh. 'Look! It should be something to set the listener's blood racing! Didn't he have two wives?'

'Yes. But not at the same time.'

'Well, what about the scene outside the jail you were talking to the author about after the interview . . . the woman being hanged and her body twisting at the end of the rope in the rain? And Hardy watching! Follow that up in your mind!'

My father wanted me, urgently, to wring her neck. My mother held me back.

'He wasn't twenty at the time. And it's a small incident in a long life.'

'Oh, *now*!' Sarah could not believe I was ready to sacrifice this sexy approach on narrow grounds of a picturesque detail lacking size or representativeness. 'Try this. But don't write anything yet.'

She was very much like Hilda Hawkins, I thought, who'd bullied me under a privet hedge in East Barton sixty years earlier, helping to lay the foundations of the aggressive masochist I'd become. Remembering Hilda, her white arms, the furious face with which she brushed aside some fastidious objection of mine to her latest proposal, that I should prove my love for her by walking through a puddle or leaping from a very high wall, I'd laugh helplessly. In the end, when we reached the moment for the writing of the trail, I'd be ready to collapse into laughter before Sarah had said a word. What she was after, it seemed, was some flash of literary knickers, produced by whatever arbitrary placing of the subject over however contrived an upward blast of air. Oh let me, when it came to this new volume of verse, this historical study, this dictionary, dip into my unconscious, keeping at bay anything that might push me in the direction of common sense, and come up with a lurid weed or two. What I did come up with was always, in her terms, hopelessly boring. She was frank about this. 'Oh, that's *boring*!' There was nothing I could do but laugh. I'd always been ticklish when invaded by rage. Here we were, under the privet hedge, and I was to go at once and cut all the pansies in our front garden, my father's most beloved flower, and bring them to her. Well, some latterday version of that.

'"The life of the man who never forgot the woman's body twisting at the end of a rope outside the jail". Now, what about that!'

I'd shriek with laughter. 'Can't say it, won't say it!'

'When I worked in local radio,' Sarah would sigh, 'we'd spend more time on the trail than on the programme – often!'

'Good Lord,' I'd say, suddenly wretched. It was time to go. Farce had devoured the scene. I'd enjoyed this work for many years, but . . . it was time to go.

If I'd been my father, I guess, I'd already be pushing the earth back on top of her in that hole in the back garden. As it happened, my mother wouldn't go so far: but I did feel her, inside me, being distinctly in favour of locking Sarah in the coal shed and throwing away the key.

Oddly, round about this time, I was provided with an unexpected view of Hilda Hawkins by Gina Flounder, who edited, in one of the local free newspapers, a page with the heading: *History from the Attic*.

When I first saw the page I thought this curious journal, one of three now pushed unsolicited through our letter box and adding to already desperate problems of disposal, and which seemed to have been put together by a set of jokey primary school children stiffened with estate agents, was offering a regular item on Greek history. That wouldn't have been entirely surprising. The strangest things were stuffed, with a rough sort of enthusiasm, into its pages. There was a guide to some obscure London art galleries: and a page of health hints supplied by an advocate of alternative medicines. (The paper had no steady policy about spelling any of these.) But Gina's page, in fact, was one that solicited old photographs from readers, who were imagined as keeping them in their attics. I remembered that my Uncle Will used to keep family photographs in the downstairs lavatory, where I found it exciting to inspect great-aunts in their youth lashed with puritanical lasciviousness into sombre gowns: I don't suppose he was the only resident of Barton to do so, but I could see that the idea of the attic being favoured led to a more attractive heading. I was quite certain that Gina had never been into an attic in her life. That wasn't her style at all.

Her page offered a repetitious diet, on the whole, week after week: lanes winding through a crush of trees that had since become streets bald with houses, or tottering inns that had stood where now were terribly untottering high-rise office-blocks. About all this, Gina adopted a jocular manner behind which lay several loose suggestions. One was that she felt herself widely loved by her readers; another, that she despised them. Using words with rapid vagueness, she humoured them for their passion for the past. Her own viewpoint, never stated but strongly to be felt, was one of scorn for any moment of history beyond, say, last December. 'Picturesque', she'd cry, of stretches of local slum; 'Quaint', of any building of two storeys or less. There was often an effect of casual insult. 'Who recognises the miserable looking man in the doorway?' she'd ask. When she posed such questions, it was as if she were taking old-age pensioners by the collar and shaking them, with rough, absent-minded good-humour. 'Any senior citizen know who the man with the big nose was who's holding the reins?' (I remembered him, though I knew better than to put my hand up: he was old Parslow, who brought round miscellaneous greengrocery in the 1920s: I could still hear the last few escaped potatoes thudding and bumping on the floor of his cart as he made his way back to his little shop.) If any reader uttered some half-throttled reply by way of a letter to Gina, always invited, nothing came of it: next Friday was next Friday, with everything forgetfully new in this corner where everything was invited to be rememberingly old. She had trouble with adjectives – except that you could imagine her amusement at the idea of being inconvenienced by such things. 'The teacher looks starchy,' she wrote of Miss Stout, standing in the corner of the classroom in the photograph, taken about 1926, which startled me as I opened the paper one day, and in which Hilda Hawkins (and, disconcertingly, I too) appeared.

Miss Stout was – as I recalled, and as she plainly looked in the photo – a soft woman. Gina must have imagined that any white blouse of the period, such as our old teacher was wearing, would have been starched, and that this stiffener would have spread into Miss Stout's whole being. Well able to control her forty-four five-year-olds, she was, in fact, a soft, warm controller. I was appalled by the school, mostly for its brutal scale and construction – the ceiling must have been fifteen feet or more above us, and heavy tiling made the lower reaches of the walls immune to damage caused by any child who'd forgotten to bring his sledge-hammer to school – but I was reconciled to it by . . . her white blouses (this is how I think of it), her plump hands, her level voice, and, I believe, her colouring. I remember a face more red than white. 'Glum expressions mingled with cheeky grins' was Gina's summary. In fact, there was deep seriousness, at one extreme, and at the other a nervous sort of smiling. The seriousness was, quite solidly, male. The girls were anxious to keep the photographer happy. They were smiling tenderly towards him. We had in front of us, on our double desks, the little battered cardboard boxes in which our work was kept. I was one of only two boys out of twenty wearing a tie. It was striped, and spoke of my mother's ambition for me. She wanted me to move into a world of ties; and the stripes, which were diagonal, would have suggested to her an elevation even greater, already a sort of grammar schoolness.

At the front was Hilda Hawkins. Alas, the rounded arms I remember, so white, so thrilling, were out of sight, clasped behind her back with what I now see as a not entirely sincere effect of demureness. She was wearing a crocheted dress,

207

high-waisted, high-necked, with what appeared to be a handkerchief pinned to it. If I wasn't also in the photo, with a full blonde cap of hair, I might have thought it was my scalp. Under her fringe, she looked out at the photographer with an expression I can still interpret: it invited him to walk through puddles without his wellingtons, throw a ball into the Corbys' garden and *go in and fetch it*, and, having cut down all his father's pansies, make a bunch of them and cut his way through the privet hedge to deliver them to his dangerous love in her crocheted dress, to be rewarded with careless exposure not only of her arms, but also her legs. I was certain that Hilda, my first, long-ago, tormenting and rounded love, was to be found somewhere at Khajuraho, in some sunny corner of that general celebration of roundedness.

Gina was wrong about the date, about Miss Stout, about the expressions on our faces. Luckily, she did not turn her inattentive attention to Hilda. That I could not have borne.

# 3

Well, I said to the ticket-collector on the pay-as-you-go train. Yesterday it cost my wife and me only four pounds forty for two of us. Now you are asking three pounds thirty for me alone. He said he understood my being startled, though he wished to be excused from sharing that exhausting emotion. There must be some explanation, though God knew what it was. And I did indeed understand that if he empathised with every dismayed passenger he'd be worn out in a week. All the same, it was odd.

'Oh well,' he said, suddenly having a purely technical thought, 'do you perhaps have a senior citizen's railcard?' And I remembered that of course I had, and that it was by producing this alongside Kate's yesterday (at her instance) that we'd secured that reduction. Here it was, I said sheepishly. He gave me the look of a man who couldn't understand why anyone should forget, especially when economies ensued, that he was a senior citizen.

He hadn't imagined how the term hurt. It was like being bluntly called an Aunt Sally; or, aside from the strict application of the title, which I enjoyed, that general name we had c. 1928 for anyone with a hint of white in hair or beard: Grandad. Inside an ageing person, such wrath at being made from day to day a less and less agreeable parcel of flesh, being out of the sexual running, being treated with essentially inhumane kindness.

It had been bad, a few days before that rail-borne humiliation, at the Rodin exhibition. Little sculptures (little for him, that is) and drawings. It had struck Kate and me, suddenly, as odd: all of us politely moving among those writhings and wrestlings and being, ourselves, so modest, so gravely attentive: at our most excited, tapping our knuckles with rolled catalogues. Good Lord, one thought, how resistant could one be to the implications of several rooms of powerful art? Our clothes should be off, we should be essaying solo contortions, or be athletically intertwined. There was a work, 'Christ and Mary Magdalene', that made me feel what it was to be a sculptor, for one of Mary's hands had driven itself into the stone and been reunited with its rawness. And that made it more amazing than ever that this sinuous excitement by which we were surrounded, this strenuous celebration of the flesh, should exist at all, and ever have came out of blank stone; and that we shouldn't be taking some sort of disgraceful cue from it.

But then, Kate and I thought – in any case, she and I would form some little sculpture that was writhing less from joyful litheness than from arthritis: *Citoyens aînés*! Ugh!

It had to be said that the attack launched by the ageing process offered surprises – many of them. 'If it weren't so depressing,' Kate had said, 'it might be stimulating.' Recently I'd looked towards the television, where a small red light showed if it was on or off. On this occasion, five small red lights provided the information, a stammer of ruby red. They floated, entrancingly. A sort of drifting brooch, I thought. I blinked to rid myself of the illusion, but it persisted.

'Ah,' said the oculist, 'that was polyopia.'

Over the years, because of the vocabulary of Bernard's craft and the random encounters of letters he dealt in, we'd come to share a view of language. Examined, black on white in this curtained room of his, it tended to the absurd.

'Yes, certainly,' he said now, 'a nineteenth century prima donna: but also the word for a condition in which several

210

images were seen where there should be one. It was a *development*.' This was an example of his own absurd use of words: he said *development*, with its suggestion of the unfolding of some splendid purpose, to avoid saying *deterioration*. The next time there was a moon, I could expect to see five moons. They would probably vary in brightness, and he explained why this was so. I enjoyed the pleasure he always provided, of not understanding him. My own anxiety was whether the number of books I had to read was likely to be multiplied by five. Only, he said (it being a reaction to light) in the case of the odd illuminated manuscript.

Years before, peering into my left eye, he'd asked if it had ever been damaged. I'd thought of my mother's story of my birth, and of the villain in it, a drunken doctor with forceps. I'd appeared with a black eye, said my mother, who'd have grieved deeply about that. Keeping clean was her often fairly desperate retort to poverty, and she detested imperfections of any kind in her children's appearance. She'd have wanted to scrub the bruise away at once. I'd enjoyed that story enormously as a child, imagining the doctor as a reeling monster, hugely hiccuping, and the forceps as a pair of pantomime pliers. Drawing on the imagery then available to me, I'd heard him singing, in rowdily slurring fashion, a hymn – probably 'All Things Bright and Beautiful'. Later, I'd taken it that my mother was exaggerating, and that the marked inferiority of my left eye was inborn.

But no, it *had* been hurt: Dr Hiccups *had* done his worst. I'd dangled from those tipsy pliers, one of its feet treading on my eye. 'All thingsh wishe and wonderful!' he'd carolled, before my mother lifted herself on her elbow (itself an elbow out of a comic after all those years of turning a mangle, you could imagine those rays emanating from it which in *Funny Wonder* hinted at great strength) and ordered him to put me down. Too late, too late! A medical clown who might well have been born in 1860, he'd pointed me already towards polyopia, somewhere close to 1990.

211

Bernard had once spoken to me with quiet awe of the space behind an undamaged, scarcely used eye, which was . . . *beautiful*, he said. A small child's eye . . . everything in its place, nothing discoloured, all bright. An intense, fresh brightness. *It sparkled.*

Once or twice recently I'd had an extraordinary sensation, as if there were a kind of splendid music everywhere, as of a multitude of events making of themselves an immense choir. It was, I thought, an ageing man's elation; and it made it seem odd, while the sensation lasted, that we should treat life as anything but an amazing crescendo. It was the last movement of a Mahler symphony, and everything had been growling and muttering *sotto voce* for twenty minutes or so as a gorgeous preparation for the final swelling which itself would occupy twenty minutes or more: a hugeness of sound approaching on tiptoe.

At other times I was pompous about our need to be resolute and stoical, and to adopt other uncharacteristic postures.

'I think,' I told Kate after one disaster (bending down and being unable to straighten up – something of that order), 'we should look at these hardbacks positively.'

'You mean setbacks,' she said.

'Oh my God,' I said. 'That *is* the end! I can't tell one word from another!'

'It's a professional mistake,' she said. 'Any writer might make it. At any time of life.'

I couldn't imagine my friend Rufus making it.

# 4

Going (actually on that pay-as-you-enter train) to watch Jill Pirrie teach, I'd run on arrival almost at once into Rufus, via his work.

'We are going to do that difficult thing – we are going to try to imagine a ghost in words,' Jill Pirrie had said.

It was a classroom, but I'd come to it as if to an alchemist's laboratory. The alchemist herself, who drew out the natural gold in the imaginations of her children, had none of the appurtenances of a worker of miracles. She was slim, dressed in green, and had been teaching for thirty years. These were the things that I observed, cautiously, as well as her lively eyes with a curious attentiveness about them, suggesting a habit of unusual concentration, and her quiet voice. Miss Baker of Barley Road, that earliest of the teachers of English who (it now strikes me) have swarmed in my life, might have been impatient with this description. Miss Baker might have wanted to know about her shoes. But that was what Jill Pirrie was very soon to say something about – the need for selection. A child (in the next lesson, ghosts left momentarily behind) had written about her first day at school, and had described her first teacher: dress, height, age. Questioned by a fellow-poet, the author said: 'I also remember – but I couldn't fit it in – she had a moustache.' Well, right, said Jill Pirrie: of course, as we all knew, as everyone in the room safely and abundantly knew, selection is vital. Even marvellous details might have to go, representing that amount of marvel that added to marvel kills light with light.

I omit the marvel of Jill Pirrie's shoes.

She didn't thrust an observation at her children, I thought – she enfolded them in it: it was hers, but it was instantly theirs. The secret behind the miracle might lie partly in this firm courtesy with which ideas and perceptions were transferred from teacher to children. Perhaps teaching at its most delicate and fruitful is always concerned, as it points out and informs, to congratulate the taught on the knowledge they now have. It's the instantaneous good manners of decent instruction.

Well, this word 'miracle'. I'd come that morning, an accepted spy in the classroom, with the distinct aim of outlawing the word. Use it, and you'd gone a long way towards making yourself believe there was no explanation. But year after year 'miracle' was the awe-struck, delighted, baffled word used by the judges in the annual competition for young writers set up by W. H. Smith, faced with poetry of astounding quality coming, in astounding quantity, from this middle school in Suffolk.

Smith's! Sixty years earlier I'd stolen a comic or two from their shop in Barton, having found I could hide, say, *Comic Cuts* under *Funny Wonder*, and pay for *Funny Wonder* only. All that at the long, slanted counter that I think of still with excitement – all those comics, newspapers, periodicals, tucked in behind one another, a long smell of ink and paper. (Behind, through fumed oak doors, silence and stationery and young lady assistants required to look as unyoung as possible, so as not to contradict the gravity of the carpets. I'd think of *that* Smith's, *c.* 1930, when I was elbowed and elbowing in today's noisy Saturday morning crush: the same shop, now unimaginably different). Socially face to face with the present managing director of Smith's, I'd confessed to my distant crime, but he'd shrunk from the citizen's arrest I was half-prepared for; the antiquity of the offence relieved him, he thought, of the need for such melodrama. 'Even my sins are old,' I grumbled to Kate. Now I was a judge where I'd been a short-trousered criminal.

You could attempt to explain those astonishing poems, I suppose, by positing something in the air or soil of that patch of Suffolk that caused true poetry to occur in children of middle school age. It seemed more likely that the source of this thrilling disturbance of the ordinary run of things – the almost *universal* ordinary run of things – lay in Jill Pirrie. And in fact you could see what she'd done. She'd laid her children open to the essential notion of similarities, and of differences made remarkable by resemblances, and resemblances made startling by differences. She'd made them extraordinarily sensitive to the power of a verb that wasn't quite, or altogether wasn't, the verb you'd expect, or was a verb used in one context that had spent much of its life in idle imprisonment in another. She'd made them aware, and had made them aware again and again, of images. Somehow she'd made them unable to tolerate idleness of language. She'd made them tremendously alert to what, when you bring words together, makes a music out of them: the echoes and hums from one word to another, and from words ten lines away to those in the line you're now writing. And she'd done all this (here was miracle tipped with miracle) without turning the children into a single standard, however admirable, poet. Within the energy she'd released, under her single impulse, her children were enabled to be perfectly individual.

It was why I wasn't, that morning, for all the inward badgering from Miss Baker, thinking much about Jill Pirrie's shoes.

I'd been astonished by my first sight of the school. I suppose at the back of my mind I'd believed it would have about it . . . at least a touch of the Brighton Pavilion. Home of such poets, it wouldn't be an ordinary school building. But it was a school building of absurd ordinariness. It was an assemblage of plain brick boxes. In its green setting, it was without grace. Trying to find the entrance (schools so often baffled as to where their

215

front doors are) I kicked myself. No miracles, no Brighton Pavilions! Concentrate on the idea of bright work being enclosed in plain envelopes!

The ghost of a place, time or a season, said Jill Pirrie now, is the very essence of that place, or time, or season. But ghosts were a cliché-ridden subject: those clanking chains, those howlings! What she was going to do was to read a story that would rid their minds of those clichés. It was called 'A Grave Misunderstanding', and was by . . .

It was by Rufus. A dog, the narrator, and his attendant person. Scene: a churchyard. Apparition: a slim, very slim, young woman, rousing the dizzy interest of the person. The dog could smell, as his foolish person could not, the flaws in that charming, floating lady: her odour was of earth and old emptiness. Her invitation to come back to her place was an invitation to enter the grave. Appalled dog, barking his warnings, infatuated person . . . 'While I read,' said Jill Pirrie, 'will you remember that this ghost is very much the essence of the churchyard.'

For Rufus, dogs were as natural a topic as tombs. He was the most mysteriously absolute person, as recognised by dogs, I'd ever known. He'd had a succession of them: on the whole, great jovial fools, extravagantly hairy. His latest, Ned, was huge and golden, and I tried never to name his type, knowing I'd not get it right. Rufus went in for dogs that were nearly, but never precisely, of a familiar breed. Recently we'd met in the Friar's Holt in Barton for lunch – though really so that Rufus could require me to read his last week's work, reacting with alarm to my every reaction. '*What's that?*' – I'd shifted my beer glass so there was less danger of its being knocked over. Rufus feared it was a gesture caused by unbearable irritation with his work. The pub dog appeared – Toby – sad-eyed, diffident. He'd walk round you, as if he'd never completely abandoned the idea of striking up an acquaintance: but at his most reckless he'd sit a good foot from your knee, uncommittedly semi-companionable. Now, he leapt lightly onto Rufus's lap, sighed, and laid his head on Rufus's breast.

I thought if he'd not taken up that position on Rufus, Rufus might have taken up that position on him.

'Ah,' said Rufus: and then, '*What's that?*' I had tried to avoid Toby's tail, which, to express his pleasure at having safely housed himself on my friend, he'd slowly brandished in my face, but Rufus, of course, had thought I was moved by hatred of his prose.

And here I was (oh, life's endless circularity!) listening to a tale of Rufus's about a dog, being used to exorcise clichés. And it had to be said that, given a little flexibility in the biological arrangement of things, Rufus could have been bottled and sold as an infallible dispersant of the over-familiar. Some of the best effects in his writing followed from his running into an imminent banality and devising some spectacular means of blowing it sky-high.

Rufus having been read, cliché exorcised, Jill Pirrie talked about the story, asked questions. Was there one sentence that evoked the churchyard within the space of a few words? Yes, where the dog said the apparition smelt of worm-crumble and pine. Smells took you back. She'd spoken before of the horror of her first term at school. If any smell reminded her of that, she'd get a lurch in her stomach. Could a ghost smell? Of course. 'We shall wish to endow our ghost with smell.' And the feel of a ghost? Yes, there was that moment when the dog leapt at the illusory lady, and 'it was like jumping through cobwebs and feathers'. Compared with a dog, what blunt perceptions men and women had!

So now . . . They should think of somewhere they knew extremely well . . . in the natural world, perhaps, or an old church; a pub; woods. Any place they might be able to evoke through a ghostly presence. Two minutes of jotting on paper.

I thought: What is here is a relaxed intensity, together with a . . . most crisp value given to time. No floundering. No uncomfortable haste – yet minds and imaginations were sprinting. So quietly and truly to make time valuable in a classroom . . . that's an achievement!

217

The two minutes over, someone had thought of Norwich Castle, another of the bailey bridge in Southwold. ('I like the precision of that.') A boy had thought of the school itself. Jill Pirrie asked if anyone had ever returned after teachers and children had gone. Jonathan had . . . He'd forgotten his PE kit, and recalled the desperate sense of silence where silence never was, and the sensation of the changing room being made uneasy by his irregular presence.

The class had become a little market of sensations, creepinesses, alarms. They considered two ghost poems written by earlier Halesworth poets. There was a sea ghost: 'The cliff crumbles like her chalk teeth.' . . . 'Her face/Lacy like fishing tackle.' . . . 'Her silk cloak and cobwebs hung from her armpits.' . . . 'Her fingernails of fish scales': And a church ghost: 'Within walls of wisdom he stands.' Could someone say something technical about that . . . be a bit clever? Yes, of course, alliteration.

And so to . . . precisely five minutes for them to begin to make their ghosts. They should forget being in Room 14 at Halesworth Middle School. 'Your words will be of no avail if they don't startle me.' The market became a workshop, devoted to startling Jill Pirrie. After which, a sharing of images. The chalk flaking on the blackboard was her skin. Her hair/Courtesy of the finest thatch. Her eyes/Segment of the sun. Her face/A lace napkin rumpled with age. Was James offering another? Well, yes, he'd been about to do that . . . but he was already beginning to rewrite it.

They turned out to have exactly nine minutes left 'to try to get into the poem.'

The next class had completed or near-completed poems to read. Meanwhile they were thinking themselves into some position that would enable them to write of life on Earth with nostalgia. Perhaps . . . you were an astronaut, circling in space; a prisoner in some underworld; an old woman in an old people's home. They'd be, said Jill Pirrie, a mixture of first day poems, and being-small poems, and astronaut poems. They had this *gardener's* sense of a variety of poetic species. Emma read

218

a poem called *'Farmyard Chatter'*, and was questioned by classmates. Where did she get the idea for her phrase, 'leather breath'? The combined smells of the farm added up to such a smell, she thought. 'Gives you a little shock,' said Jill Pirrie. The class quivered with knowledge of what it was to administer a shock through words. 'Tissue-paper cows digesting grass.' *Tissue-paper?* Well, if it was windy they seemed to be faintly swayed by the air.

In a fish poem, where did an image for the fins come from? 'Well, that,' said the candid poet, 'was from a different fish.' 'That's a reasonable part of your power,' said Jill Pirrie. 'To mix experiences! To combine fish!' Michelle was already in space. 'An astronaut sits in an eye/Watching the earth.'

If I were limited to two plain comments on poems from Halesworth, I'd point first to the essential gift they display, that would be striking in a senior poet and is quite astonishing in poets aged between eleven and fourteen, of such accuracy and originality of perception as leaves the memory littered with phrases. Well, there's the pig on stiletto heels, as one example where there are thousands. And then I'd point to the total absence from this abundant poetry of the easily or self-infatuatedly poetic. I'd yet to read a Halesworth poem that didn't reach earth in a statement that might have thrilled for the way it was expressed, but was full of a sometimes quite dour good sense.

What they'd been shown was how to look, truly look, and then how, drawing exclusively on this experience of looking (increasingly habitual), to find words for what they saw. And you startled because what you saw, if this was the order of your inspection of the world, was always startling.

'It's not in the National Curriculum,' said someone in the Halesworth staffroom. '*Nothing* in the National Curriculum is worth doing', said another.

Over lunch I thought of a phrase for Jill Pirrie. She was a helplessly happy teacher. She said yes, she was – and, of course, a performing teacher, having her say as part of the opera that every lesson was. ('Opera' is my image. Singing splendidly, her own use of language often unaffectedly noble, she was a cause of singing in the children. And they caught from her, what clearly they wanted for themselves, seriousness.) But under the new order of things, her being a performing teacher was a cause of inspectorial frowning. The cant word now was 'facilitator'. It was what a teacher had to be: marginalising herself, and causing children to invent their own education. Well, we agreed, facilitation – though there had been more graceful words for it – had for a very long time been an element in teaching. But an *element* – not the whole of teaching, and a small part of the teaching of some. I thought she had 'facilitated' the children to arrive at the words 'alliteration' and 'onomatopoeia' as definitions of practices already arrived at. The substantial element in her work, lay in that display of hers, the now immensely seasoned display of herself as someone to be startled, refreshed, rescued from cliché by her children's use of words.

The Poet Laureate, chairman of the W. H. Smith judges, had said he felt a kind of awe in face of the idea that Jill Pirrie's example might have revealed something awfully important, and that if we took it seriously, the whole of teaching might have to be changed. Elbow to elbow with the unassuming phenomenon herself, I thought there was little enough in what she did that could be turned into procedures transferable to others. You could make a list, of course. There was . . . creating, in the classroom, intensity of a comfortable kind; never letting a lesson, any more than a poem, go dull or dead, sowing an occasion with shocks; and there was ensuring that time, without painful urgency, had a clear, constant value.

But you were left with the problem that these prescriptions were really effects of the teacher's entire nature. The educational world often assumed that good teaching could be brought about by the imitation of good teachers, and there was a dreadful limit to that; because good teaching in the end is a consequence of what the good teacher irreproducibly is.

220

She'd been introduced, Jill Pirrie told me, to the prime author of the new order in education, better described as disorder, and he'd smiled and asked at once: 'Do you teach grammar?'; and as she gave her necessarily complex answer, the smile faded, the eyes narrowed.

The new order, she said, was so time-consuming in terms of its mere administration, the ticking of targets (pages of 'targets' for every child, as if they'd been dartboards), the filing of acts of facilitation, that you could fail to get round to teaching at all. Suppose she hadn't thirty years of experience behind her, and hadn't the determination that sprang from that! How intimidated she might be, how she might be persuaded to teach poetry once a month, or perhaps never.

I told her of an occasion when, in a radio discussion with education as the subject, we'd been asked what reform, even revolution, we'd bring about if it was all to be done by magic wands. I said I'd like to ensure happiness in the classroom. I was fallen upon at once. Good Lord, cried a man carefully grey, we'd had enough talk of *jollity* in schools. The time for *high jinks* was over. (He had this curiously hectic notion of what happiness was.) Learning was no joke. This idea that there might be something agreeable in it had brought us close to the brink (he didn't say of what), but thank Heaven, such notions had been swept away for ever, to be replaced by a suitably miserable realism. Let us, he said (employing a sequence of euphemisms so as to sidestep the actual use of such terms as 'downcast', 'joyless' or 'profoundly depressing'), let us pursue the new path, of cautious wretchedness and avoidance of any kind of elation. Later, travelling down from the studio in a lift with him and other fashionable educators (themselves much given to attack on 'fashionable educators' who somehow combined being all the rage with having been swept into the dustbin of educational philosophy) I made myself as prepared as a pacifist may be for physical scrimmage.

And I told Jill Pirrie how, not long before, I'd interviewed the minister who'd presided over this pretence that educational advance lay in our being, as teachers and parents and children,

221

systematically unpleasant, dull, as carefully drab as my apoplectic adversary on that radio programme had set out to be. I thought ill of the minister for being, with such bustling ambition, so ready to suggest that the most complex of human enterprises, carrying with it a long and subtle history of thinking and rethinking, of bright ideas and blank ones often repeated in a cycle of experiment, achievement and failure (the printed literature stretching back over two millenia), could be busily turned in the finally correct direction, with a preoccupied smile, by a place-holder patently eager to hurry on to hold other and even better places.

He had put a book together, and I was to talk to him about it. It was, I thought, like interviewing a large glossy balloon made of thick rubber. You tried to impinge upon this balloon, to affect it in some fashion, but it wasn't possible. As you asked a question, the balloon received and deadened the impact of it, without at all attempting to identify its particular character as a question; it was an all-purpose sort of deadening activity, that went habitually into action whenever it detected (by the oral shape, I guessed) a question. I had never had such a curious sensation of not actually meeting a man in whose company I found myself. Or of literary questions being fended off, or transformed at the very moment of apparent answer, as if they were political questions.

I remembered my friend Maurice Lee, in a television debate, offering ideas as he always did, ideas that smiled and were warm, and how in that setting, which implied the superiority of cold if not frozen opinion, he was bested again and again, in terms of chill logic, by another debater who drew his ideas, stiff with frost, out of the refrigerator of his mind. I thought it should have been taking place in Maurice's huge farmhouse kitchen; and Maurice should, whilst talking and listening, have been hurling bits of this and that into pan or saucepan, tasting, exclaiming, as I'd seen him do time and again. I thought of the warmth that was implied when you said people had bedroom eyes: in that way, Maurice had classroom eyes. His educational ideas were like his dishes, you tossed in this and

222

that and tasted and swore and sometimes it didn't work out and you threw it away and started again.

Imagine discussing education in terms, not simply of happiness, but of bedrooms and bean soup, in that grey radio discussion!

Oh education, poor education! I thought, in Jill Pirrie's company, of my son Tom, struggling with the truth of it a hundred miles from Halesworth. When we talked of teaching, he and I, both deeply familiar with the educational dugouts, both moved by memories of the best moments when the mere delight of being human and in need of education had overtaken us in the presence of some group of children, themselves unfashionably delighted, I'd be reminded of Siegfried Sassoon's poem about the two foot-soldiers deploring the general:

'But he did for them both with his plan of attack.'

And when they turned to education on television news programmes! That use of the very vaguely suitable visual material! 'Today the leading teachers' union . . .' At once a classroom appeared; a teacher; children; a blackboard; a lesson, in mid-development. The news item faded from my attention. 'Today the leading teachers' union revealed that they had secretly manufactured a nuclear bomb and were proposing to drop it on the Department of Education and Science if their pay demands were not instantly met.' So it might have gone on, and I'd not have noticed, for I'd be watching that teacher . . . that (as they thought) stock illustration of the activity of education. Interesting that he should think it a good idea to wear that particular beard! Nice/nasty use of the blackboard! Watch that boy in the third row! Bright, very bright, but showing every sign of devoting his brightness to the cause of anaarchy! '. . . a day's strike next Tuesday . . .' That particular arrangement of desks – how would he justify that? Oh, *don't* cut it off now! He was just about to . . . surely he wasn't just about to do *that*!

I found myself worrying greatly, from time to time, about the effect of peripherally relevant visual aids on our view of things. Well, especially on mine. I was sensitive to what they did when it came to education, simply because after my years of teaching no classroom to me could be a mere background. The foreground: that was where classrooms always were and would be!

It was rather as if . . . a reference to some pay settlement for the Army were accompanied by scenes of mayhem: howitzers hurling shells, crumpled corpses, any military scene out of the immense dreadful stock of such things.

# 5

In 1940, my diaries remind me, a most unlikely alliance was brought about by a dispute over the contents of the meagre military cupboard with the aid of which the conquest of Barton was to be balked. This alliance was between my father and our English master, Williams. It wasn't an historical landmark in a year oppressively overstocked with those; but on a domestic scale, it was as astonishing as the Nazi-Soviet pact had been.

Their relations had seemed beyond all repair. Williams having advocated that I go to university was atrocity enough; but on top of that I'd turned to him at moments when a son might conventionally have been expected to turn to his father. And Williams being small, Welsh and witty – all that was against him. My father had always had, not particularly hidden away, the conviction that the Welsh were a race who sought to mask their treacherous intents with music. 'All *little* Williams cares for,' he'd say, 'is Number One. If only you could see that he doesn't care about *you*! If you get to university, it's one up for him, isn't it? That's all he's interested in.'

And there it was. Behind Williams' generous friendship had lain, in my father's view, this tautological desire for Number One to be one up. So I was astonished to overhear him say, at the time of the formation of what was at first called the Local Defence Volunteers: 'I've got an ally in Williams, I think.' Suddenly my old teacher was not even the dwarf my father had always implied he was. The withdrawal of the scathingly stressed adjective 'little' was as if he'd failed to speak of one of my friends as 'young'. '*Young* Fletcher,' he'd damagingly say, packing into the word a tremendous suggestion of irreparable callowness, '*young* Best.' Youth, like shortness of stature, was enough to make everything one did, or said, ludicrous. 'These *young* people,' he'd sometimes say to my mother, simply meaning me.

'What jest has history up her sleeve?' I asked my diary.

The fact is that my father and Williams were now colleagues in the LDV. To the office intrigues that had concerned him ever since he became a civil servant, my father was now able to add a thickening crop of paramilitary conspiracies. These seemed to spring from differences as to what weapons might or might not be requisitioned, and where they might be kept, and who might have this or that sort of access to them; and the division of opinion appeared, from what I overheard, to be related to a further set of adjectives and descriptive phrases, among them 'fat', 'council employee' and 'mother's boy'. I couldn't imagine that the man who'd introduced us to Shakespeare was inclined to attach simple meanings to simple words, but the fact was that my father and Williams were of one mind as to the requisition, housing and availability of weapons; and, I came to suspect, much else. Enemies in respect of my wretched and successfully foiled hope of going to university, my father and Williams would have been at one in disliking persons given to falling back on some hinted importance related to official position or (I remember one of my father's chief hates) size of residence.

I have a note of the alarm I felt, knowing Williams was now in possession of a revolver. He was extravagantly absent-minded, and had famous mishaps in the classroom with the impedimenta of education. I was reminded of him when I read of the sculptor Giacometti, at a time when all his work in plaster began fair-sized and then, to his dogged astonishment, insisted on being reduced until it was half an inch high: his travels round Paris, it was said, could be traced by the plaster-white imprints of his footsteps. Williams ran through chalk in much the same way, snapping it, dropping it and treading on it, putting it in his pockets and crushing it there. Tom Sadler and I once saw a photograph of the Cerne Abbas giant, that ithyphallic figure cut out of a Dorset hillside and outlined in chalk, and we thought it was not unlike – though of course Williams was the reverse of a giant, dwarfed by an early illness, and never carried a club. But the chalk, as Tom Sadler said, made it him to a T. I worried a little for my father, so often now in the company of such a man armed with a revolver that might be no less dangerous for having been in mothballs since the First World War. I had, given our old relationship of teacher and pupil, an uncomfortable inclination to confiscate the weapon.

I was reading *Robinson Crusoe* again, after hearing Desmond McCarthy talk about it on the wireless. 'A brave coward,' said McCarthy, 'makes the best hero for a book of adventure.' Alarming adventure was clearly what lay ahead of us, and if I had any aspiration in respect of it, it was to cultivate the bravest cowardice of which I was capable. Defoe said he wrote the book to stimulate 'invincible patience under the worst misery,' and that seemed to make reading it a timely exercise.

Oh what a strange moment that was! With all behaviour in suspense, and horror catching its breath before it took everything into its grip. It was now that something curious happened to the relationship between Jenny Lawrence and me. Someone in the reporters' room at the police court asked if we were in love, and I'd found myself nodding. Jenny was present and offered no denial. There followed some weeks when we must have had something epithalemic about us, for everywhere complete strangers went out of their way to greet us as lovers. One afternoon when we were in search of a priest, for news-gathering purposes solely, we found ourselves in a great garden, attached to the local Methodist headquarters. 'You can look at the gooseberry bushes,' said the caretaker at the church, directing us across the road: it was a low version of the sort of comment we'd become accustomed to. Entering the garden, my diary says, was like a moment out of *Alice in Wonderland*. War seemed to have been at work already: the greenhouses were empty, ransacked. Bushes had burst out of their careful shapes, and we had to push our way between two overbrimming weigelas. And so to the lawn, where, among stripes of light and darker green, a gardener was pushing a lonely mower. He had a saturnine face. I was reminded of him nearly half a century later when gardeners phantomly appeared and vanished in the hotel garden in Agra. After telling us the minister wasn't there, after all, he went on mowing; as he did so, murmuring: 'Bride and bridegroom . . .'

The strange thing is that Jenny and I said nothing about it to each other. It was as if we'd pretended not to notice we were drowning. I remember that the unreal elation we felt seemed to depend on our saying nothing, nothing at all. Nothing much united us: but I conclude now that we were briefly united in some phenomenal fashion by the nature of that moment before history began to scream, and of that desperately beautiful spring and summer.

To add to the queerness of it, Jenny had a colleague on the *Palmers Park Journal* who was clearly in love with her in some absolutely non-phantasmal fashion. Paul Desmond was known as Des, and the very name seemed sensible in a way that made it a reproach directed against the folly that enfolded Jenny and me. I was fond of Des, a pleasantly solid, red-haired young man, who was amused by much that happened and laughed in helpless gusts that often stood in for some statement or comment he was too tickled to put into words. You'd come from some ludicrous scene in court, not seldom a magistrate in a fit of moral apoplexy imposing a sentence much beyond his powers, so that he had to be put right by an embarrassed clerk of court; in the reporters' room Des would clutch you and shake with laughter, and nothing needed to be said. But I knew he was worried about the illusion into which Jenny and I were locked. Its unreality must have dismayed him, deeply; and in my turn I was worried about being a cause of dismay to so honest a friend. 'Somehow it doesn't seem a world for honesty any more,' I wrote in my diary.

And then Jenny went on holiday for a week, and when she returned it was all gone, the mad magic had blown away; it was as if we'd walked across that row of dots in Eliot's poem that, as it seemed to me, split 'A Cooking Egg' into two barely related parts. And Des vanished, too, being taken beyond laughter and destroyed in North Africa.

My friend Ben Fletcher, soon to join the Navy, wondered aloud if Hitler might be . . . a necessary purge? Terrible to say . . . but might there be something in it? 'So many things on our side are so bad,' he said. 'We have this half-liberty. We are corrupted by this dreadful Empire. Apart from its hour of horrible cruelty, might not the tempest that Hitler's raising alter the world for ever, and for good? – Because we can reply to him only by converting half-liberty into whole liberty.'

That, I guess, was another of those elations and simple extravagances of feeling that were flying around, offering themselves at a moment for which, as it happened, Ben and I had words we owed to Williams: actually, to *Poems of Today, Book Two*, studied by us, under Williams' eye, with great intensity. 'In dreary, doubtful, waiting hours,' Ben would quote from Julian Grenfell's *'Into Battle'*, 'before the brazen frenzy starts . . .' We'd murmured the lines to each other on the brink of school exams, but there was nothing facetious about the quotation now.

I was deaf, needing my ears blown out. I had a young man's furious distaste for himself, sharpened by the general occasion. 'Left alone, I would become a creeping and verminous hermit, causing disorder but unable to create order.' (It seems severe, but I imagine I had evidence of this dismal proclivity.) Sometimes in a bus between Barton and Monmouth Hill I'd pretend I didn't know there was a war, and would wonder how I'd recognise its existence. 'But it's like my deafness: grown habitual. The obvious marks, of course, the white dashes on the roadway, the now-dusty posters, shouting of out-of-date proclamations, enjoying a stale courage: the blank sockets of the signposts.'

'Every morning is lovelier than the last,' I wrote: and 'Oh this lovely world! How can I complain, waking to find myself alive in it!' I dreamt that I met Tess Grayson, and she said: 'Yes, he is still the same: still making unnecessary notes about very small matters.'

I made a note of being with Jenny and passing two men we knew to be Belgian refugees. One said of her to the other: 'Beautiful, *beautiful* . . . !'

I find this entry in my diary for September 7, 1940. It is the writing of a twenty-year-old with literary ambitions, who wanted to say everything gloriously, and so, much of the time, anxiously overwrote. What seems to me interesting, fifty years later, as the groaning branch that the twig turned into, is that when it came to the dropping of bombs, his incorrigible wish to swagger with words had to come to terms with an experience that shocked everyone who passed through it into some variety of awe. So he swaggered, shocked to whatever is the core of anyone's being. I enclose in brackets the words I would now remove, as being unnecessary when the barest statement had the character of rodomontade. (The last being a word he would greatly have approved of).

'Tonight,' he wrote, 'I find myself unwilling to write. It is an anatomy of horror, like an old book of skeletons.

'I was to go to a horticultural show. Jenny would be there, and I was wearing a sky-blue shirt. Out of these facts I made a small pleasure. An air raid warning came, and it was to an almost vacant street, its only occupants looking up at the sky, that I went. The bus suddenly jerked to a stop. I looked up. Across a field, brown flat wings like a bat's, came an aeroplane: then soared up to show its circles. Late and after the show came Jenny, so she needed my notes. She was in a bright summery frock. We walked up the hill. When we got there – two little fires, far away on the rim of the city: bright, cardinal. We moved a bit, and there was a much bigger one, in the region of St Paul's: an outrageous swaying of considerable flames. We felt sick, and went into a café. We had been there some time, it was darkening, when the whistles went. Jenny began to tremble. I finished dictating quickly, and as calmly and gently as I could because she was trembling so much. We went out, silent under these horrific events. The sky was a spreading pink pool, curiously vague and peaceful for a reflection of the fire we could see, now so high-tongued, so livid that we seemed to hear it crackling. The city churches stood out black against it. The whole valley seemed aghast with flame. We stood in the muffled darkness, Jenny silent, feeling herself, I knew, so out of place, so silenced by the contrast between her summery dress and her girl's speech, and this flaming abyss, this silence pierced by searchlights, this silence of men sternly enduring the bitter fruits of our folly. She shivered, there was between us the silent relationship of brother and sister: and I was glad to see her on her way home on her bus.

'Fear there must be. But I wanted to calm and control people. Panic is an inflation, a self-indulgence. I seemed to see panic, a flying, whispering thing in a cloak. A man came up and said: "The swine! We oughtn't to take any prisoners . . ."'

And the next night, when I was at home: 'The warning has gone again, like the punctual pain of a sick man. It's of a hospital ward that I think: all seems sick, a huge sickness with few doctors and antics from the patients . . .

'I've thought a lot of Jenny today: made so silent by the malignity in the air of last night, so small and fragile in the darkness in her bright frock; standing close to me in the darkness . . .

'When my father isn't here, as tonight, I am left technically in charge. This is a theoretical state, demanded by my mother: it means being the masculine presence, interpreter of noises.

'All the time I don't want to write anything about this except that it is horrible and not to be borne. But it is queer sitting here and feeling sure that anything I think about it is heartlessly rhapsodical compared to the actual experience of being

231

bombed, that terrible unthinkable event that happens on every one of these nights – the crash and flash and the house falling in upon you and a hundred wounds smashing the frail body. Men who had respect for the frailty of the body, to whom it was a vision and a joy, would not in this [bestial] way traverse the skies, tormenting defence, ready to drop their [diabolical] missiles at random.

'Mother and Betty are lying by the wall, on their mattresses. Mother in a grotesque woollen cap, her anxious face peeping from it like the face of a diver from his helmet. Her eyes close – they open again – she listens: I have to remember to be patient. "No, it's not gunfire" – she believes me. But her eyes wander in her head as she follows the buzz of the aeroplane round and round the sky, a wasp in the darkness.

'Oh, those two galleys bearing the proofs of the foolish things I'd written about the raids. I have no speech of my own. My sentences are wooden blocks, subject followed by predicate always, stiff and overbearing . . .

'This, of course, is being written to the usual squibs and rockets – as if a child had thrown a match into a box of fireworks. The wire protection of the windows shakes with a dry twang . . .

'My father, returned, look up towards that endless buzz and cries: "We'll retaliate all right. Don't worry! *Don't worry!*"'

And the next day, in Monmouth Hill:

'War and peace. In peace, people might be going anywhere. In war, they are all levelled and imprisoned by the same dull destiny. I heard a woman saying of her maid's reaction to the raids: "But she feels differently to us. On a lower plane."

'I behaved badly to Jenny. "It's been a terrible morning," she said. "You've been so niggly."

'"I am mean and spiteful," I chanted. The centre of MH was closed for a timebomb that had fallen against a bank building and was slipping inwards.

'This is what it is to live amid toppling towers.'

# 6

I thought of such scenes, inevitably, when we watched *The Trojan Women* at Epidaurus, nearly fifty years later.

Kate and I had once had the idea of keeping a notebook, listing the things we'd never thought we'd do, but did. It would have been a companion to the 'We must . . .' notebook we actually started keeping, but quickly discontinued. *That* followed from our irritation with ourselves, saying forever: 'We must do this, go to that, not miss the other . . .' yet (for mere want, we thought, of reminders) unerringly missing the other, hardly ever going to that, rarely doing this. Keeping the notebook was simply an unbearable way of calculating the number of times a moment of absolute enthusiasm led nowhere at all. We wrote a final page of entries that it might have ineffectually contained had we been born at other times, ending: '*Don't* miss the first night of *Hamlet* . . .', and then burnt it.

There'd have been an entry in that other notebook for what we were up to now, crossing gorse-covered moorland in a bus on the way to Epidaurus. Hadn't expected gorse: hadn't, when we arrived on the scene, expected such a large operation of reception and control: so many cars and buses and coaches, so many car- and bus- and coach-parks, so many policemen. So many paths among so many trees before, with stunning suddenness, we saw the theatre. It was like that moment in

233

Nepal when round a corner turned out to be the Himalayas. Round *this* corner was the familiar great scallopshell; except that it didn't look instantly great – neat, rather, tucked into place on the hill. Becoming aware of its immense size was something that happened slowly, as we took our seats close to the stage and looked up towards the figures in the highest reaches of pale stone.

We'd paid as much as we could, wanting to be sure of seeing and hearing. It turned out we'd qualified also for strips of foam to make the long sitting less painful. But most of these privileges became neither here nor there at a marvellous moment when the lights were dimmed for the play to begin. At once there was an immense rustling swarm and, turning startled towards it, we saw that everyone in the upper tiers was moving rapidly down to fill every empty lower one. It was a great winged movement, as if a huge pale bat had rearranged itself lower on some tremendous surface. One moment, an audience scattered over the shell: the next, a quite different conformation, all of us crowded as close to the action as possible. It was the first *coup de théâtre* of the evening. *The Trojan Women* was a bonus; but even if that had been suddenly cancelled, we'd have had our money's worth.

'The Trojan play to end all Trojan plays,' says Peter Levi. The towers have toppled and the world of the Trojans is now emptied: it contains neither hope nor mercy, but the absence of these must still be the theme of appalling ceremonies, rigorous debate, dreadful *post mortems*. Hecuba the queen has become the property of Odysseus; Cassandra, her mad prophetic daughter, is Agamemnon's. All this, cries Hecuba, for one woman, one wedding. That woman appears, Helen, arms bound, and there is an exchange between them, one of those implacable debates, every turn of which is a wound inflicted on those already dead. In this production the chorus of women who with lamentations mark the desolations of the story as they accumulate, now marked the terrible give and take of this discussion, creeping towards Helen, fascinated, or crawling away from her in revulsion. Music came from drums, a clarinet, a deep pipe. In the growing darkness of the tale, the growing darkness of the evening seemed another actor. There is in the play the remorseless slaughter of a child, and as it came to that, we heard the weeping of babies and small children, present in the audience in extraordinary numbers. Into such a knot of attention were we drawn that I remembered only afterwards what elsewhere would have seemed a startling distraction: a breakaway flame from one of Cassandra's torches set light to the shoulder of Hecuba's gown, and the herald Talthybios stepped forward to beat it out, most briskly.

In Athens, where we'd spent a night on our arrival in Greece, it was hot beyond belief, and, with the poisoned air of their city boiling, even the Athenians were gasping. But to hardly bearable heat, which was beyond their control, they added hardly bearable noise, which was not. There'd been a basketball match, Greece v Yugoslavia, and it had been televised – and Greece had won. This must be celebrated by driving cars and motorbikes round and round the city at full pelt, hooting continuously till long past midnight, making mad circles of sound – deafening ones in the centre surrounded by fainter and fainter suburban uproars – but none of it as faint as one might have wished. In Napflion a few days later another victory, or the same one retelevised, led to a similar demonstration: the whole town, having for an hour or so been a motor horn, became a whistle, then a single great shout, and finally, towards dawn (as it seemed), a delirium of police sirens. What, we wondered, did Greece lack, that it must have all this? Though perhaps it could be said otherwise: What does Greece have, that it must have this, too? Not a people who would allow the world to end with a whimper.

The birds in the morning were as noisy as the citizens. We'd lie in bed expecting them at any moment to leap on their infinitely unsilenced motorbikes and go snarling through the air . . . Not that Mr Growser had come with us. Waking in Barley Wood would seem bland after this. Our reticent robins.

In the north, we made our noise indoors. Here, the main room in which life was lived was the entire outdoor scene, and sounds must be enlarged to match. It was what I'd felt in Africa. The idea of holiday was tied up with some notion of increased sound. You could feel the need of it by its absence in the ruins of Tiryns, built out of stones the handling of which must have called for gangs of giants: it was thought some lord of the place might have been the prototype for Hercules. The odd thing, here and at Mycenae a few miles away, was the silence: that golden silence, disturbed only by the shuffling feet of sightseers. What equivalent of roaring round and round the town on motorbikes would once have filled the air on jubilant occasions, or even lesser ones?

It was our pleasure to have, up the road from our hotel (you could stare into it from the little balcony of our bedroom), a football stadium. An afternoon match, in which large sections of the audience seemed perpetually on the move, circulating in bristling patrols and discussing the unfolding game with rivals, ended with a long verbal dispute under police supervision. It was down-market drama clearly in the tradition of *The Trojan Women*. There was the conflict, and then there was the furious analysis of the conflict.

I was re-reading *Middlemarch*. Somewhere in it George Eliot said the easy-minded knew vinegar only when the sourness was forced upon them. I'd worried sometimes that I was myself hopelessly easy-minded, liking the world so much and more inclined to like people than not. My father, who'd taken it from his mother, needed to discover an unpleasant explanation for everything that happened, and for every piece of behaviour. My mother had wanted very much to like people and happenings, and my father would be enraged by her apologies for the conduct of neighbours. I'd concluded (after seven decades) that ill-nature and good-nature were equally defective, as instruments for the inspection of life. Best was to be . . . sourly sweet, sweetly sour. Not that it helped to know this. The essential bent given to us was not capable of much alteration. If my memory of the young Tom Sadler was a true one, he didn't intend or wish to become a hermit: but that's what he'd become.

And, given the wickedness of the world, its daily evil, the huge sum of human indifference and cruelty, there were times when those furthest from being easy-minded must despair because they were not able to despair.

I'd not run into Tom since that encounter in the shopping precinct. But I'd had news of him from another old friend, who said Tom had made virtually a real hermit of himself. 'Miserable old bugger he's become!' And I thought that must have been out of some deep dread of life. His wife (so I interpreted my impatient informer) was a prisoner of that dread, and Tom longed to have his children, too, behind bars: but they'd escaped. I remembered visiting his home when we were boys – but rarely. It had not been welcoming, and I'd taken away a sense of Mr Sadler very matter-of-factly not much liking Mrs Sadler, and Mrs Sadler in some unfussy fashion finding Mr Sadler uncongenial. Tom's over-sweetness of address at school, that had so infuriated Sergeant Clinker – had that been bred out of some forlorn hope that he could transform all that dry dull unhappiness?

I thought, trying to catch at a clue, of the Tom Sadler I'd walked those unwarring lanes with, in the early months of 1940. How we turned and turned in the wake of our childhood and youth!

With Epidaurus round the corner, it was a moment to observe that after that fiery scene in 1940, when the city was set enormously on fire by what essentially was a droning high in the air (I think it was that monotone that so maddened my mother, in her refuge under the living room table: murder should have some more remarkable voice), I never again in my remorseless diarying gave much space to introspections or utopian moralisings. Reality took over. Facts and details, things said, seemed at last more important than great general statements, ignoble in their attempt at nobility.

A few weeks ago I'd interviewed the poet Roy Fuller, in his mid-seventies writing sonnets about (what was Tess Grasyon's phrase?) 'very small matters'. He said he wished in his earlier work he'd been more particular and less general. 'You can make a poem out of any small fact now?' Yes, he said. But he thought he might have written too often about the 53 bus. I write, I said, far too often about Barton High Street.

Going to bed in Napflion, I took two necessary medicaments, a spray and a pill, together, and the result was extraordinary. I was compelled to write page after page of *Middlemarch*, in what seemed exactly George Eliot's manner, agonising over aphorisms, moving the characters through what in televisual terms were shadows of their original behaviour; I was shackled to someone else's novel, and knew perfectly well that it had no need of my labour. I may have fallen asleep; I awoke . . .

. . . a monument to siccity, says my diary, demonstrating that George Eliot still had me by the collar.

In the heat, we plotted our way from the shade of a tree to any other shadow that offered. The best time was evening, when it was marvellously warm only, and the sea practised its nightly trick of feigning transparency, and the world and his wife (but often, we suspected as we sat at the harbourside, someone else's) became silhouettes.

'*Flax*,' said a caption in the little, perfect museum, which displayed a certificate of its perfection signed by Richard Hoggart. '*The tiring process of its cultivation and elaboration, referred to by the people as the trials of flax, consists of rippling, retting, scutching and hackling.*'

'Just like life itself,' said Kate.

# 7

The girls from the grammar school Kate had attended, a late
19th-century appendage to the boys' school, and in which my
elastic wife had suffered the subduing effect of a remarkably
inelastic uniform that suggested a close association between
propriety and pleats, now treated their loins as if they'd been
cakes, and provided them with what my mother would have
recognised as cake frills. Others wore skirts that had the
character of minimal black elastic bands, and would have made
the movement of their legs impossible had these been skirts
that in any way involved the legs. I thought I might mention
this, if I ran into her, to our neighbour, Gwen Finch, who
was in her ninetieth year, had been headmistress of a girls'
school, and ruefully enjoyed the outrages brought about by
change. Gwen was a sort of mild Miss Growser, brandishing
her parasol as indignantly as she could, given her tendency to
a stern sort of giggling. I expected, anyway, she was woken in
the morning, as we were, by the voices of young women who'd
taken their dogs for a walk across the fields opposite us.
Arriving at the four-barred gate which was directly over the
lane from our bedroom window, they'd intermit astonishingly
audible conversation ('I said to him, I'm not going to do that,
if you've been to Lanzarote you don't want to go there again
in a hurry, do you know what I mean?') with coarse shouts
designed to flush their dogs from various corners of the field:

'Caesar! Pompey! Cato!' It wasn't possible to be sure about these names, for the immense volume of the shouts was not matched by clarity of articulation, but it always sounded as if the cast of Shakespeare's Roman plays was being warned of curtain-up. Looking out some mornings, half-expecting the field and lane to be full of persons falling on their swords under the eye of *au pairs* of enormous size, I'd be surprised to see a small mild dog or two and a number of young women of slight build who'd flung on, for this early occasion, fishermen's thigh boots, hasty tutus and t-shirts proclaiming their intention of doing unimaginable things to themselves or others.

Gwen was deaf, but she must have heard a little of that. She must have looked out, at times, and wondered what had happened to the gym-slip.

And then we were at her funeral. That tall woman with an ironical face (and, I'd thought more than once, an ironical walk) had missed ninety by a month or two. 'Gwen was a very private person,' said the priest in the little local church, where she lay in her inappropriate coffin. I always found myself ludicrously enraged by the spanking newness of coffins. The impossibility of their ever getting to look used was against them, surely. They had the appearance of the most deeply uninteresting sort of new furniture. For Gwen it seemed particularly unsuitable: it was a funeral cliché, and she was not given to clichés.

She'd set the priest a problem, having made it clear that she wished nothing to be said about her on this occasion, no biography. Even saying she was private was to break faith with that demand for final, absolute privacy. She'd not thought anyone would come, anyway. She'd outworn all her close contemporaries. Intent on having no nonsense about anything, she was not going to fool herself about the interest her death, absurdly belated, as she thought, would rouse.

I'd always enjoyed meeting her for the few refreshing sentences she'd offer; the refreshment lying in that freedom from nonsense. Being as old as she'd become had itself encouraged nonsense, she thought, and she'd been sharp, once, telling me of an acquaintance who'd drive ten miles twice a week to bring her delicacies of food, or books. Gwen was particularly independent of mind in the matters of diet and literature. But it was being regarded as someone to be tenderly conducted towards the exit that irritated her. I used to imagine the fastidious way she'd have treated staff and children, when she was a headmistress, and how that sensible manner of hers would have been unexpectedly smudged, now and then, with laughter. She'd never married. Perhaps, to her, love had seemed a kind of nonsense. Certainly it would have threatened a spectacular breach of privacy.

At her funeral, at which she'd hoped to become anonymous but hadn't, I thought I didn't really regret the joke I'd made at our last encounter. I'd noticed that W. H. Smith's, victim of my infantile malefactions, was now speaking of *clearance event* when plainly it meant *sale*. 'I suppose when we go it will be a *disappearance event*,' I said, and Gwen made a wry face. Anyway, as a jovial remark that could have been better timed, it wasn't in the same class as the one made by an aunt of Kate's, whom we all knew to have months at most to live, when she begged Kate to back her in persuading her husband to buy a new suit: 'You never know when he'll need it — a funeral, or something.'

And here we were, at Gwen's disappearance event.

If it had been possible I'd have consulted her about that problem that, as it seemed to me, had arisen in Gina Flounder's free newspaper. Among the small items of news, planted here and there among the pages, I'd noticed a recurrent event for which the sub-editor could think of one headline only: FLASHER STRIKES. It was so precisely what a flasher didn't do that I had a professional inclination to come to the sub-editor's aid, but could think of nothing much beyond FLASHER FLASHES. Gwen would have been delightedly appalled to be consulted on such a matter. Half of her would hardly believe that subjects that for much of her life had led to a great clapping of hands over other people's eyes might now be brazenly discussed in terms of the language to be used.

Half of her would react as she had done to being woken in the middle of the night by what turned out to be an obscene telephone call. She'd deeply resented it, she told Kate, who'd said such calls could be . . . brutally shocking. Oh no, said Gwen, it wasn't that – it was having her sleep interrupted that had annoyed her.

We spoke that verse that finds matchless prose for the statement that three-score-years-and-ten are your best hope: you can live beyond them, but it is not to be recommended, it will be gnashing of teeth and failing to meet deadlines and perhaps behaving in an odd manner at the microphone. It didn't seem, for all its splendour, quite the verse for the funeral of a woman who'd almost achieved four-score-years-and-ten and made, if wry, still deeply interested use of the last score.

It didn't seem, Kate and I thought, a few months away from our seventieth birthdays, an ideal verse to be uttered in our hearing, either.

# 8

But there was my mother's hundredth birthday to celebrate, before that.

Owing to what she'd have regarded as a very silly misjudgement by the Fates (women who like her had left behind them a long trail of empty cotton reels), she wasn't present. I'd have given much to have had a photo of her, as a baby, as a child. But they'd had no money for photographs, and no habit of it. In the earliest picture I had she was twenty or so, in a group of women at a Church Army convalescent home in St Leonard's. Though they were mostly old, they were arranged like schoolchildren, in obedient rows. My mother was at the back, hands behind her, jaw jutting. I imagined she might have learned that posture, hands stowed away, at the workhouse school she'd attended for a time and been sorry to leave, the uniform was so clean and crisp. But there was an obstinacy about her, something I remembered in her when she was my young mother, inside respectful poses a readiness to be difficult – and, of course, that jaw! She'd have needed some obstinacy, perhaps, to get to the convalescent home (the nearest to a holiday that could ever be hoped for, she said), and more to stay – and that, and other qualities to ensure that her mother came with her. My grandmother, Jessie, was in the front row, a small crushed woman, who before long would be going to the Middlesex Lunatic Asylum for Paupers, Colney Hatch (later made polite as the Friern Hospital), where she'd stay for the rest of her life, being given to hopeless melancholy. It was what happened when the crushing went a bit too far. In Jessie's case, I've always supposed that was when her husband, the grandfather I'd never known, vanished into prison.

What bare scenarios! Difficult not to feel that, in that direction, my origins amounted to an almost absurd minimum of harsh facts. Not so much a family tree as the ashes of a few family twigs.

For Lizzie and Jessie, it had been a farthing world. I remembered my mother's purse, the one she had when I was a child – black, with heavy brass catches, and worn brown lining. I remembered her fingers feeling among the coins, in a shop. She thought through the painful economy of the week by way of that touching of coins, calculating and re-calculating what she had, what she could surrender, what she must keep. Any coin that found its way into her purse became an anxiously familiar creature. I thought of the misery with which she must have felt in that brown lining for some coin, even a farthing, that might have been overlooked (as if that were ever possible) when in my first term at the grammar school I'd come home without a cap. It had been tossed irretrievably by a fifth former into a garden beyond the school wall, and another must be had, at once, for being without a cap was high treason, homicide, the most fearful crime imaginable. You could be hanged, drawn and quartered for it. At that time, a few months out of Barley Road School, I'd not have been surprised had it turned out that this Elizabethan foundation, all thorns and portcullises, was permitted by ancient charter to carry out such a punishment. There'd be a special assembly and the headmaster would offer his familiar lament at the presence among us of persons not capable of being moulded into gentlemen. Then a brisk execution, carried out by the school porter, whose disgruntled expression would have been a silent statement of *his* familiar lament that he was supposed to do this, that and the other (not just hanging but drawing and quartering as well) in addition to getting things ready for school dinner. Form IIA would be

244

restless for a while after that, discussing their grandstand view of Blishen's guts, but old Mullet would soon nag them into their usual puzzled morning attempt to find a footing in maths, that treacherous marsh into which the simple streams of arithmetic turned out to have led.

I already knew that to say 'My mother can't afford another cap' would have been to invite strokes of comedy from masters or prefects. Having a mother was an unfortunate fact about which gentlemen were reticent.

I remembered a moment from my mother's last years, when she was in that *institution*, as she insisted on calling Cedar House, the polite home for the elderly she'd settled into. Finding herself in a flat specially created for her in Buckingham Palace, with the Queen running in and out with gossip and little gutter cakes (my mother's obstinate term for *gateaux*), she'd have settled for the same description. An institution was whatever place the elderly found themselves in, as the result of a process not absolutely voluntary. In the small brown room to which her world had dwindled, she said to my sister: 'Look what I've got in here!' and opened a cupboard. It was laundered sheets she had in there, hidden behind the bottle of brandy which (though we all knew about it, and indeed had given it to her) was itself hidden behind a layer of those objects she was still willing the world to know she possessed. Of these last, the number was constantly decreasing. She was caught in that final year or so in a fever of concealment and disclosure. She hid objects, or thoughts, only so that she could set out to astound with their suddenly confessed existence. Now she said to Betty, of the sheets: 'Put them in your basket and take them home! Quick!' And when Betty demurred, and asked where they'd come from, Mother was startled and confused: to the question which she'd not imagined being asked, she had no answer. Betty said she began delivering a lecture on the subject of honesty, but then, confronted by this open-mouthed ancient child who was her mother, could say no more. She put the sheets on the end of Mother's bed, for the attention of the staff, and they spoke of other things. And talking it over we

245

realised that here, in this last shaft of time through which our mother was plummeting, was an echo of her days as a housemaid, nearly eighty years earlier. Then it must have been common practice to take what you could from the posh house you worked in and smuggle it out. In that farthing world of hers, it made the most obvious and desperate good sense. And here, at Sawdust House (as she called it when she wasn't calling it Soda House or Seidlitz House – for her, words had always danced round other words, with a general tendency to change partners), she'd found bed linen at her mercy, and had excitedly stored it away. Betty's refusal to have it was enough to halt the activity. She became deeply puzzled and turned to other things.

And I wondered how much of our behaviour, as we aged, was composed of echoes of our deep past. If she hadn't left school at twelve, had read books or gone to the theatre, my mother might have had some ironical grasp of what was happening, and been a little more ready for such scrambled seizures of memory, those gusts of ageing bewilderment that blow the contents of our heads in every direction. As it was, Lizzie aged ninety had lapsed back without a struggle into Lizzie aged nineteen.

Oddly, on that hundredth birthday of hers, I remembered the most absurd of the many resemblances between us, one that had worried her, for its possible effect, when I was small. On her left foot she had six toes, the last three webbed. I had three webbed toes, and six altogether, on my right foot. It was not impossible to use this eccentric foot of mine as the starting-point for 'This little pig went to market' and so on, and my mother made a point of doing it, but halfway through, the narrative was obliged to fake things a little. I was oddly proud of the blemish. And much of the literature I read suggested that to be without some such flaw might be a flaw in itself, and lead to the abandonment of all hope of wealth and status. (A small resident of Manor Road, Barton, in the 1920s, was surrounded by models of improved status. There was no way for him but up. I had dreams of being Mr

246

Richardson, who lived in one of the biggest houses among the generally big houses that trudged heavily up the hill with their accompaniment of gardens and garages and orchards and conservatories, we being a lower-middle-class semi-detached smudge at the bottom. Mr Richardson owned Horlicks, or Bovril, or a toothpaste, some huge possession of the sort – the story as it reached juvenile ears varied; and he appeared to be solitary, with no companion so banal as wife or child, but a chauffeur who drove his Rolls Royce, a car so silent I believed it might not require such a coarse propellant as an engine). You had some small oddity, always sited so that it was only by intimate accident (in the last chapter or the last-but-one) that a more profitable identity was established for you. It was usually a matter of some strawberry-shaped mole. In my far more interesting case, when by a fortunate turn of narrative I was spotted by an opportune lawyer with my socks off, the cry arose: 'This is indeed the Marquess of Aberystwyth! Observe the six toes, three webbed, a tradition for many centuries in that family!'

As the years passed, and it became clear that I wasn't to be – perhaps the ennobled owner of HP Sauce or a range of fish paste – I was left simply with the psychological consequences of having webbed toes. Here was evidence of the deep grooves that may be scored in our awareness when we're very young. In my sixties, as I attempted to settle to sleep (so that I could dream about losing my briefcase), I was still compelled to go through a ritual that had its roots in childhood. It was totally irrational and could not be brought to an end by reasoning. I had to ensure that those toes that were separate had not, since my last check, a few minutes or sometimes a few seconds earlier, got themselves slily webbed. The need was at its worst when I was very tired or nervous, but it could strike whatever my condition. Suddenly, as I was beginning to slip into sleep, and when the smallest move would spoil everything, I was seized with the horrid wish to reach down and begin the foolish, *foolish* work of separation. If I tried to resist, then the sensation of webbedness became unbearably plausible. I would

247

feel my toes growing together. No good, as I knew, to lecture myself on the famous absence from the list of human diseases of any sudden tendency for toes to unite. I had to check. And at times, it has to be said, this deep doubt of my ability to maintain essential crevices *as* crevices meant that I was compelled to ensure that, as I lay there, I hadn't, instead of my usual and useful arrangement of buttocks, developed a single seamless buttock.

I remember bitterly the effect when I was a boy of having that last uncertainty. The need to check could arise anywhere: in the classroom, in a crowded street. I achieved over the years as furtive and dissimulated a form of inspection as could be worked slowly for in such a difficult case. Even carried out with this tortuous indirectness that I'd invented, there was a simple indelicacy involved, close to grossness, that caused me much misery.

Somehow, though I was on intimate terms with her for sixty-one years, I never thought of asking my mother if she'd experienced similar consequences of our webbed state. But then, there was so much I didn't ask her. I knew her so well, and knew her barely at all.

# 9

Kate was first, by nine days, to be 36,816,480. When I told her that that, by my calculation, was the number of minutes in seventy years, she was incredulous. There must have been more, she said, as if she'd been keeping a tally of these tiny divisions of her existence.

'I can only ask you to observe,' I said, 'that over this period our hair – yours and mine – has turned white with shock.'

'I can imagine you as an old man,' Jenny Lawrence used to say. It was when I was being, her word, niggly. I'd be a shrivelled old grumbler, she meant, being unpleasant about people's verbs of motion, and as tetchy as if the world was being burnt around us. I'd be absolutely Mr Growser. Saying you could imagine friends when they were old was then a game of improbabilities, an extravagant form of chiding. Ten years later, when she'd been devastated by tuberculosis, she said at one of our last meetings that she clearly wouldn't make old bones, and within months she'd made young ones. I suppose among the feelings I have about life is one of apology to Jenny, for so much outlasting her; and also for not ending up as the short-tempered old man of her imagining. I wish it was possible to go back to Monmouth Hill in that hateful year and to be a little more patient when she invited me to amble with her to police court, or to surge forth with the ABC teashop as our destination.

Williams had got no further than sixty-six. I sometimes thought of an evening when I was seventeen or so and he'd walked me round Barton ('You need some fresh air – your worthy father will be blaming me for your bookman's complexion') and, after mesmerising me with his stories of poets glimpsed in bookshops or overheard on unidentified lawns, he advised me that there were other goals in life than the making of money. It wasn't the first time he'd pointed this out, and I was always puzzled: for he spoke urgently, as if within minutes of leaving him I might surrender to some scheme for fairly rapid self-enrichment. In that penny world of 1937 I had no difficulty whatever in avoiding materialism as conscientiously as any human being ever had. 'Not every writer makes as much as J. B. Priestley' was one form in which Williams cast his warning. I'd guiltily search my soul for any, however faint, desire to be like Priestley. Literary aspirants in the mid-thirties knew better than that. He was middle-brow, and that's all one needed to say about him. Williams would be accusing me next of wishing to write like . . . Robert Louis Stevenson or Charles Lamb – other names then despised. I was as hurt as I ever allowed myself to be when the wound was inflicted by this man to whom I clung as my one clear guarantee that another sort of life was possible, and that I wasn't cut off from Aldous Huxley and D. H. Lawrence by some impenetrable barrier.

We'd reached, that pre-war evening, the front gate of Williams' lodgings where he suffered from a landlord who, under surface respect, clearly held that being a schoolteacher was to be little more than an overpaid clown. When I visited Williams his landlord would say, in a tone intended to suggest fatigued astonishment: '*Still* trying to teach *him*, Mr Williams!' 'And one or two others,' Williams would rejoin. Now we leaned against the gate and Williams attempted to express the intensity of his resolve not to become well-to-do. 'You know, Edward,' he said. 'I have no desire whatever to be one of your £1000-a-year men.'

I walked home thrilled by this avowal. In a year or so I was to join the *Monmouth Hill Gazette* and, for the first six months, pay ten shillings a week for the privilege of working there. Mr Trout, the editor, claimed that I was being trained as a reporter. If I laugh at that hollowly now, I remember that I laughed at it, hollowly, even then. I was, in fact, between the autumn of 1938 and the spring of 1939, one of your minus-£26-a-year men. That was going a bit far in the direction suggested by Williams. I've thought, sadly, over the years, that in urging the path of the ill-paid highbrow rather than that of the shamefully well-rewarded middlebrow, he hadn't me in mind at all. He feared it might happen to him; that fleshpots might be offered and all his guardian spirits, Shakespeare, the poet Vaughan, his old schoolfriend Dylan Thomas, might not save him from succumbing to the lure. In the sixth form Marlowe's *Doctor Faustus* had been a set book, and, making a grille of his fingers, as he always did when he had some impropriety to propose, Williams peered out at us and suggested ('You'd better not repeat this to your worthy fathers') that the temptation we'd all be most likely to give way to was that of seeing Helen of Troy – or, ah, some . . . Betty of Barton, perhaps, he hoped he caused no offence by choosing that name – in, ah, her deshabillé. (A favourite word of my mother's, who called it diss-a-bill.) 'Liquefaction', Williams murmured, and spoke Herrick's lines to us about his Julia and her clothes: somehow he seemed to be suggesting, what I've often thought, that liquefaction would do for Julia undressed as well as Julia dressed. It was certainly a word for many of the figures at Khajuraho. But the general plight of Faustus, as the tempted man, clearly fascinated Williams; he circled round and round it, in the classroom and on those evenings when I'd visit his digs and his landlord would pretend to believe that I was Williams' only pupil. And Williams would play Chopin waltzes for me, and I'd yearn for a creature composed of Helen of Troy and Betty of Barton and Virginia Woolf and Katherine Mansfield and Ginger Rogers and a girl whose name I didn't know and who lived further up Manor Road on the left – all of them, pending the fusion I desired, forming an attentive audience for the music as stumblingly played by Williams (but

251

I thought no professional pianist could have made it more soulful) but being unanimously naked, liquefactory.

And the sorrow of it is that Williams' true temptation, to which he succumbed, was one not discussed in *Doctor Faustus*, and was never mentioned between us. It was the temptation of spending his whole life talking, planning, scheming, beautifully and ineffectually arranging and proposing, for others often, but also (alas, alas) for himself.

An effect of having lived in the same town all your life: its streets being full of the surprising ends of stories. *There* went John, who as a young man was always in the first flush of an affair, or its last. There were never, for him, any intermediate flushes. He had two gifts of equal force, for precipitately falling in love and falling precipitately out of it. His praise of a lover gained was as unreal as his dispraise of a lover lost. His amorous energy and versatility were much-envied, and we thought indeed there'd be no end to it, he'd be bounding for ever from love to love. Now he was solitary with uneasy eyes, who laughed as if he did not believe in laughing. There was Brian, who had always loved to be bored. I could remember him being furious in a field on the edge of Barton, sixty years ago, because some faint edge of excitement had entered into our traffic with the local brook. He liked in the morning to dam it, and in the afternoon to undam it. We had introduced some element as of naval warfare, involving broken-off branches. Brian was passionate about tedium, even then; and on that distant occasion left our company, vowing to have nothing to do with us ever again, and indeed we didn't see him for a couple of hours. Now he had arthritis, and seemed to have nothing else. There was another friend notable for his dislike of drama in real life; we'd met in the first form at the grammar school, and he'd at once found me over-excited, as in my turn I found him under-excited. He was a deeply cool spirit. In 1940 he'd been certain I was over-dramatising, as usual, about the fall of France, and bet me sixpence it wouldn't surrender on the day before it did. He'd made the fondest of marriages, given backbone by the wry amusement with which he and his wife observed each other. She said their lives together might have been more thrilling; though thinking wistfully that was so was not the same as actually wanting it. She had a curious absent-mindedness when they walked together, he said, and if he stopped to look at something she'd walk on without noticing he was no longer with her. It had sometimes occurred to him that, if he wanted to, and he didn't, he could have run away from his wife simply by standing still. He thought little of the past, and recalled Sergeant Clinker in an unspecific way, contending, however, that my feelings about that old tyrant of the Friday afternoon playground were exaggerated. But then he'd always held that writers were persons who, in order to make their material strong enough for their purpose, subjected it to extremes of recollection and preservation, as meat is allowed to get high, so that it was no less distant from reality than a jugged hare was from a live one.

We'd meet in the Friar's Holt and would sometimes make observations there based on an old perception of ours: that you might hope for a profounder understanding of what people were up to by looking at their lower halves. If you wanted instances of the apparent story going round locked to the hidden story, see how, as they stood at the bar, their heads, shoulders, faces, voices, made one sort of declaration about their business, while the language of their legs was sometimes remarkably contrary and often dissident. A voice was composed, but the foot twitched, angrily. There was eagerness in the face, but the legs were listless. Up above, deep concentration on what was happening; but down there, what inattentiveness of hands scratching, fingering buttocks, diving into pockets and exploding out of them again. There were times when, suddenly unable to take my eyes away from this giveaway landscape of lower limbs, I'd felt human physiology might be divided as maps are in atlases, into the political and the physical. On the whole, upstairs were your politicos, downstairs your wholly physical characters, a fidgeting of knees, a sometimes desperate tangling of legs. Yet who could say that the one or other of these halves was the truer person?

Peter thought I exaggerated the distance between tops and bottoms, but was drily interested. But then he believed I exaggerated the darkness of my father's nature. 'Always got on well with him,' he'd say, as if I'd simply lacked his diplomatic and father-handling skills. Oh Peter, I'd think, you weren't his son! 'I liked his jokes,' Peter would say. Well, I did, too, increasingly, in recollection . . . his old persistent jocularities, the nearest in fact he came to jokes. 'I believe you – thousands wouldn't,' he'd say. Or 'I see, said the blind man.' Asked by an over-energetic small son to do what he didn't want to do 'Got a bone in my leg.' As jokes they weren't much. I'd love them for themselves, for the sweetness in him they spoke of; but also, and more and more as time went on, for the sign they gave that for the moment he'd been shanghaied by benignity. My mother might take the opportunity of defending a neighbour and my father would let it pass. 'Stuck-up sort of bugger, if you'll excuse my French.' Then a grin. I saw what Peter meant. He had an urchin's grin on a face that, as he was disastrously aware, might have stood in as an Identikit portrait for famous handsome film stars of the time, Clive Brook, Ronald Colman.

What I found difficult now, as I confessed to Peter, was keeping abreast with experience. For me that had always amounted to maintaining my diary, but now I'd flinch from the daily effort, and let it drift, there was too much life, and I was like Jill Pirrie's children, I was averse to succumbing to cliché, if it could be helped, and that meant great labour. Sitting in that classroom at Halesworth, I'd envied the children's unwary use of energy. Now I kept little notebooks, and soon there'd be heaps of them, alongside that ridiculous row of diaries. It was as if Miss Baker at Barley Road had said, not 'write what you see in the picture' but 'write what you see in life', and so the exercise had never come to an end. Peter thought it was about time I realised that I'd always exaggerated one's need to be a recorder. Had it struck me that since we first met I'd consumed probably a small forest of paper?

# 10

The latest thing in Bush House was lavatorial confusion. Some problems of plumbing, clearly complex, meant that there were lavatories familiar as GENTS that were now LADIES, and vice versa; and that, to prevent simple ease of transposition, there were some (but unreliably) that remained as they had been. It was a building in which people were inclined to attend absent-mindedly to such a need, their heads full of programmes or of fury with colleagues. So you were where you shouldn't be, or were running from landing to landing.

In such time as I had to spare from that sort of thing, I did a programme with Sir Huw Wheldon, who turned out to have precisely my old headmaster's habit of saying things in twos and threes. He'd chosen a favourite book, and I was to discuss it with him. So now, after an exchange of feelings about the book before the recording, he cried: 'I trust you! I trust you! I trust you! I don't know why I trust you, but I do! You are a better reader than I am!'

'Oh, that couldn't be so,' I said.

'It's so! It's so! It's *so*! I can feel it. Good reader myself, but – I trust you!' The producer diffidently reminded him that when the recording began, we should both be sitting square on to the microphone. Huw Wheldon was appalled. His eyebrows leapt. He made enormous gestures of refusal. 'No! No! No! You can't get the best out of people if you ask them to stare at each other! I want to loll! Blishen wants to loll! We want to loll!'

Aware of the misery on the producer's face, I attempted to express my willingness not to loll. The producer said: 'These are the studios we are allocated – with these microphones, and –'

'No! Don't tell *me* about allocations! You have to insist! No, don't tell me! I know all about this! Eh?' The producer agreed that Sir Huw knew all about this, but – 'I'll do it now, but you must do something about it! You must do something about it!'

I asked him what he'd like me to call him. Educator and broadcaster? 'No! I don't care for either of those terms! No, they won't do, will they? They won't do! They won't do!' I thought I'd lost his dramatically declared trust, but he was spankingly genial. 'What I like is – Take this down – "Was a very well-known broadcaster in this country; not only made his own programmes but in the course of time" – that's the phrase I like – "in the course of time became managing director, that is Head" – in the United States, you know, they say "managing director" – you have to spell it out – "of BBC Television."'

And I thought what enormous and serviceable self-confidence he had, and how useful it would be to have some of that; and perhaps (but I wasn't very hopeful) it might arrive as a result of being seventy.

On the eve of my own birthday I had a dream in which an important role was played by a physically large member of the political party I supported; on his back he had a knapsack in which there were pies, cakes and fruit. As we spoke he was struggling to add to these. Kate and I were running away, I said, and were anxious to find somewhere to live, at least temporarily. Yes, he said, having difficulty with a quiche; he looked up at the tremendous hillside beneath which we were standing, and which increased in size as we gazed at it. Usually when he'd begun to talk he was difficult to stop, but now he merely said 'Yes', again; and I then observed that Kate was

256

scurrying along the road that at that very moment had placed itself at the top of the hillside. To say she was a long way away didn't cover the case at all, but at once I was on the road, too, and running after her. I wished she had waited before starting out on her own. The road lengthened, and there was now no sign of her. I was scurrying, too, but the road grew longer still and reversed its direction. I had once more that sensation of the geography arranging itself so that no encounter was possible, nor arrival at any destination at all. Things lost were lost.

And this time, it seemed, I'd lost Kate.

I woke in a panic, but it wasn't true. Among all the oddities, I thought, was the way we took sleep for granted. There was Kate curled up in the nightly trance without which she would not survive. I suspected her of having better quality dreams than mine – the cast list, from odd mentions, sounded spectacular – but she was evasive about this.

I lay there remembering the past day – including a train journey in which I'd avoided Arnold Pribble only by behaving, on the platform and then most of the way to London, as if I were six inches shorter than I was, and even older. I thought I'd given an impression also of being bearded. There was still that huge blue declaration on the embankment just before you drew into the station where I alighted. In the comics of my childhood a door never opened but there was a mat with WELCOME printed on it. Those were clearly the front doors of life, and the convention helped to make you feel you'd been generally invited in. Life said 'Come in', and there was the everlasting living room, the never-failing dining room, the guaranteed bedroom, and the usual offices (clearly and dependably marked). Now, I thought, I had made my way round to the back door, and it said frankly: PISS OFF EVERYONE.

Think of something else, I told myself. But it was some process other than thought that brought to mind a moment during the coldest winter of the century, as they said it had been, a few years back. It had been a sudden astonishment, the garden seeming subject to an invasion of angels, a score or more seagulls swooping down on a tray of food Kate had put out, but not alighting. There was this instant great grey hullabaloo of wings, breathtakingly filling the scene, and then instantly gone. It had lasted a split second.

How many split seconds in seventy years?

Keep thinking of something else, I admonished this antique and failing diarist in whose skin I lived. So he thought of a moment when a grandson – not yet in the business of appraising old age or life itself, but concerned only with the character of a winter afternoon – had said:

'It is not quite too dark.'